Culture and
Customs of
Korea

Culture and Customs of Korea

∽∘∾

Donald N. Clark

Culture and Customs of Asia
Hanchao Lu, Series Editor

GREENWOOD PRESS
Westport, Connecticut • London

Library of Congress Cataloging-in-Publication Data

Clark, Donald N.
    Culture and customs of Korea / Donald N. Clark
       p.   cm.—(Culture and customs of Asia, ISSN 1097–0738)
    Includes bibliographical references and index.
    ISBN 0–313–30456–4 (alk. paper)
    1. Korea—Civilization. 2. Korea—Social life and customs. I. Title. II. Series.
DS904.C4492 2000
951.9—dc21   00–021074

British Library Cataloguing in Publication Data is available.

951. 9
CLA

Library of Congress Catalog Card Number: 00–021074
ISBN: 0–313–30456–4
ISSN: 1097–0738

First published in 2000

Greenwood Press, 88 Post Road West, Westport, CT 06881
An imprint of Greenwood Publishing Group, Inc.
www.greenwood.com

Printed in the United States of America

∞

The paper used in this book complies with the
Permanent Paper Standard issued by the National
Information Standards Organization (Z39.48–1984).

10 9 8 7 6 5 4 3 2 1

Copyright Acknowledgments

The author and publisher gratefully acknowledge permission for the use of the following material:

The *sijo* poems in Chapter 3 from *Seoul; Past and Present; A Guide to Yi T'aejo's Capital*, by Allen D. Clark and Donald N. Clark (Seoul: Hollym Corp., 1969), pp. 24, 34, appear by permission of the Royal Asiatic Society–Korea Branch.

Sŏ Chŏngju's poem "Grandmother" from *Unforgettable Things*, translated by David R. McCann (Seoul: Si-sa-yong-o-sa, 1986), p. 21, appears by permission of Si-sa-yong-o-sa Publishers.

Unless otherwise noted, all photographs appear by courtesy of Donald N. Clark.

In Memory of Kim Jai-hyup

Contents

Illustrations

Series Foreword

GEOGRAPHICALLY, Asia encompasses the vast area from Suez, the Bosporus, and the Ural Mountains eastward to the Bering Sea and from this line southward to the Indonesian archipelago, an expanse that covers about 30 percent of our earth. Conventionally, and especially insofar as culture and customs are concerned, Asia refers primarily to the region east of Iran and south of Russia. This area can be divided in turn into subregions commonly known as South, Southeast, and East Asia, which are the main focus of this series.

The United States has vast interests in this region. In the twentieth century the United States fought three major wars in Asia (namely, the Pacific War of 1941–45, the Korean War of 1950–53, and the Vietnam War of 1965–75), and each had profound impact on life and politics in America. Today, America's major trading partners are in Asia, and in the foreseeable future the weight of Asia in American life will inevitably increase, for in Asia lie our great allies as well as our toughest competitors in virtually all arenas of global interest. Domestically, the role of Asian immmigrants is more visible than at any other time in our history. In spite of these connections with Asia, however, our knowledge about this crucial region is far from adequate. For various reasons, Asia remains for most of us a relatively unfamiliar, if not stereotypical or even mysterious, "Oriental" land.

There are compelling reasons for Americans to obtain some level of concrete knowledge about Asia. It is one of the world's richest reservoirs of culture and an ever-evolving museum of human heritage. Rhoads Murphey, a prominent Asianist, once pointed out that in the part of Asia east of Afghanistan and south of Russia alone lies half the world, "half of its people and far more than half of its historical experience, for these are the oldest living civilized traditions." Prior to the modern era, with limited interaction and mutual influence between the East and the West, Asian civilizations developed largely independent from the West. In modern times, however, Asia and the West have come not only into close contact but also into frequent conflict: The result has been one of the most solemn and stirring dramas in world history. Today, integration and compromise are the trend in coping with cultural differences. The West—with some notable exceptions—has started to see Asian traditions, not as something to fear, but as something to be understood, appreciated, and even cherished. After all, Asian traditions are an indispensable part of the human legacy, a matter of global "common wealth" that few of us can afford to ignore.

As the result of Asia's enormous economic development since World War II, we can no longer neglect the study of this vibrant region. Japan's "economic miracle" of postwar development is no longer unique, but in various degrees has been matched by the booming economy of many other Asian countries and regions. The rise of the four "mini dragons" (South Korea, Taiwan, Hong Kong, and Singapore) suggests that there may be a common Asian pattern of development. At the same time, each economy in Asia has followed its own particular trajectory. Clearly, China is the next giant on the scene. Sweeping changes in China in the last two decades have already dramatically altered the world's economic map. Furthermore, growth has also been dramatic in much of Southeast Asia. Today war-devastated Vietnam shows great enthusiasm for joining the "club" of nations engaged in the world economy. And in South Asia, India, the world's largest democracy, is rediscovering its role as a champion of market capitalism. The economic development of Asia presents a challenge to Americans but also provides them with unprecedented opportunities. It is largely against this background that more and more people in the United States, in particular among the younger generation, have started to pursue careers dealing with Asia.

This series is designed to meet the need for knowledge of Asia among students and the general public. Each book is written in an accessible and lively style by an expert (or experts) in the field of Asian studies. Each book focuses on the culture and customs of a country or region. Each volume starts with an introduction to the land and people of a nation or region and includes a brief history and an overview of the economy. This is followed by chapters dealing with a variety of topics that piece together a cultural panorama, such as thought, religion, ethics, literature and art, architecture and housing, cuisine, traditional dress, gender, courtship and marriage, festivals and leisure activities, music and dance, and social customs and lifestyle. In this series, we have chosen not to elaborate on elite life, ideology, or detailed questions of political structure and struggle, but instead to explore the world of common people, their sorrow and joy, their pattern of thinking, and their way of life. It is the culture and customs of the majority of the people (rather than just the rich and powerful elite) that we seek to understand. Without such understanding, it will be difficult for all of us to live peacefully and fruitfully with each other in this increasingly interdependent world.

As the world shrinks, modern technologies have made all nations on earth "virtual" neighbors. The expression "global village" not only reveals the nature and the scope of the world in which we live but also, more importantly, highlights the serious need for mutual understanding of all peoples on our planet. If this series serves to help the reader obtain a better understanding of the "half of the world" that is Asia, the authors and I will be well rewarded.

Hanchao Lu
Georgia Institute of Technology

Acknowledgments

THIS BOOK owes much to the advice and support of colleagues and friends during periods in Korea teaching at Yonsei University and doing research supported by grants from the Korean-American Educational (Fulbright) Commission and my home institution, Trinity University. Among the many mentors and friends who have contributed to my understanding of Korean history and society are builders of the Korean studies field such as Professors Edward Wagner of Harvard, Koh Byong-ik of Seoul National University, George Paik (Paek Nakchun) of Yonsei University, and Chun Hae-jong and Lee Kwang-rin of Sŏgang University, as well as numerous contemporaries in the field in various disciplines, in both Korea and the West. While their influence is everywhere in the book and I am indebted to all of them, I hasten to add that responsibility for the interpretations (and errors) is wholly my own.

The firsthand material about life in Poksu district was acquired during the year my wife and I spent there in the Peace Corps and on subsequent visits. Korean friends have given me a profound appreciation and respect for Korean life and culture over the years. I dedicate the book to the memory of the first of these, Kim Jai-hyup, whom I met in Seoul while when I was a student at Seoul Foreign School and he was attending Kyŏngbok High School, in 1960. Jai-hyup was the first to introduce me to Korean family life, the cultural richness of the city of Seoul, the fascinations of Korean markets and the delights of Korean restaurants, and the world of Korean ideas and thought. We kept in touch through college, graduate school, and our early years in academe and remained close friends until his early death from cancer in the 1980s. His passing took not only a personal friend but a productive scholar, then businessman, and finally, through the public affairs group that he co-founded, contributor to better understanding in U.S.-Korean relations.

I am grateful to Wendi Schnaufer and Barbara Rader of Greenwood Press for their patience, persistence, and constructive criticism over the many months of writing and production, and to series editor Hanchao Lu for his comments and support throughout the process. My wife Linda, always my best and most supportive critic, likewise deserves deep thanks. Many of the insights about life in Poksu came through her access to village women, her memory, and the notes and records she kept during our time in the countryside.

In general I have used the McCune-Reischauer system for romanizing Korean throughout the book. I have made exceptions where certain names are known outside Korea by variant spellings as in the cases of Presidents Syngman Rhee (McCune-Reischauer Yi Sŭngman), Park Chung-hee (Pak Chŏnghŭi), and Kim Il-sung (Kim Ilsŏng), among others.

Chronology

2333 B.C.	Traditional founding date for the earliest kingdom of Korea, founded by the legendary Tan'gun.
1122 B.C.	Traditional date for the migration from China to Korea of the Chinese nobleman Kija and his 5,000 followers, establishing the city of P'yŏngyang.
108 B.C.	The Chinese Han dynasty establishes commanderies in Korea. The longest-lived one, Lolang, continues in existence as a virtual Chinese colony until A.D. 313.
57 B.C.	Traditional founding date for the Korean kingdom of Silla, in southeastern Korea. Two other Korean states are included in the Korean Three Kingdoms: Koguryŏ (37 B.C.) and Paekche (18 B.C.).
A.D. 372	Traditional date for the entry of Buddhism into Korea. In Koguryŏ, a Confucian school is founded.
A.D. 668	The kingdom of Silla completes the unification of the Korean peninsula with Chinese help, overcoming first Paekche, in the southwest (A.D. 663), and then Koguryŏ, in the north (A.D. 668).
A.D. 918	Founding date for the kingdom of Koryŏ. Koryŏ completes the reunification of Korea by accepting the surrender of the last Silla king in 935.

1392–1910   Korea is ruled by a succession of twenty-seven kings from the Yi clan of Chŏnju. They call the kingdom Chosŏn, usually translated as "Land of the Morning Calm."

1446   King Sejong (r. 1418–50) announces the invention of the Korean phonetic alphabet known as *han'gŭl*.

1592–98   Korea suffers an invasion by Japanese armies sent by the warlord Hideyoshi on an expedition to conquer Ming China. The invasion is halted by a combined Sino-Korean force and a long stalemate follows. The Korean admiral Yi Sunsin develops a metal-clad warship known as the Turtle Ship, to harry Japanese supply lines. Eventually, after Hideyoshi's death, the Japanese withdraw from Korea, leaving the peninsula in disarray.

1700s   *Sirhak*, the Korean school of "practical learning," takes shape, involving the "investigation of things" and proposals for social and institutional reform. Korea also produces important new works of art and literature such as the genre paintings of Kim Hongdo and Shin Yunbok, and new-style novels in *han'gŭl* are written by women of the royal court. Eventually, certain *sirhak* scholars establish a Korean branch of the Catholic Church.

1876   Korea, sometimes called the "Hermit Kingdom" for its policy of seclusion from foreign contact, is "opened" when a Japanese naval expedition forces the Koreans to sign a modern treaty for trade and diplomatic contact.

1882   Korea and the United States sign a treaty, Korea's first with a Western country.

1890s   A Korean religious movement called the "Religion of the Heavenly Way" (Ch'ŏndokyo) is behind a peasant movement known as the Tonghak ("Eastern Learning") Movement. Korea requests Chinese assistance to put down the rebellion, Japan intervenes to block the Chinese, and the Sino-Japanese War of 1894–95 results. After the war, Korea loses its status as a tributary state of China and the king of Korea declares his country an "empire," the Empire of Taehan.

1904–5	Russia and Japan go to war over their rivalry for hegemony in northeast Asia. After difficult fighting on land in northern Korea and Manchuria, the Japanese succeed in sinking the main Russian fleet on the sea. The war is mediated by President Theodore Roosevelt, and Russia is eliminated as a contender for influence in Korea. In November 1905, Japan forces Korea to sign a protectorate treaty, turning over Korea's foreign affairs and defense to Imperial Japan.
1910	Japan annexes Korea and makes it a colony. The Korean government is forced to sign a treaty giving their country to Japan, and Japan rewards important Korean officials with titles and cash grants.
1919	The Korean population rises in protest against harsh Japanese rule during funeral observances for the former Korean king. Japanese colonial authorities are caught by surprise and react with great violence. Over the course of the "March First Independence Movement," as it is known, an estimated 7,000 Koreans lose their lives.
1920s	The Japanese soften their colonial policy in Korea, assigning a relatively liberal navy admiral to govern the country. His "cultural policy" permits the Koreans to publish newspapers and enjoy limited freedom of expression. Korean Communists join with other nationalists in a political organization that is allowed to flourish briefly, but it comes apart because of the internal conflicts between the Communists and other Koreans.
1930s	Japanese rule resumes its military discipline as Korea is turned into a staging area for the Japanese war in China (1937) and eventually mobilized for the all-out Pacific War. Koreans are drafted as laborers and then as soldiers in the Japanese military.
1943	In Cairo, Allied leaders Franklin D. Roosevelt, Winston Churchill, and Chiang Kai-shek agree that after Japan's defeat in the war, "in due course" Korea should be free and independent. However, no concrete plans are laid to move Korea from colonialism to self-determination. Instead, the Roosevelt administration thinks in terms of placing Korea under an international trusteeship.

1945   When Japan suddenly surrenders in August 1945, the
            United States and the Soviet Union decide to draw a line
            across the peninsula at the 38th parallel and to occupy Ko-
            rea in two zones, the Soviets in the north and the Americans
            in the south. The two powers then take charge, eject the
            Japanese, and serve as "trustees" over Korea until a national
            government can be created. Koreans protest the trusteeship
            idea. In the north, the Soviets quickly create a left-wing
            government under Korean Communists. In the south, the
            Americans are slower to abandon the trusteeship idea.

1947–48   After fruitless talks between the United States and the So-
            viet Union over how to constitute a unified Korean gov-
            ernment, the United States turns the Korean "problem"
            over to the United Nations. The United Nations organizes
            elections in Korea that actually take place only in the
            southern zone. The representatives who are elected draft a
            constitution and elect a president, the American-educated
            Syngman Rhee (Yi Sŭngman). To answer the newly es-
            tablished "Republic of Korea" (ROK) in the south, the
            Communists in the north establish the "Democratic Peo-
            ple's Republic of Korea" (DPRK).

1949   American occupation forces withdraw from South Korea
            but remain nearby in Japan. The last Russian forces
            withdraw but remain nearby in coastal Siberia near Vlad-
            ivostok. In China, the Chinese Communists defeat the
            Nationalists in a civil war and establish the "People's Re-
            public of China" (PRC) with its government in Peking
            (Beijing).

1950–53   In June 1950, after several years of trying to undermine
            the conservative political leadership in South Korea, North
            Korean leader Kim Il-sung launches a full military invasion
            to reunify the Korean peninsula under DPRK control. The
            Americans, who appear to have renounced any further role
            in Korean affairs, decide to answer the invasion by re-
            introducing troops. They organize an international peace-
            keeping force under a specially created United Nations
            Command (actually commanded by an American general,
            with American and South Korean forces as the main ele-

ments along with Great Britain and many others). This force halts the North Korean invasion and eventually turns the tables with a counterinvasion of the north. Fearing that the DPRK, a Communist ally, will be completely destroyed and that the Americans might actually invade China itself, the Chinese Communists intervene in November 1950, forcing a disorderly retreat on the United Nations Command. After heavy fighting, the war settles down on a line across the middle of Korea. Truce negotiations begin in the spring of 1951 and drag on in an atmosphere of frustration and enmity for more than two years. On July 27, 1953, the shooting is stopped by an armistice agreement that establishes a four-kilometer-wide Demilitarized Zone across the entire peninsula very close to the original boundary of the 38th parallel. The two Korean republics begin the laborious process of reconstruction after suffering terrible physical destruction and the loss of more than 2 million citizens on both sides. Chinese losses are in the hundreds of thousands. Americans suffer 34,000 battle deaths and 20,000 more noncombat fatalities, and the British Commonwealth suffers the loss of 1,263.

1952–60   In South Korea, President Syngman Rhee is elected and reelected president. The 1960 election turns out to be so corrupt that the citizenry erupt in massive demonstrations that succeed in ousting him from power. A constitutional change and a new civilian government follow but are not able to make much headway against South Korea's intractable economic problems.

1961   Elements of the ROK Army take power in South Korea in a military coup. They suspend the constitution and rule by martial law. In 1963, they turn the government back over to civilian leadership, but having retired from the army themselves and having run in the elections, the military men retain control of the South Korean political system and economy.

1963   The South Korean government launches an aggressive program of export-led economic development, seeking loans from Japan and other countries to finance its projects.

1965   South Korea settles its differences with Japan arising from the colonial period and accepts financial help. Japanese companies enter into joint ventures with South Korean companies, some of which eventually evolve into the conglomerates called *chaebŏl*. Although many Koreans worry about Japan's possibly taking over their economy, the government under President Park Chung-hee contains their objections and pushes his plans through. Through government control of the banking industry Park ensures that certain selected Korean companies will receive favorable financing to help them grow.

1966   South Korea contributes two army divisions to the American war in Vietnam. Koreans take this as repayment of their debt to the United States for saving their republic from Communist takeover in the 1950–53 war with the north. The United States pays all costs of the Korean troop deployment to Vietnam and awards lucrative construction contracts to Korean companies, greatly increasing the flow of valuable international currency into the Korean economy. Korea begins to enjoy a "Vietnam Boom."

1969   President Park Chung-hee rams through the national legislature an amendment to the South Korean constitution that will enable him to run for president for an unlimited number of terms.

1971–72   After nearly losing the presidential election to his rival Kim Dae-jung, and after having been shaken by U.S. President Richard Nixon's sudden change of policy toward Communist China and the apparent American debacle in Vietnam, President Park Chung-hee declares a state of national emergency and assumes the authority to rule South Korea by decree. He decrees an end to criticism of himself or his government. People who object or oppose him are arrested and some serve long prison terms.

1970s   The South Korean economy racks up an impressive record of progress and growth. Korean companies are weaned away from foreign management and financing and begin thriving on their own. South Koreans enjoy an unprecedented standard of living, while in North Korea, where recovery from the war was better than in the south during the 1960s, the state-controlled Soviet-style economy begins to lag.

1979   After a wave of labor unrest as South Korean workers demand a fairer share of the country's increasing wealth, President Park is assassinated in an attempted "palace coup" between factions of his own administration. The South Korean army launches an investigation, and in December the general heading the investigation, Maj. Gen. Chun Doo-hwan, forcibly takes control of the South Korean military and makes himself the strongman. The civilian government can do little to stop him.

1980   In May, after weeks of demonstrations against Chun's grab for power, an outbreak of protests in Kwangju, in southwestern Korea, leads to massive army intervention and the death of hundreds of civilians. Although General Chun succeeds in suppressing the Kwangju uprising, South Korean citizens in general are outraged. Though he engineers his own selection as president of the next civilian government later in the year, he never recovers legitimacy as a national leader.

1980s   South Korea continues its march to economic prosperity. The International Olympic Committee awards the 1988 Summer Olympic Games to Seoul. In 1987, after years of endemic but illegal student protests against the Chun regime, the Korean people rise up to demand free and democratic elections at the end of the year. The Chun government capitulates; however, Chun's handpicked successor wins the election nevertheless when opposition candidates split the majority vote between them.

1990   President Roh Tae-woo, General Chun's chosen successor, uses his power to launch a policy of "Nordpolitik," opening Korea's doors to trade with the socialist countries. In developments that are astonishing to people accustomed to the barriers of the Cold War, South Korea begins diplomatic and trade relations with the Soviet Union and

China. The North Koreans feel betrayed by their Soviet and Chinese allies, but they can do little to change the situation.

1991   South and North Korea both are admitted to the United Nations as regular members. In October, the United States announces that it has withdrawn all its tactical nuclear weapons from the Korean peninsula. In December, North and South Korea sign a nonaggression agreement and a promise to resolve their differences through dialogue. They also agree that the Korean peninsula should be freed of nuclear weapons.

1991–95   The West discovers that North Korea is building a structure that is probably a nuclear fuel reprocessing plant capable of producing plutonium for nuclear weapons. Through several years of tense political jockeying and delicate diplomatic negotiations, an agreement is concluded in October 1994 whereby the United States will lead in solving North Korea's need for nuclear power by organizing a financing consortium to build two new nuclear power plants powered by reactors that are not as likely to produce weapons-grade nuclear fuel. The cost is borne mostly by South Korea and Japan, and the consortium is called the Korean Peninsula Energy Development Organization (KEDO). Construction begins at a coastal site in northeastern Korea. The agreement is to follow a series of steps whereby North Korea freezes construction on its reprocessing facility, submits to continuous monitoring by the International Atomic Energy Agency (IAEA), abandons construction of its relatively unsafe nuclear reactors, and accounts for all its spent nuclear fuel to show that it has not built any atomic bombs. The last step in the program is to be the installation of the core elements of the two new reactors, but only after North Korea's full accounting for all elements of its existing nuclear program and the establishment of "transparency" to assure the effectiveness of international safeguards.

1992   In South Korea, Kim Young-sam is elected president, the first nonmilitary chief executive in thirty years.

1994   In July, North Korean leader Kim Il-sung dies. The North Korean system goes into mourning, led by Kim's son and successor Kim Jong-il.

1997   In South Korea, longtime opposition leader Kim Dae-jung is elected president, only to face the worst economic crisis in the republic's history. A hurried bailout by the International Monetary Fund brings the financial crisis under control, but long-term solutions require restructuring of many vested interests in the South Korean economy, including reorganization of the powerful *chaebŏl* conglomerates. Kim Dae-jung's leadership skills are sorely tested as he tries to balance the forces in the crisis and find a solution. By the end of 1998, the crisis appears to be ending and South Koreans are beginning to relax.

1998   North Korea test-fires an advanced missile over the Japanese islands into the Pacific. The DPRK claims it was an attempt to launch a satellite in honor of Kim Jong-il's confirmation as head of his late father's regime, but Japan, South Korea, and the United States see it as a dangerous step that destabilizes the region's security and threatens peace in the region. The Japanese are particularly upset and interrupt negotiations on trade and recognition with the north. Hardliners in the United States and South Korea paint North Korea as a "rogue state" and argue that trade and humanitarian aid are only making the north more of a military threat to its neighbors.

1999   Through a painstaking process of negotiations North Korea is persuaded to drop further missile tests. The north, however, complains that the United States has not lived up to its promises under the 1994 agreed framework, particularly in its slowness to lift economic sanctions against the DPRK. The West reads North Korea's behavior as threatening and President Bill Clinton assigns former Defense Secretary William Perry the task of studying the North Korean "problem" and reviewing American policy. Perry eventually delivers a report that calls for a dual approach: continued military deterrence along with the creation of incentives to cooperation. South Koreans meanwhile step up their contact with North Korea under President Kim Dae-Jung's "Sunshine Policy." Large numbers of South Koreans take tours of the Kumgang mountains, an environment of storied beauty in Korea that has been closed to them for more than fifty years. South Korean companies also conclude investment deals with North Korea. A significant economic stake in peaceful trade between North and South develops.

2000   President Kim Dae-Jung presses his positive approach to North Korea in public statements, and in the spring there is the sudden announcement of plans for the southern leader to visit his counterpart Kim Jong-il in P'yongyang. After careful preparation the meeting takes place in June. It is the first time that leaders from the north and south have met since the division of their country in 1945. The visit takes place in an unexpectedly cordial atmosphere, with the personalities of the two leaders setting a tone that raises spirits and hopes that at long last the intractable problems of separated families and mutual hatreds can be solved. President Kim Dae-Jung and Chairman Kim Jong-il sign documents affirming their intention to work toward reconciliation, not along lines of German reunification but more as a confederation, Chinese style, of "one country, two systems." They agree to implement a program of family reunifications at an early date, and Chairman Kim accepts President Kim's invitation for a return visit to Seoul in the near future.

1

The Story of the Korean People

KOREA IS A NATION that was little known to the outside world until it burst into the news in the middle of the twentieth century as a major trouble spot in the Cold War. The Korean Conflict, which lasted for three years from 1950 to 1953, established Korea as a battleground in the worldwide confrontation between democratic capitalism and Communism, and it remains a place where the tensions persist even after the fall of Communism in Europe and the dissolution of the Soviet Union. Because of Korea's strategic position on the edge of the "free world," it is easy to overlook the historic and cultural features of Korean civilization that make it an intrinsically interesting place to study and visit. Despite the war and continuing division of the country into northern and southern republics, and despite the long years of poverty and struggle that followed the cease-fire in 1953, the two parts of Korea are poised to play a significant role in world affairs in the twenty-first century. South Korea is already one of the world's most energetic trading economies. North Korea has attracted attention as a country determined to assert its independent course, demanding respect and recognition as well. Both sides share many centuries of cultural heritage, and that common heritage is the subject of this book.

North and South Korea together have a surprisingly large population for such a small landmass. Twenty-two million live in the north (the Democratic People's Republic of Korea, or DPRK) and 45 million—more than twice as many—live in the south (the Republic of Korea, or ROK). The 67 million Koreans live on a peninsula that is the size of the American state of Minnesota, with 2 million more living just across the northern border in the

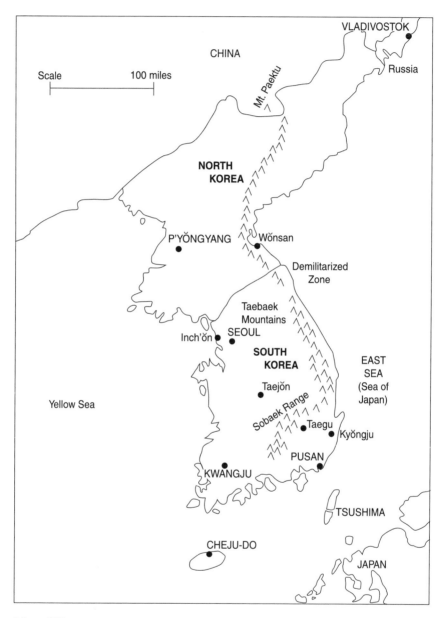

Map of Korea.

northeast Chinese provinces of Liaoning and Jilin. If one adds to this the most significant overseas Korean communities that include 750,000 ethnic Koreans in Japan and about a million in the United States, the population of "Greater Korea" exceeds 70 million. The population of China, Korea's closest neighbor, is many times greater. Japan too has a much larger population. But there are more Koreans than there are people of any European nationality except Germans, and Koreans outnumber the people in every South American country except Brazil. Thus in terms of population, Korea is a significant world civilization. However, until modern times, the Koreans kept to themselves, did not export their culture or religion, and never sought trade or colonies in faraway places. Until the late 1800s, in fact, Korea's seclusion was so tight that the outsiders who knew of it often called it the "Hermit Kingdom."

Koreans traditionally have made their living by farming, and until 1950 most Koreans lived in farming villages. When the economy started shifting toward manufacturing, Koreans began migrating in large numbers to the cities where there were factory jobs. As the cities grew and demanded more services and many new kinds of labor, they attracted even more people from the countryside. The cities started requiring every kind of skill and type of work, and within only a few years the proportions had shifted from an 80 percent rural to an 80 percent urban population. Much of this shift was concentrated on the capital city of Seoul and its suburbs, which grew from a population of 300,000 in 1950 to 11 million in 1995.

The influx of millions of people to the cities made Korea's urban areas dynamic centers of energy and creativity. It also took the pressure off the countryside, where large families historically had had trouble making ends meet. As wealth increased in the cities, a rural development program in the 1970s and 1980s helped equalize the standard of living in Korea's villages. New technologies and farming techniques made better food available across the country. People all over the world bought Korean products and money flowed into the Korean economy. Growth was not without its price: the cities became almost unbearably congested and polluted, and not everyone shared in Korea's new prosperity. But by the year 2000, Korea as a nation was enjoying an undreamed-of standard of living.

KOREA'S PLACE IN EAST ASIA

This success story with all its ups and downs is part of Korea's modern history and only happened within the past forty years. Before that, life in Korea was highly traditional and Koreans were still in their "hermit" mode.

Yet over the course of centuries, even in isolation from the outside world, the Korean people succeeded in developing a unique way of life. Though it existed in the shadow of China and drew on the Chinese for protection and many of its cultural patterns, Korea had its own language and customs, its own unique family system and way of life. At the same time, the Koreans admired Chinese culture and imitated it to an extent. For example, Koreans always used the elegant Chinese written script called "characters," a way of writing symbols for words instead of using an alphabet. They did this because Chinese characters were full of meaning and beautiful to look at. However, when they read the characters out loud or interpreted their meaning, they did so by speaking Korean words. For example, the historic name for Korea is "Chosŏn," the Korean pronunciation of a Chinese word, "Chaoxian," which is written with two characters that together can be roughly translated as "Morning Calm," or "Land of the Morning Calm," and their meaning is the same whether a Korean sees them and pronounces them "Chosŏn" or a Chinese sees them and pronounces them "Chaoxian." The Japanese, who use Chinese characters in the same way, would pronounce the name slightly differently, as "Chōsen." This way of using Chinese characters in different languages is what defines most clearly the Chinese "family of nations," to which the Koreans belong. Other "family members" are the Japanese, Vietnamese, Tibetans, Mongolians, and other Central Asian peoples. Though they may have had little to do with each other, they all looked up to the Chinese, regarded China as the apex of human civilization, and were happy to adapt desirable Chinese ways of doing things.

The Koreans are descended from people who migrated throughout the northeast Asian territory that encompasses today's Russian Far East, the Chinese northeast (known as Manchuria), and Siberia. These prehistoric ancestors lived in the Stone and Bronze Ages for many thousands of years before beginning to record their history in written form. From their tombs and the cast-off debris of their settlements we know that they used fire and tools, hunted animals and fished for food, and honored their leaders. Some of the things they left behind resemble similar objects in Siberia and northeast Asia. That fact, together with the fact that the Korean language resembles languages in northern Asia, leads us to believe that the earliest inhabitants of the Korean peninsula were of Siberian origin. They might have been related to the people who crossed the land bridge to Alaska. But their migration happened so long ago that we cannot call them "Koreans" any more than we can call the early travelers to Alaska "Americans."

"Korea" as a nation occupying most of the Korean peninsula did not begin until A.D. 668. Between the Neolithic (Late Stone Age) period and that year of unification, several different areas of Korea saw the rise of small states, some of them kingdoms, in which culture and customs developed that continue to mark Korean civilization as unique today. Tribal organization, status consciousness, and the transition from hunting to farming all were part of Korean life at that time. The language developed then, as did early forms of Korean art that we can still study today, in the form of pottery and stone carving. Later on, distinct kingdoms gave rise to organized monarchies, a class system, and a tradition of education. By 668, Koreans had created a mature national culture within defined national boundaries.

Between 668 and the early twentieth century, the Koreans living on their peninsula had three successive governments, all of them under families of kings (dynasties). Each of the three, called Silla, Koryŏ, and Chosŏn, achieved a new level of social, political, and economic development and brought "Korea" closer to what we see today. Many of Korea's institutions were adapted from examples observed in China. High officials called "ministers," who managed specialized functions of government such as finances and justice, assisted the king of Korea. In order to wield power, Korea's officials had to pass tests to prove their intelligence, education, and fitness to rule. Certain families contributed large numbers of these officials and thus became a kind of aristocracy. These aristocrats were known as the *yangban* class, and they were the richest and most respected (and sometimes feared) people in the country. People respect their descendants even today, and most Koreans consider their attributes—elite educations, property ownership, political power, and social prominence—the most important things to be pursued in modern life.

Korea has one of the highest levels of education in the world, with middle school children ranking first in the world in math and science. Elementary schooling is compulsory, and more than 90 percent of all Koreans can read. Many speak another language, whether English, Japanese, Chinese, or Russian. Korea has a relatively young population; 50 percent in both parts of the peninsula are younger than twenty-five. Koreans are also "homogeneous"; that is, they are of a single racial type, with few identifiable minorities. There are small Chinese communities in the biggest cities, but no Japanese and very few Americans or Europeans, though there are thousands of American soldiers who spend short periods in Korea as part of their military service. These, of course, are not counted in Korean population figures.

THE KOREAN PENINSULA

The Korean peninsula extends southward from the mainland, between China and Japan. The waters surrounding it moderate and determine its weather, which is hot and humid in the summer and cold and dry in winter, following the weather pattern known as the monsoon. The warmth and rains of summer make Korea an ideal place to grow rice, and irrigated paddy lands are visible everywhere in the country. In fact, because Korea is so mountainous and populous, it seems that every square inch of land is used for growing something. Tiny fields appear to crawl up the mountainsides, growing potatoes and leafy vegetables that do not require flat land. In addition, since the introduction of plastics, clear vinyl greenhouses have become a familiar feature of the landscape, sheltering fruits and vegetables from the wind and cold and lengthening the growing season. Plastic greenhouses are just one of the many dividends of economic modernization, bringing better food for everyone.

The sea has determined not only Korea's weather but much of its history as well. Korea's location on a peninsula has been an important factor in defense, isolating the population and protecting them from all but the most determined invaders. Except for the Japanese who invaded Korea in the 1590s, all Korea's enemies have attacked from the north across the Manchurian border. Nomadic peoples who are remembered for having invaded China often "rehearsed" their attacks by invading Korea first. Such were the Khitans in the 900s, the Jurchen in the 1100s, the Mongols in the 1200s, and the Manchus in the 1600s. Each invasion disrupted Korea's harmonious relationship with China and its other neighbors and provided a new chapter in Korea's history, reminding the Korean people of their vulnerability within the region. Though the encounters were painful and destructive, they helped shape Korean civilization by teaching the Koreans to depend on themselves. They also created a certain fatalism in the Koreans, a historic sense of suffering and endurance that more recently has helped them get through the hard times of the twentieth century.

The Korean peninsula is 85,300 square miles in size (220,847 km²) and roughly 600 miles long from the Manchurian border to the southern coast. The land border is 636 miles long (1,025 km), most of it with China but the last 11 miles of it at the eastern end, with Russia. The border follows two rivers, the westward-flowing Yalu and the east-flowing Tumen, both of which arise from springs on the slopes of Mount Paektu, the sacred peak that is part of the "Ever-white Mountains" on the northeastern border. Southward from this mountain mass juts the backbone of Korea, a range called the T'aebaek Mountains. This range runs the length of the Korean peninsula, dividing it into a sharply defined coastal area on the east and a series of broad valleys to the west.

Korea's spiny terrain has always hampered communication between different parts of the country and created more or less distinct regions within it. Until railroads, highways, air travel, and mass communications started breaking down the regional divisions of Korea in the twentieth century, the mountain barriers were a dominant feature of Korean civilization. However, at the same time, the existence of separate republics in North and South Korea has made it impossible to benefit from improved communications. This unhappy circumstance is the result of the Cold War in the twentieth century.

While it is true that the Korean people have lived as a single nation since the seventh century, the conditions and limits imposed upon them by their geographical situation have largely determined the course of their national life. The seas and the foreign peoples around Korea have served to isolate and confine the Koreans in their native land. And the mountains have channeled the population toward the south and southwest, making South Korea twice as populous as the North and requiring intense efforts at land cultivation and the production of food. The fact that the mountains become more rugged and the valleys less hospitable in the northern half of the country helps explain why, even today, North Korea cannot feed itself even though it has only one-third of the nation's population.

Instead, North Korea has other assets. Minerals abound in the mountains. Indeed, the first hint of Korea's existence in Western historical sources are Arab references to a storied kingdom of "Sila" somewhere east of China that was rich in gold. In the 1890s, European and American investors found veins of gold in the mountains of northern Korea and spent forty very profitable years digging it out. There is also copper, iron, lead, and one of the world's most concentrated supplies of tungsten, which is used for filaments in lightbulbs. North Korea's interest in nuclear energy is due in part to the fact that it has much uranium.

During the first half of the twentieth century when Japan ruled Korea as a colony, the government developed North Korea as an industrial area and South Korea as an agricultural region. The north got dams that produced electricity for the whole country. The south got roads and railroads that connected agricultural areas to the national market, helping feed the whole country. This regional interdependence magnified the disaster of national division after 1945, when the Communist-controlled north was cut off from the American-backed south, effectively separating the heavy industrial base from the breadbasket. It took many years for the south to rise above a survival-level existence, industrializing from scratch. And after more than fifty years North Korea still has not developed a healthy and balanced national economy.

GEOPOLITICS

Korea's position between China and Japan has been described by outsiders in terms of "geopolitics," the interplay of geography and politics. Looking at the map of Korea, they have described it variously as a "tiger" approaching Japan or as a "dagger" pointed at Japan. These images suggest that Korea is somehow a threat to Japan or useful to Japan's enemies. This was one reason behind Japan's takeover of Korea between 1905 and 1945. On the other hand, the threat sometimes went the other way, as when Japan used Korea as a route to get to China, when it invaded the mainland in the 1590s. Japan used Korea in similar fashion in the 1930s, when it turned its peninsular colony into a staging area for the invasion of China in World War II.

Korea's most unfortunate experience with geopolitics came after World War II, when the United States and the Soviet Union split the peninsula in half and installed rival governments in South and North Korea. This was done as part of the competition between the United States and the U.S.S.R. during the Cold War and it set the stage for a bloody civil war in 1950–53, a war that killed 2 million Koreans but failed to reunite the country. Half a century later, even after North and South Korea developed separate economic political systems and the south grew rich, and even after the United States and the Soviet Union ceased being enemies, the Korean people are still having to struggle with the consequences of their national division.

CHOSŎN: THE LAST GREAT KOREAN KINGDOM

Until the twentieth century, Korea was a self-sustaining kingdom with its own monarch, bureaucracy, public institutions, and social structure. The stability of Korea's system is suggested by the fact that the last dynasty of the monarchial period lasted an astonishing 518 years from 1392 to 1910. This stretch of time is known as the Chosŏn dynasty, using the ancient name that the Koreans themselves used to refer to their country at the time. The twenty-seven kings of the Chosŏn dynasty were all members of the Yi clan of Chŏnju, descendants of the dynasty's founder, Yi T'aejo (r. 1392–98). Because so much of Korea's modern consciousness is rooted in the patterns of the past, it is important to understand the framework of the dynasty and some of the basic ideas that regulated Korean life under the Yi family kings for more than half a millennium.

When King T'aejo founded the Chosŏn kingdom in 1392, he began by adapting many of the institutions of the preceding Koryŏ system. However, he also changed many things. One reason for the overthrow of Koryŏ and the founding of Chosŏn was the corruption in the Koryŏ court that came from favoritism toward wealthy landowners who used their riches to manipulate the royal government. The founders of the new government of Chosŏn seized the great estates, measured the land, and levied taxes on it to finance the state. They also distributed some of it as rewards to supporters of the new dynasty. The government of Chosŏn also began a campaign against Buddhist institutions, believing that the great temples and monasteries simply had too much power and had misled the people into spending their time and money seeking salvation from the Buddha instead of working, producing, and serving the greater good.

The new king was supported by officials who had passed the Chinese-style civil service examinations that were first held in Korea in 958. The content of the examinations stressed social responsibility based on the Confucian classics, and officials educated in this mode were steeped in a version of Confucian philosophy that set high moral standards for all aspects of life, including government. For hundreds of years, Confucianists had looked down on Buddhism as a tool for distracting the masses from the work at hand, which was building a society based on justice and propriety using humanity and conscience as guides instead of the spirits, or gods. Confucianists disliked the way Buddhist monks withdrew from society and lived in monasteries instead of providing examples of correct leadership and behavior. Monks did not marry or have children, for example, appearing to disrespect their parents by not carrying on their family lines. The Confucianists thought it wasteful for temples to use the hard-earned contributions of ordinary people to create luxurious displays, gilded images of Buddha, and expensive religious festivals. They were offended that some of the biggest Buddhist temples were so rich they had to train guards to protect their material assets. Thus, though some of the early Chosŏn reformers were actually Buddhists in their personal lives, they agreed that the organized Buddhist religion had to be suppressed, its temples confiscated, its monks and slaves "returned to their former occupations" (i.e., farming and taxpaying), and the remaining Buddhist clergy banished to a few temples in the mountains.

Another aspect of making Chosŏn a "neo-Confucian" state was rectifying its relationship with China. A new Chinese dynasty, the Ming, had arisen at approximately the same time in the aftermath of the Mongol collapse. In the 1390s the kingdom of Chosŏn sought a peaceful relationship with the Ming. King T'aejo sent tribute to the Ming emperor and promised to live peacefully, making no alliances with the emperor's enemies or doing anything that would seem improper for a "younger brother" country. The Koreans voluntarily assumed this subordinate position as a matter of Confucian propriety, and they were not ashamed to copy Ming laws, the Ming way of measuring days, months, and years, and even Ming clothing styles. These were signs of "serving the great," which Chosŏn regarded as the proper stance for a civilized but weaker kingdom hoping to survive on the fringe of the great Chinese empire. It was Korean policy to give China no reason to invade, or interfere, in Korean affairs. The best way to do this was to assure the Chinese that they would never be a threat or source of trouble. By giving the Chinese no reason to interfere in their internal affairs, the Koreans thus purchased their autonomy, or right to rule themselves. They were then free to continue building their own Korean culture to a very high level.

Another aspect of Chosŏn neo-Confucianism was the encouragement of learning. King Sejong, the most celebrated of Chosŏn's twenty-seven kings, who ruled from 1418 to 1450, is remembered as a scholar-king, a sponsor of important new studies in history, literature, astronomy, and philosophy. King Sejong's most important contribution was the invention of an alphabet for the Korean language, a system of writing that provided a phonetic symbol for every sound in the Korean language. The alphabet, known today as han'gŭl ("Korean writing") has nineteen consonants and ten vowels that are combined into clusters and pronounced as word syllables. The idea of writing syllables came from Chinese, but where Chinese syllable-words are expressed in symbols that are sometimes actually pictures of things, Korean syllables are simply maps of sounds, as in our own writing. To read Chinese one has to associate a visual symbol with a word. To read Korean one has to associate sound with a word. The difference is something like the two ways we write numbers: "2" or "two." The numeral "2" is a symbol that stands for a number. The word "two" is a sound that means the same thing.

The han'gŭl alphabet, of course, was invented not by the king himself but under his direction, by a group of advisors known as the "Hall of Worthies," or Chiphyŏnjŏn in Korean. Sejong was one of the best-educated Chosŏn kings, one who could hold his own with the most erudite scholars in his realm. He enjoyed bringing wise men together and challenging them to invent new things or engage in important scholarly projects. One of his scholars, Chŏng Inji, wrote a multivolume history of the entire Koryŏ dynasty entitled Koryŏ-sa. Others invented a clock, a rain gauge, new ways of calculating mathematics, and musical instruments. The most significant technological innovation was the invention of copper type that could be moved around in lines on a tray to print different things. The Koreans' supply of movable type was used to print eight different works between 1403 and 1484. King Sejong's proclamation of the han'gŭl alphabet, presented in an explanatory text entitled *The Correct Sounds for the Instruction of the People*

(*Hunminjŏng'ŭm* in Korean), was one of the works printed with movable copper type.

During the Koryŏ period it had become customary to refer to the wealthy ruling class as the *yangban* ("two branches") class, referring to the two types of officials, the civil and the military. To become a *yangban* a man had to be appointed to government office, and to be appointed he had to either pass the merit examination or be chosen as a special favor by the king or other high official. The civil "branch" was more important than the military, and by the early Chosŏn period, it was better to have passed the examinations than to have been appointed on some other grounds. Nevertheless, appointments-by-favor were common, especially for officials who had stood loyally beside the king during a crisis, or had helped him take the throne when there were several contenders. These loyal defenders were called "merit subjects," and they were richly rewarded by the kings they helped. There was considerable tension between the examination passers and the merit subjects, and they often argued and struggled for power and the king's attention.

King Sejong died in 1450 and his son King Munjong, a man who was in poor health, reigned only two years before passing away. Sejong's twelve-year-old grandson then was next in line, and he mounted the throne as King Tanjong. However, Sejong had had several sons, some of whom were still alive. One of them, Prince Suyang, resented the fact that the throne had passed into his brother's lineage and believed that he deserved a chance to rule in his dead brother's stead. Prince Suyang therefore had the young King Tanjong kidnapped and murdered, and then seized the throne for himself, reigning under the title of King Sejo. Many proper *yangban* officials were horrified that a king, however young and undeserving, had been murdered and they regarded Sejo as a wrongful king and a criminal in fact. Though Sejo arrested and punished many of his critics, the *yangban* disagreed about whether he was entitled to the throne. At issue was the question of whose descendants would succeed to the throne in future generations. At issue also were questions of loyalty and propriety: whether Sejo had proven himself disloyal to his own father by challenging the succession.

To Confucianists especially, these questions were important. The Chosŏn dynasty had begun when Yi Sŏnggye, a Koryŏ general, usurped the Koryŏ throne, grabbing power for himself. Now, just a little more than half a century later, the legitimacy of the ruling house was again in doubt because the king had taken power by violence instead of by legal means. This was one of several political and moral problems that weakened the Chosŏn monarchy and caused rifts within the *yangban* class. Groups of *yangban* joined one side or the other and fought each other bitterly, refusing to hire each other's younger members, purging members of the other side, and seeking revenge when the power changed hands. The kings, being at the center of many of the controversies, were unable to stop the quarreling, which worsened as more *yangban* passed the examinations and became eligible for appointment to only a limited number of jobs. Once again, as in the Koryŏ period, who a person was, or whether a person had a powerful patron, became more important than the moral qualifications that were desirable in wise and effective leaders.

The remarkable power of the *yangban* as a group reflects the corresponding weakness of Chosŏn kings. Kings started out seeking support, first from the emperor of China, who had to approve the accession of all new kings in Korea, and then from factions of the *yangban* who were needed to carry out the king's will in government. The *yangban* cliques perpetuated themselves through academies called *sŏwŏn*, where young scholars were trained to support their elders' ideas and political positions. A *sŏwŏn* graduate was expected to be a loyal follower of his mentor, who most likely had spent some time at the group's *sŏwŏn* teaching and telling stories about what had happened in Seoul. The mentor was regarded as a kind of godfather, and he protected his followers and maneuvered them into government jobs. Strong mentors with active *sŏwŏn* academies thus spread the contagion of factional fighting in the government.

The Chosŏn kingdom experienced its worst crisis, however, in the form of yet another foreign invasion. In 1592, after subjugating the feudal lords of Japan, the warlord Hideyoshi set out to create a great empire that included Korea and China. To reach China, Hideyoshi's armies had to land near Pusan in southeastern Korea and advance through Korea to the Chinese border. Korea was caught unprepared for the invasion and had to ask for assistance from the Ming court in Peking. Chinese armies intervened in Korea and stopped the Japanese advance, turning the peninsula into a battlefield. The Koreans themselves resisted, first with their own army, then with local militia units organized by local *yangban* and sometimes even by Buddhist monks, though they were most often defeated by the better-trained Japanese.

Along the southern coast, however, a Korean official named Yi Sunsin carried on a most effective naval campaign that sank many Japanese ships and disrupted the Japanese supply lines. Admiral Yi put copper canopies over the decks of his wooden boats to protect them from Japanese arrows and the burning projectiles that the Japanese used to set enemy boats on fire. Then, using oarsmen below decks, he maneuvered his boats close to the Japanese vessels and attacked them with great effectiveness. The copper canopies resembled the shells of turtles, so Admiral Yi's boats were called "turtle ships"

Hyangwŏn-jŏng Pavilion in the Chosŏn-era Kyŏngbok Palace, Seoul.

(*kŏbuksŏn* in Korean). Admiral Yi is remembered not only for his invention but also for his daring. He used his knowledge of the coastline to trick the Japanese into entering traps where they were more easily destroyed. At the end of the war, in 1598, Admiral Yi was killed in the middle of his greatest battle. He died a hero to the Koreans, and he is remembered as their finest example of military prowess and honest sacrifice. Today his tomb is a national shrine and his statue stands overlooking the main crossroads of downtown Seoul.

THE LATE CHOSŎN PERIOD

The war with Japan lasted from 1592 until 1598 and ended only after Hideyoshi died and his successors abandoned his plan to rule the mainland. Korea suffered greatly from the war. Many Koreans died in the fighting, and others were captured or kidnapped and taken to Japan. There was much vandalism and looting. Many of Korea's remaining Buddhist temples were ransacked and burned, their precious gold-leafed images and paintings being stolen not only by the Japanese enemy but also by the "friendly" Chinese. In Seoul itself, when the king and royal court fled the city just before it fell to the invading Japanese, Korean citizens reacting to being abandoned by their ruler attacked the central palace and set it ablaze. It is said that the fires that burned the palace's documents collection were set by Korean slaves who wanted to destroy the records that marked them as members of the country's lowest class.

The war in Korea coincided with the rise of a powerful new Manchurian state under a gifted leader named Nurhachi. Nurhachi and his sons unified the nomadic tribes formerly known as the Jurchen, organized them into fighting units, and made plans to conquer the fast-fading Ming dynasty in China. Before they did that, the Manchus, as they were called, subjugated the Koreans by invading the peninsula, first in 1627 and again in 1636, and forcing the king to swear loyalty to them. Then, with Korea under control, they found an opportunity to invade China and overthrow the Ming government in 1644.

Having to bow to the barbarian Manchus was a bitter defeat for the Koreans, but they had little choice. The Manchu invasions, together with the Japanese invasions of the 1590s, caused a serious disruption of Korean society and were a blow to the state of Chosŏn. Despite this, however, the Korean system proved resilient. Though the *yangban* as a class continued to dominate society, imposing the rigid system of values known as neo-Confucianism upon themselves and others, in the eighteenth century there were important innovations. The long and peaceful reigns of kings Yŏngjo (r. 1724–76) and Chŏngjo (r. 1776–1800) were a time of artistic and literary creativity. The Chinese-style landscape and portrait paintings that were prized by the *yangban* were supplemented by a new, commoner-style "genre" painting showing ordinary people engaged in daily life. These genre paintings today are some of the most descriptive documents about Korea in the 1700s.

The era also brought advances in literature written in *han'gŭl* script. This followed many years during which King Sejong's alphabet was little used. Korean writers, most of them *yangban*, had actually scorned the alphabet as too easy and too limiting, and they had continued to write in the much more difficult Chinese characters that were so hard for ordinary people to learn. It took many years and a great deal of money to learn to write Chinese well. Few people who were not *yangban*-class men could afford this kind of education. Accordingly, the few who could write Chinese were able to use literacy and their writing ability as a social barrier, protecting their privileged position while denying basic communications skills to the less fortunate.

In the eighteenth century, however, the educated women who belonged to the royal family, along with other cultured women of the *yangban* class, began to write their own literature, not in Chinese but in the Korean *han'gŭl* alphabet. Their works were diaries, memoirs, and stories about palace life, written in the Korean language and far more expressive of the emotions and conflicts that were so authentically part of daily life. Certain commoners also learned *han'gŭl* well enough to write stories and novels. These works survive as commentaries on the conditions and injustices of life in the *yangban*-dominated Chosŏn kingdom, and by the nineteenth century, *han'gŭl* had become a tool for non-*yangban* to communicate and even organize rebellions against their rulers.

Within the *yangban* class, too, there were spontaneous impulses to reform. The Chinese founder of neo-Confucianism, Chu Hsi (1130–1200), had taught that truth could be found through a better understanding of reality—"the investigation of things," as he called it. Certain Korean *yangban* were dissatisfied with the stuffy customs of their own class and they sought new ways of thinking about reality. They organized a school of thought all their own, called *Silhak* ("practical learning"), which became interested in Western scientific ideas that were being studied by the Chinese in Peking. These ideas had been brought to China by Jesuit missionaries, and they involved astronomy, mathematics, and other studies of the natural world as well as philosophy and the Christian religion. The "practical learning" scholars advocated realistic answers to the problems facing Korea, suggesting applications of Western science and technology. They also went far toward adopting the Jesuits' understanding of the spiritual dimension and even founded their own branch of the Catholic religion in Seoul, which turned out to be the beginnings of Korean Christianity.

THE "OPENING" OF KOREA

Korea remained isolated from the outside world through most of the nineteenth century, content to maintain its special relationship with China and to be left alone. There were outbreaks of dissatisfaction, however, in the form of peasant revolts. An uprising of unhappy miners in northwestern Korea nearly became a civil war, and in the 1860s a religious leader in the southwest founded the "Religion of the Heavenly Way" (Ch'ŏndokyo), recruited thousands of peasants, and briefly threatened central control over his region. There were attempts by British, French, and American naval vessels to pierce Korea's shell and open a dialogue, but these ended in failure. In 1876 the Japanese sent a warship that forced the Koreans to sign a treaty opening trade and diplomatic relations with Japan. Additional treaties followed in the 1880s, with the United States, Great Britain, Germany, Russia, and France, among others. Western missionaries, Protestants and Catholics, took up residence in Korea's main cities and towns, founding churches, starting schools, and building clinics and hospitals. A handful of brave Western investors put their money into Korean gold mines and railroad concessions.

By the turn of the twentieth century, several Western countries had established a small stake in Korea. Their interests, however, were small compared with those of Japan, which looked on Korea as a strategic territory that could not be allowed to fall into the hands of a potential enemy. In 1895 Japan won the Sino-Japanese War and forced the Chinese to renounce their historic tributary relationship with Korea. In 1905 Japan won the Russo-Japanese War and forced the Russians to declare an end to their interests in Korea. These Japanese victories, together with Korea's own military weakness and the lack of any outside power that was willing to step in and defend Korea, set the stage for Japan to assert a "protectorate" over Korea. In 1910 Japan completed the process of conquest and forced the Koreans to sign another treaty ceding their country to Japan as an outright possession. From that point forward until the end of World War II, Korea was a colony of Japan.

COLONIAL KOREA

Japan's reasons for taking Korea were not limited to national security. The Japanese believed their country to be overpopulated, and the mainland of Asia was one obvious place to send people and seek resources for their continuing economic modernization. Even as they took Korea, some Japanese planners had their eye on Manchuria and even dreamed of moving into China and eventually creating a Japanese-led empire of "Asia for Asians."

During their first decade as Korea's colonial overlords, the Japanese changed many things. They abolished the monarchy, bribed many of the *yangban* to win their support, rounded up and shot many former Korean soldiers who had become part of a resistance movement, and tried to intimidate everyone who did not accept or support their dominance. At the head of the colonial government was a governor-general, an army officer who was in effect the new king of Korea. He ruled as he saw fit, with little supervision from the Japanese government in Tokyo. He took a land survey that resulted in many Korean farmers having to sell their land, usually to Japanese who came over from the more crowded Japanese islands. To enforce his edicts he used a military police force known as the *kempeitai* and a system of courts that paid scant attention to human rights. Korea was reorganized to serve Japan, and the Koreans themselves were reduced to being low-paid workers in their own country.

In 1919, a coalition of religious leaders organized a peaceful protest against the harsh policies of the Japanese colonial government and demanded independence for Korea. The *kempeitai* and Japanese army cracked down on the protests and for nearly a year there were periodic clashes between the people and Japanese troops. The Independence Movement cost the lives of more than 7,000 Koreans, but it did bring about a softening of Japanese colonial policies. During the 1920s the colonial government was headed by a more humane governor-general who allowed Koreans to gather and speak and publish their own magazines and newspapers. He improved education and allowed Koreans to join religious and even political organizations. Koreans used this period to discuss how they should continue pushing for independence. Some argued that the Japanese were too strong to be defeated and would have to be accepted while Koreans tried to preserve their culture through studies of history and literature, and by educating young Koreans to work toward liberation. Others argued that the only way to get rid of the Japanese was to take weapons and fight. They worked to organize associations, whether legal or illegal, that empowered farmers, workers, and small bands of guerrillas who did the fighting. Both the "cultural nationalists," as they were called, and the advocates for armed struggle raised funds for their movements from abroad. The cultural nationalists were supported by overseas Koreans in China and the United States. The armed revolutionaries were supported by people in the Soviet Union and Communists in Manchuria and China.

During the 1930s, Japan itself abandoned democracy and an earlier commitment to peace and began to prepare for a war to promote its idea of an empire of "Asia for Asians." Korea became a base for this effort, a staging area for armed forces as they invaded, first, Manchuria, and then, in 1937, China itself. To support their war the Japanese mobilized the Korean people as laborers, taxpayers, and ultimately as soldiers. They transported many Koreans to Japan to work in mines and factories while Japanese workers were drafted for military service. Women also were put to work, mostly in factories. Some were sent abroad along with Japan's army to serve the troops in the field as cooks, laundresses, and some as "prostitutes" or "sex slaves." The Japanese called them "comfort women."

Part of the mobilization that the Japanese forced on the Koreans was meant to make them better subjects of Japanese emperor Hirohito. They were ordered to go to shrines and pay respects to the spirits of the war dead and Japan's national heroes. They were ordered to speak Japanese and stop speaking Korean. They were ordered to change their names and begin identifying themselves as Japanese and not Korean. The cultural nationalists who had been trying to keep Korean culture alive were arrested and forced to speak out in support of Japan's imperial plan. And during the war itself Koreans were forced to make great material sacrifices, enduring food rationing and contributing pots and pans and even their jewelry as the war gobbled up every bit of metal that could be located in the Japanese empire. When clothing wore out it simply was patched and patched again until the Koreans were wearing rags. When shoes wore out people made straw shoes or went barefoot.

DIVIDED KOREA

In August 1945, Japan surrendered to the victorious Allies and lost its empire on the Asian mainland. Korea was liberated, but the Allies decided to take charge of it, occupy it with troops, remove the Japanese, and preside over the creation of a new Korean government. This was to be done in two occupation zones, north and south, to be occupied by the Soviet Red Army and the United States Army, respectively. The border between the two zones was to be the 38th parallel of north latitude.

The United States proposed the 38th parallel as the boundary between north and south Korea as a temporary line. Along with the Soviet Union it intended to create a "trusteeship" in Korea, protecting and preparing the Koreans for self-government. The Americans and Russians who made these decisions in fact knew little about Korea and did not consider the fact that the Koreans already had governed themselves for many centuries. They simply assumed that they would need some supervision. The Americans also wanted to occupy southern Korea in order to block the advance of Soviet troops toward Japan, which was its main interest in the area.

For three years between 1945 and 1948, the U.S. Army ruled South Korea and the Soviet Red Army ruled the north. Under their rule, the Korean people dealt with the legacy of the Japanese colonial period as well as the postwar military occupation and the division of their country. There was considerable anger in Korea between people who had resisted the Japanese and been punished and others, who were called "collaborators," who had cooperated with the Japanese and had even prospered before liberation. The Koreans themselves set up "people's committees" all over the country and tried to knit them together into a national government. The United States and the Soviet Union established military occupation regimes that overrode the authority of the people's committees in the two zones and substituted Koreans of their own choosing as candidates for leadership. In the south, the U.S. military government supported Syngman Rhee, an American-educated Christian leader with a reputation for having resisted Japan in his youth but who had spent most of his adult life in the United States. In the north, the Soviets presented Kim Il-sung, an ethnic Korean who had fought the Japanese as a guerrilla and had spent the war years in the Soviet Red Army. However, since Kim Il-sung was a Communist, he was completely unacceptable to the Americans. And since Rhee was anti-Communist, he was unacceptable to the Soviet Union and the Korean Communists.

The Americans and Soviets had originally agreed to negotiate until they found a way to create a coalition government. The negotiations, however, stalled in 1946 and broke down completely in 1947 as neither side was willing to give in to the demands of the other. The United States therefore called upon the United Nations to engineer the reunification of Korea under one national government. This was a natural step for at least two reasons: the United Nations had been created specifically to handle problems like Korean reunification, and the United States had great influence with the UN and could probably work through the UN to get a settlement close to what it wanted. The Soviet Union and Kim Il-sung, on the other hand, saw the move as an attempt to impose an American-controlled settlement on Korea and refused to have anything to do with it. When the United Nations proposed a nationwide election, one in which the south would have twice as many voters as the north, the northern side rejected the plan. When the United Nations announced that it would go ahead with the election in the southern zone, even if it meant creating a government over only half of the country, the Russians and North Koreans denounced the Americans for trying to split Korea forever, and tried to disrupt the election. When the election took place anyway, a government was created for the Republic of Korea in the south, with Syngman Rhee as president. The United States and most members of the United Nations recognized the ROK, which was American-supported and friendly to capitalism, as the Korean people's only legitimate government. The northern side meanwhile created an alternative Democratic People's Republic of Korea with its government in the ancient city of P'yŏngyang. The DPRK was oriented toward Communism, maintained close ties with the Soviet Union and the socialist countries, and was led by the Korean Workers' Party under Kim Il-sung.

As the pro-capitalist and pro-Communist parts of Korea drew apart, people crossed the line to live in the side they preferred. In North Korea, many kinds of people were made to feel threatened, including former Japanese collaborators, wealthy landlords and business people, and Christians, who were organized in opposition to the Kim Il-sung government. These people carried what they could and crossed over into southern Korea, often leaving property and family members behind. They were very angry with the Kim Il-sung government and hoped for its early demise. Their politics in the south were passionately anti-Communist and they were intolerant of anyone who thought good of Kim Il-sung and his Communist backers in China and the Soviet Union.

Kim Il-sung, for his part, continued to fight the splitting-off of South Korea as a separate country under American sponsorship. He sent armed agents into the south to try to disrupt the 1948 election. When that failed, Communist elements in the south revolted and had to be crushed with military force. The Americans donated their weapons and equipment to the brand-new South Korean army and pulled out, hoping that the South Koreans could sustain themselves. Kim Il-sung meanwhile lost many skirmishes with the southerners and by the end of 1949 had only one choice left: a full-scale military invasion of South Korea in hopes of a quick reunification.

Kim ordered his armies into action across the line on June 25, 1950. This invasion began the Korean War, a three-year episode that cost more than 3 million human lives including more than 2 million Koreans, 900,000 Chinese, 54,000 Americans, and several thousand from the various countries that joined under the United Nations flag to punish the North Koreans for attacking their "neighbor." North Korea drew support from the Soviet Union, which supplied tanks, airplanes, petroleum, weapons, and ammunition, and it was saved from complete destruction in the autumn of 1950 by the intervention of hundreds of thousands of army "volunteers" from the People's Republic of China.

Kim's invasion succeeded for a few weeks, though it failed to capture all of South Korea. The Americans, meanwhile, organized a counterattack that succeeded in wiping out most of the North Korean Army and enabled them to occupy much of North Korea by November. It was at this point that the Chinese entered the war, not wanting to see the destruction of a neighboring Communist country, feeling that they owed a debt to the Korean Communists who had helped them win their own civil war in the 1940s, and fearing that the Americans would invade them next. The Chinese intervention changed the direction of the war again, forcing the Americans, South Koreans, and United Nations halfway down the Korean peninsula more or less to the 38th parallel, where the war settled down to a two-year stalemate. It ended with a truce on July 27, 1953.

When the dust settled and the dead had been mourned and buried, Korea remained as before, divided along a line that lay fairly close to the original 38th parallel. Along it ran a four-kilometer-wide strip called the "Demilitarized Zone" (DMZ), signifying the separation of the two warring armies.

The two sides had promised to refrain from provocative actions, but almost immediately they commenced harassments that have continued in both directions until this day. Meanwhile at a special "truce village" called P'anmunjŏm, in the DMZ, the two sides have traded accusations and occasionally tried to make progress toward reunification, for nearly fifty years without result. As long as the Cold War continued, China and the Soviet Union backed Kim Il-sung's North Korea while the United States backed South Korea under a succession of presidents and generals.

THE SOUTH KOREAN "ECONOMIC MIRACLE"

In 1961, elements of the South Korean army seized power in a coup d'état. The coup leader, General Park Chung-hee, vowed to lead South Korea out of the poverty and suffering that had plagued the people since the war. Promising to turn South Korea into a dynamic modern country, he cracked down on corruption and exhorted his people to work hard and save for the future. He and his army cohorts founded a political party and ran in civilian elections, reorganized the government, and tackled the difficult job of getting the economy moving. Park created a central Economic Planning Board (EPB) and used his power to open doors to foreign money, borrowing capital and negotiating for aid from the United States and Japan. Beginning with this, the EPB mapped out a series of five-year plans that set ambitious targets for production. Using the slogan "Production, Exports, Construction!" the government made the Korean economy produce goods that could be sold abroad, earning foreign exchange that could be used to buy imported raw materials, machines, and advanced equipment for further production. The Park government also sent Korean workers abroad to Europe and the Middle East to earn money in places where labor was scarce. In the 1960s Korean troops also fought in Vietnam, their expenses being paid by the United States. These multiple sources of revenue from outside Korea "primed the pump" of the Korean economy and made it possible to exceed the Five Year Plan targets time after time.

The government also stressed rural development through a program called the "New Community Movement." Aimed at increasing agricultural productivity and raising the standard of living in the countryside, the New Community Movement made credit available to farmers, supplied them with seed, fertilizers, and pesticides, installed electricity and safe water, promoted public health, paved roads, built schools, and improved transportation and communications. These improvements, together with the trend toward urbanization, dramatically increased per capita production in the provinces and narrowed the gap in living standards between Koreans who lived in the cities and rural villages.

The enormous sacrifices required to accomplish these things were not evenly distributed despite the government's best efforts. Many Koreans suffered under brutal working conditions. The rate of injuries and accidents among those who did "3-D" kinds of work (difficult, dirty, and dangerous), workers such as miners and those who worked in urban sweatshops, was very high. One type of worker was especially exploited: the teenage girls fresh from middle school whose good health and quick reflexes made them excellent factory hands. These girls normally worked long hours for low pay and often were expected to send their wages home to their families, sometimes to finance their brothers' educations, until they quit work to get married. Korean workers were discouraged from organizing unions or engaging in any kind of collective bargaining. Indeed, their low wages were a key to South Korea's economic progress.

On the other hand, the Park government tried to engineer the success of Korea's biggest companies by having government-controlled banks make them government-guaranteed loans. These companies quickly became conglomerates called *chaebŏl*, which were made up of families of companies. The Hyundai *chaebŏl*, for example, included automobile, construction, shipbuilding, and retailing components. Samsung, which started out in textiles, developed an electronics manufacturing specialty that became known around the world, first for televisions and microwave ovens, and then for semiconductors and other high-tech computer components. Demand for Korean products overseas helped free Korea from foreign aid and then enriched the *chaebŏl*, enabling them to buy up smaller companies and grow big enough to control a significant part of the national economy.

When workers saw the wealth that was accumulating in the *chaebŏl* they demanded higher wages. The Park government, however, resisted any loosening of control over the workforce. It argued that worker unrest was a threat to national security that would destabilize the country and invite intervention by Communist North Korea. Park used the national security argument to make himself a virtual dictator by 1974, ruling by decree and outlawing all criticism of himself or his style. In 1979, in the middle of a wave of worker unrest, he was assassinated by one of his own deputies. There followed a brief period of democratic reform before another army general, Chun Doohwan, seized power for himself. When civilians marched in the streets to protest Chun's coup, he ordered army units to attack them. After a massacre in May 1980 that killed hundreds of protesters in the city of Kwangju, the Korean people glumly allowed him to postpone democratization.

South Korea endured Chun Doo-hwan's dictatorship from 1980 until 1988. Meanwhile, the people continued to work hard, the *chaebŏl* continued to grow, Korean products were sold all over the world, and the standard of living rose dramatically. Koreans were also proud to have Seoul chosen to host the 1988 Summer Olympic Games. Much of their energy was channeled into making the games a kind of "coming-out party" for Korea. In 1988 the world saw the games hosted in a city that had completely recovered from the war and was serving as the heart of a thriving modern country.

A year before the Olympics, however, mass demonstrations and demands from people in every walk of life forced the outgoing Chun Doo-hwan to allow a basic change in the national constitution that opened the way for unprecedented freedom. Instead of being chosen by a government-controlled electoral college, the next president would be chosen by popular vote. Among the other democratic changes, perhaps the most important was the easing of restrictions on the press. The result was a more responsive and responsible political system. And while a former army general won the 1987 presidential election, in the 1992 and 1997 elections the winners were leaders of the opposition who were famous for standing up to Park and Chun in the struggle for democracy during the long dark years of military rule. The election of Kim Dae-jung as president in 1997 was especially significant. Kim Dae-jung had been a nemesis to the military leaders who had preceded him. He had opposed Park Chung-hee in two elections, nearly winning one. Park had imprisoned him and Park's police had tried to kill him more than once. Chun had him sentenced to death in 1980, and it took an international outcry to get the sentence lifted.

After years as an outsider, Kim Dae-jung triumphed in the 1997 election only to be faced with the most serious economic crisis in South Korea since the Korean War. He had spoken for many years about the need for "economic democracy" in his country and had criticized the cozy symbiosis that had existed between big business and previous governments. This marriage of government and big business had led to "crony capitalism" and a series of bad economic decisions which precipitated a crash in the autumn of 1997. Just days before Kim's election, Koreans were obliged to watch in humiliation as the outgoing government sought billions of dollars of bailout funds from the International Monetary Fund (IMF) to cover the bad debts that had financed some of the cozy dealings of Korea's biggest companies. In return for the bailout, the IMF had demanded control of certain elements of the

Korean economy such as banking. When he took office in early 1998, President Kim Dae-jung was forced to begin his presidency by asking the people to accept painful levels of unemployment, the closure of badly run banks and businesses, and a sell-off of ill-conceived ventures by the big Korean conglomerates such as Hyundai and Samsung. The strong medicine took effect within a year of the crash, and by mid-1999 the Korean economy was well along on the road to recovery. Though many Korean workers had not yet found jobs, the signs pointed to a better-run Korean economy in the next century, and there was plenty of reason to hope that the country would return to its former level of prosperity. President Kim Dae-jung deserved part of the credit for this, but once again it was the Korean people themselves who proved it had the discipline to meet the crisis with their own hard work and determination.

NORTH KOREA'S POSTWAR EXPERIENCE

North Korea's leader Kim Il-sung blundered when he decided to invade South Korea in 1950. He did not expect the United States to again come to South Korea's defense, but he was mistaken. Kim should have realized that the recent triumph of the Chinese Communists under Mao Zedong and the continuing need to defend Japan from Communist influence would have left the Democratic administration of President Harry Truman no choice but to intervene with American forces if North Korea invaded the South. By the end of 1950 Kim's plan had proven to be such a disaster that the Chinese Communists had to enter the war to rescue the DPRK from oblivion. After the Chinese intervention, the war settled down for two and a half years of bitter fighting that ended only on July 27, 1953, with the truce that created the Demilitarized Zone.

By the end of the war the North Koreans, though still tough and determined, were completely unable to provide for themselves. Aid from other Communist countries helped the North Koreans regain their balance. The Soviet Union and China played the biggest role in North Korea's recovery. Other countries also helped. East Germany, for example, raised funds and sent supply trains to help one city in particular, the port of Hŭngnam, which had been blown up by the Americans during their retreat in December 1950. Today the German plan for the rebuilt city of Hŭngnam is still visible in the way the streets and many major buildings are constructed. Like South Korea, which received massive aid from the United States and United Nations as well as private groups in the West, North Korea was fortunate to have many outside friends who helped it recover from the war.

After the Korean War disaster, Kim Il-sung moved to protect his reputation and authority by purging other North Korean leaders who criticized him. Seeking to remain neutral in the developing theoretical argument between the Soviet Union and China, Kim invented a philosophy called *Juch'e*, meaning "self-reliance," to indicate his country's determination not to be drawn into the Sino-Soviet dispute. Seeking to walk a fine line between them, he insisted that North Korea could do everything it needed to do on its own, without relying on foreigners. Of course this had not been true in the past. Foreign aid had been essential during and after the war. But Kim meant that from the 1960s on his people would make what they needed, themselves. The *Juch'e* idea became an important national goal, and people were encouraged to work harder to throw off the need to depend on outsiders, however friendly they might be.

Until the economic slump of the 1990s, the *Juch'e* ideal was a weapon in North Korea's propaganda war with the South. The South was portrayed as dependent on America, a puppet government that exploited its people and organized the southern economy to provide cheap goods to rich Americans while depriving its people of a decent life. This was a caricature, of course, but it stung the South. Many South Koreans took the accusation to heart. University students in particular seemed to admire Kim Il-sung's patriotic determination to make North Korea an independent country reliant on no one.

It has been said that the story of North Korea is the story of its leader, Kim Il-sung. This is because Kim used his own personality as a rallying point for the demoralized North Korean people, inspiring them to Herculean labors in the effort to rebuild their country. By the early 1970s, the North Korean economy was humming, with heavy industry and agriculture leading the way. North Korean products were bartered to China and the Soviet Union in return for oil and other strategic commodities the North Koreans lacked. Its per capita income was higher than in the south, and in Cold War terms it seemed that the socialist/Communist part of Korea had outdone the capitalist/democratic part of Korea.

However, the pattern of economic development in North Korea was different from that in the south. Using guidance from the Soviet Union, the North Koreans emphasized heavy industry and agricultural development and neglected consumer production. The North Korean emphasis on heavy industry did not raise the standard of living of ordinary people as quickly as it rose in the south. The reason is that ordinary workers did not buy locomotives, steel, and railroad track. In the south, the factories made products for export but they also made products that ordinary people could use, from clothing and cosmetics to televisions and automobiles. The two economies were structured differently, and dramatically different experiences occurred in each.

North Korea's biggest economic problem had always been its lack of farmland and the part of Korea lying north of the 38th parallel has always depended on imports from abroad or from the south, which was now cut off by the border, to feed its population. The idea of *Juch'e* self-sufficiency in agriculture was attractive to North Korea's leadership but ultimately it proved impossible to achieve. Instead, North Korea supported itself by bartering raw materials to other Communist countries, using exports of metals, timber, and coal to pay for food and oil, and by selling heavy manufactures such as railroad equipment and military hardware in foreign markets. This worked for as long as there was a community of nations willing to barter with North Korea. However, when Communism fell in Europe in the early 1990s the former socialist countries stopped making special arrangements to benefit the North Koreans. The former Soviet Union demanded money in exchange for the vital oil resources it had been sending. China did likewise. Meanwhile, the West continued its long-standing trade embargo against North Korea, refusing to extend credit or needed materials to help it develop its economy. The result is that North Korea experienced an energy shortage followed by a shortage of everything that required energy. The economy began to contract. The existing rationing system turned into a government demand to cut daily meals from three to two, and the country's dream of *Juch'e* self-support collapsed into a nightmare of shortages and even starvation.

The North Korean people, by all accounts, are a hardworking and loyal population whose patriotism is a significant part of the story of their country's survival. They revere the memory of their leader Kim Il-sung, who died in 1994, and they respect his son, Kim Jong-il, who succeeded him. However, Kim Il-sung allowed the people's respect for him to develop into a remarkable personality cult. Statues of Kim Il-sung, some of them fifty and sixty feet high, were erected all over the country during his lifetime. The people were told to wear Kim Il-sung buttons on their clothes to indicate their loyalty. Kim paid visits to factories and farms and gave "on-the-spot-guidance" when it is doubtful that he knew much about the technical work he was advising. Kim held the position of president, head of North Korea's Communist Party, and head of the armed forces. The top university was named for him, as were many other institutions. History was rewritten to say that Kim had liberated Korea from Japan in 1945. His family members assumed top positions. His son became known as the "party center" of the ruling party, and the "Dear Leader," while Kim Il-sung was referred to as the "Great Leader."

As a result, by the early 1990s, North Korea was the "country of Kim" rather than a real socialist state. When he announced that his son, Kim Jong-il, would succeed him, many dismissed North Korea as a weird Communist monarchy. As explained in Chapter 2, however, this easy dismissal of North Koreans as fanatical followers of Kim was too simple. In fact, Kim Jong-il was someone to be taken seriously, an experienced party operative with a considerable following and track record within his own country. His father groomed him for leadership, and the transition after Kim Il-sung's death in 1994 went much more smoothly than Western observers expected. Clearly, the "Kim dynasty" enjoyed deep and wide public support. While the rest of the world seemed mystified by events and trends in North Korea, the north demonstrated surprising resilience as a system. Kim Jong-il spent more than three years mourning his father and with proper attention to the Confucian ethic of filial piety (see Chapters 2 and 5), he refused appointment to his father's official positions. Meanwhile, despite the cruel shortages of food and energy that plagued the daily life of the Korean people, Kim Jong-il and his supporters consolidated their power. In 1998, after showing due reluctance, the younger Kim accepted his father's title of Great Leader and became General Secretary of the ruling political party. However, he left the post of president vacant in memory of his father as if to suggest that the late President Kim continues to occupy the position in spirit.

THE PROBLEM OF REUNIFICATION

Since the end of the Korean War, the problem of reunification has been uppermost on the Korean agenda. The opposing systems in North and South Korea are incompatible, however, and reunification almost certainly would mean destruction of one in favor of the other. The North Koreans attempted reunification by force and it failed, in the Korean War. Since then, diplomacy and the well-meaning efforts of foreign governments to mediate the disputes between North and South have resulted in very little. The two halves of Korea remain divided, mutually antagonistic, and heavily armed for a possible renewal of the war.

The two Koreas have made many proposals over the years for reunification. Most of these have been put in terms that are really meant to force the other side to say no, so the proposing side can blame the other side for blocking reunification. But there has been progress. South Koreans are helping North Korea with its energy supply and South Korean companies are eagerly exploring ways to invest in the North. North Korea, however, continues to consider the South Korean government as illegitimate and a mere puppet of the United States. The North wants a peace treaty with the United States, and to deal with America on an "equal" basis. The United States and South Korea want the issues resolved in talks between the two Korean sides, without any foreign powers. Failing that, they want China and the United States to sit with the North and South Koreans while the Koreans work it out among themselves. The issues are complicated and progress is frustratingly slow. Year by year, however, it seems that contacts and shared interests between the two Koreas are on the rise, and there continues to be hope that as the war recedes into history the Korean people can find their way to a reconciliation.

2

Thought and Religion

KOREA IS A COUNTRY of many religions and belief systems that fall into three main categories: "established," "newly rising," and "popular." "Established" religions include Buddhism, Confucianism, and Christianity. "Newly rising" religions include the Unification Church and several other sects that are derived from Christianity, as well as variants of Buddhism and the unique Korean Religion of the Heavenly Way (Ch'ŏndokyo). "Popular" religions include shamanism, which is the latter-day manifestation of the ancient spirit worship that has been part of Korean life since the dawn of civilization.

Additional belief systems derive from Chinese popular religions such as the cult of Guanyu, the God of War, and popular sects of Daoism. A commonly found vestige of Korean popular religions is the pair of carved posts, resembling totem poles, that are often found at entrances to parks and villages, one reading "Great General of All Under Heaven," and the other reading "Great Female General of the Underworld." Though the poles are now mere decorations, they refer to a tradition of guardian gods that were stationed to defend the premises from evil spirits.

In North Korea today, the state officially discourages the practice of religion, regarding it as unscientific, superstitious, and a vestige of the feudal past. A certain number of North Korean citizens continue to practice Buddhism, Protestant and Catholic Christianity, and the Korean religion called Ch'ŏndokyo, but they have to belong to state-sponsored religious organizations that are closely monitored by the government. Religious practice outside the bounds of these organizations is regarded as subversive and the practitioners run serious risks. It is also much harder for an avowed religious believer to advance in North Korean society, since careers are generally open only to those who support the regime and, in many cases, those who are active members of the ruling Korean Workers Party. Any discussion of religion in Korea today therefore must be confined almost entirely to South Korea, where religious belief and practice flourish and a wide variety of denominations, sects, and cults have developed without significant government control.

Religious statistics in South Korea are inexact but most observers agree that approximately 25 percent of the population is Christian, another 25 percent are Buddhist, perhaps 2 percent identify themselves as Confucianist, and another 2 or 3 percent belong to one or another of the Korean newly rising religions. However, while many Koreans feel compelled to pick one or another label when they are surveyed, in fact many do not belong to any single tradition but think of themselves as belonging to several at once, being comfortable with a mix of symbols and rituals that would seem incompatible to a Westerner. For example, most Koreans in their family lives are highly influenced by Confucianism—reverence for ancestors, respect for elders, and a consciousness of the mutual duties and obligations to relatives. Some may also feel deep affinity for the beauty and serenity of Buddhist temples and worship and may even visit Buddhist temples to pray. Korean Christians, having joined a religious tradition that is less tolerant of other faiths, might shun Buddhism but they are much less likely even to be aware that they are guided throughout their lives by Confucian rules and understandings. But there are also Christians who have thought a lot about the mixture of Western religion and their own identity and conclude that their beliefs contain elements of shamanism, Confucianism, Buddhism, and Christianity all at the same time. In fact, there is a vibrant discussion in Korea concerning this very thing: the "Koreanization" of Christianity.

KOREAN IDEALS AND VALUES: THE CONFUCIAN TRADITION

Confucianism is a value system that seeks to bring harmony to the lives of people in communities—the family, the village, and the state. As such, it is arguably not a religion at all but rather a type of humanism aimed at social ethics rather than spiritual issues such as life after death. However, it is more than a mere set of rules for daily living. It also recognizes behavioral norms and morals and distinctions between right and wrong, and associates these norms with a transcendental moral order in a way that approaches the religious. Confucianism also places great stress on the continuity of the family and the connections between ancestors and descendants, so that the living are connected to their forbears through what has sometimes been called "ancestor worship." This too has tended to make Confucianism seem like a religion.

Confucius (551–479 B.C.) lived in the Chinese feudal state of Lu during a time of incessant warfare among the small kingdoms and estates that had not yet been unified into the centralized empire we call "China." For Confucius and the thinkers of his time, society's main problem was the violence and the counterviolence that always seemed to follow as those who had been defeated came back in search of revenge. The people who suffered most were the innocent farmers and simple people who were robbed, killed, and carried away as slaves in these endless rounds of warfare. Like many other thinkers of his time, Confucius was troubled by this pattern and wondered how it could be stopped. Confucius' ideas on this subject constituted much of what he taught his students in lessons that are recorded in a book of his dialogues entitled *The Analects of Confucius*.

Confucius, whose name is a Latin form of the way he was known in Chinese, which was "Gong Fuzi," literally "Master Gong," taught that people are *not* created equal and do not become equal throughout their lives. Rather, when they are born they are weak and need parents. When they are in school they are bigger or smaller or older or younger by age than other students. When they marry, wives are subordinate. With friends they have mutual duties and obligations. And as citizens they are subject to the authority of the government, king, or emperor. Throughout a person's life, he or she is always defined in relation to everyone else. As time passes, the relationships change. Sometimes they even reverse, as in the case of grown-up children who end up taking care of their aged parents. But there always is an element of reciprocity—a set of mutual obligations. Parents protect and teach their children and children should learn and obey their elders. Older siblings should set good examples for younger children and younger children should follow. Friends should be able to depend on each other throughout life. Husbands should love and provide for their wives and wives should love and obey their husbands. And everyone should obey the king who protects the people and provides for them. These paradigms are often referred to as the Confucian "five relationships": ruler/subject, father/son, older/younger, husband/wife, and friend/friend. In all of them but one—the relationship between friend and friend, assuming the friends are of exactly the same age, gender, and social rank—the relationships are *un*equal and require that the weaker party voluntarily submit to the stronger while the stronger exercises nurture and protection over the weaker.

Confucius taught that if individuals would be conscious of their own place in society and the nature of their relationships with others, all need for violence would vanish. People would accept what they have and not attack each other or steal. Rulers would be generous and just and there would be no need to rebel. The strong would lead by moral example and others would gladly follow them out of respect. Thus harmony would prevail whether on a societal level, as in the state, or on a familial level, in the home.

In seeking to harmonize the relationships among people, Confucianism lays a heavy burden on individuals. First of all, an individual's selfish desires are not as important as what is good for the group as a whole. A person is expected to think first about what the group or family or community needs, and if his or her own needs conflict with what is good for the group, the group comes first. Second, Confucianism teaches children that they owe an unpayable debt to their parents. In Korea, the debt is called *ŭnhye*, meaning "grace," referring to the gracious bestowal of life and nurture by parents. As an old proverb puts it, "Your debt to your parents is deeper than the ocean and higher than the mountains." This *ŭnhye* exists before the child is even aware of it, when the parents clothe and feed and nurse and teach the infant who otherwise would die without their help, and the child can never escape it.

Confucianism is a very old way of thinking but it is seen everywhere in China, Japan, Korea, and other societies that have been influenced over the years by Chinese ways of thought. In today's Korea, for example, children learn before the age of ten that their lives are not their own but belong to their families. It is very unusual for a young Korean to make an important choice alone, without taking into account what his parents and other important family members think he should do. Questions of what to study, where to go to college, and, above all, whom to marry, are all decisions that are made with the advice of parents. This is because education and marriage are family issues, affecting the young person's ability to earn and provide for aged parents and the next generation of the family lineage. The young person *owes* it to ancestors and parents not to make decisions selfishly or without taking their wishes into account.

No Confucian family ritual is more significant than the annual *chesa* or ceremony honoring the spirits of the most recently departed ancestors. When a grandfather dies, for example, his gravesite is chosen with great care, using ancient principles of geomancy and fortune-telling that take into account the hour of the man's birth and death, the signs of the zodiac, and the contours of the land around his fields. When the spot has been determined, a funeral is staged that allows friends and family to come together to express their grief publicly. A year after the funeral, the family gathers again for the ritual of the *chesa*—to remember the grandfather and to hold a feast, including a symbolic offering of food to the departed spirit. Someone may address the spirit in an attitude like prayer, the act that makes the *chesa* seem like ancestor worship to Westerners, even though it is more properly understood as a ceremony honoring the *memory* of an ancestor. The real purpose of the *chesa* ceremony is to remind everyone of the continuity of the family and of the debt that is still owed by younger generations to those who went before.

Another sign of Confucianism's influence in modern Korean life is the bonding that goes on between schoolmates, and in school between teachers and students. Powerful loyalties bind classmates to each other, ties that remain in effect all through life. This means that fellow alumni help each other find jobs after graduation, encourage and help each other's children much like godparents, give each other advice, and help each other when there is trouble. Another kind of school tie is the lifelong relationship between students and their teachers, beginning with the extreme respect shown teachers in the classroom and continuing after graduation, as younger people continue to revere those who taught them, asking their advice and making sure they are properly honored as they grow older.

A variation on the theme of loyalty in school is loyalty in an organization during a person's career. A bank trainee, for example, is taken in hand by a mentor and taught the business, and this relationship turns into a variant of the "older brother/younger brother" tie. A carpenter's apprentice, perhaps a boy without parents or education, is taught how to work with wood, and he becomes, in effect, the carpenter's son. The carpenter/teacher may actually take responsibility for finding the apprentice a wife from among his acquaintances' families. The obligation for a young worker to live up to the standards set by an employer is a serious one, and it often brings forth levels of commitment and productivity that amaze people in other countries. The loyalty of workers to their companies, their willingness to put in long hours, and their sacrificial teamwork all add up to what is sometimes called the "Confucian ethic," a kind of secret weapon that has enabled South Korea, along with Singapore, Hong Kong, and Taiwan (the four "minidragons") to outproduce much wealthier societies and compete for top ranking in the list of world trading powers. Confucianism is even visible in hard times, as in 1997–98 when several of the "minidragons" suffered economic reverses. People took their inability to pay debts, or the economic miscalculations of their leaders, or the exposure of corruption in their systems, as collective problems or a kind of group shame, and they vowed together to work even harder to make up the lost ground.

In all these cases, the key component is a mutual caring and responsibility,

Government officials in traditional court costumes at the annual ceremony honoring Confucius, in Seoul.

or, looking at it another way, submission and authority, learning and teaching, submitting and protecting. And, as any Westerner would note, a feature of the entire system is the limits that it places on the individual's freedom of action and rights to make decisions for oneself. Only when older and in a position of responsibility does a person acquire authority, only to find that the authority is limited by the responsibility to provide care and nurture for those who are younger and weaker.

Leadership is an important part of social organization, and traditional Confucianism has always taught that leaders should be chosen for their moral qualities as well as for their ambition and ability to lead. Since the inequalities between people are facts of life, there are naturally some who are more fit to lead than others. One of the Confucian texts puts it this way: "Some men are born to labor with their hands; others are born to labor with their minds."

Finding good leaders is a key task for any society. In Confucian societies such as China and Korea, education was a prime qualification for leadership. This education was acquired at great effort and expense in village schools and in district schools under the stern discipline of learned teachers. In China, and also for almost a thousand years in Korea, the government staged examinations for students to test their mastery of the ideals they had studied in the Confucian classics. For most of the Chosŏn dynasty (1392–1910) there were lower examinations in the Confucian classics and in Chinese literary arts, the latter leading to a coveted *chinsa* ("presented scholar") degree. Passers of the lower examinations next engaged in higher studies and took preliminary higher examinations in their respective provinces and then a capital examination in Seoul, at the end of which the top qualifiers were immediately appointed to government posts. The various civil examinations (*munkwa*) were held every three years and on additional occasions as needed. There were also military (*mukwa*) examinations.

Passing the examinations, even at the lower or preliminary levels, was the chief qualification for membership in the aristocratic ruling class called the *yangban*. Any successful examination candidate was regarded with awe by family members and neighbors and enjoyed great social status, even if he did nothing more than reside in the ancestral village and teach in the local school, using his tuition income to buy land and maintain his family in comfort. Competitors for advancement in the higher levels of the examination system were objects of even more pride and celebration, with their *yangban* status rubbing off on relatives. Thus it was in everyone's interest to invest in education and success in the examinations. At the pinnacle of the system, official appointees were put into positions where they enjoyed substantial incomes from fees and gifts as well as their salaries, income that they typically reinvested in more land, increasing the basis of their family's wealth.

The examination system was based on the Confucian idea that a society's most moral people should be its leaders, and that moral knowledge was best acquired through a study of philosophy, history, and literature. Becoming saturated with moral messages from the past was the best preparation for an uncertain future in which no one knew what would happen or what decisions would be required—except that in all things, the leaders would need to base their actions and decisions on sound moral judgment. The Confucian tradition had a name for this ideal kind of leader: the "princely man," one who was truly worthy to be respected and followed by others. Today, there remains a great reverence for highly educated people in Korea, even though their educations may be in such modern (and un-Confucian) fields as English literature, political science, medicine, and engineering. The idea that education connotes moral knowledge and the right to be respected and followed by others is deeply rooted in the Korean value system.

These are ideals, of course—the way Confucianism is *meant* to operate as the ethical core. It must be added that, human nature being what it is, there are abuses. In fact, the abuses are quite common. However, the consensus among Koreans and others who adhere to Confucian norms is so universally understood that the abuses stand out as violations all the more clearly. For example, in modern times not all leaders have been moral people. In South Korea, leaders and presidents are supposed to be elected after submitting themselves for popular approval through the vote. When this pattern is abused or broken, the leader loses legitimacy and is not regarded as a proper ruler. An example is the way General Chun Doo-hwan seized power in 1979–80 in South Korea. He used units of the army to overthrow his own commanding officer and then, when the people marched in the streets to object to his tactics, he cracked down with military force on civilians, killing several hundred. Though people were terrorized into accepting him as president later in the year, he was never regarded as "legitimate" even though his government accomplished many positive things during his time in office. He remained in power only through his overwhelming military power—power wielded by other army officers who were loyal to him in a Confucian style, as "younger brothers"—all of whom, in the end, were swept out of power in a wave of public rage. General Chun was actually sentenced to death for his actions—though he was later pardoned to spare the country the agony of seeing an ex-president put to death.

Confucianism, therefore, is a living system of values in Korea, and whether or not it is a "religion" is less important than the fact that Koreans understand its precepts as a guide for their own lives. Indeed, it fits well with other religions. Christian churches, for example, are run very much according to Confucian rules governing mutual expectations and obligations among members, and between members and their religious leaders.

KOREAN RELIGIOUS IDEALS: THE BUDDHIST TRADITION

Buddhism began in India around 500 B.C. with the life of a prince named Siddhartha. Siddhartha was raised in luxurious surroundings and his parents meant for him to become a great ruler. However, as a young man he began to wonder about the meaning of life and embarked on a quest to discover why there was so much pain and suffering in the world. During his quest he separated himself from family and friends and tried solitude. He renounced material possessions and tried poverty. He even renounced health and tried to discipline his body in search of enlightenment through pain.

Siddhartha became a Buddha ("Enlightened One") in a flash of insight one day while meditating. He immediately gathered his disciples and began to teach them what he had learned. The core of his teaching came to be known as the "Four Noble Truths of Buddhism," which are: first, that it is the fate of all living beings to suffer throughout their lives; second, that the suffering has a cause, which is desire, or greed; third, that the suffering can be stopped if a person wants to stop it; and fourth, that the way to stop it is to follow the "Eightfold Path," a list of eight kinds of concentration to guide daily living, including "right views," "right occupation," "right speech," and "right meditation." These "right" things all are unselfish ways to live: to be considerate and sacrificial toward others, to tell the truth always, and so forth. The goal was to reach a saintly state of being called "nirvana," which really meant escape from the endless cycle of rebirth and suffering that Buddhists believe is endured by all living things. Nirvana is a difficult concept. Sometimes it is described as simply extinction, but it is really more like the achievement of great peace and unity with the cosmos, a blending of one's being with all of nature, something like a drop of rain water merging with the sea.

Buddha's prescription for living grew out of a long tradition of thought in India that included the concept of reincarnation, a limitless sense of time, and a rich artistic heritage. Buddha's sermons were gathered as teachings and studied by disciples, and the disciples were the core of what became the Buddhist priesthood, or *sangha*. Buddhist priests preached and taught at specific locations that evolved into temples. Some of the teachers were very famous and they elaborated Buddhist ideas into a large collection of stories and illustrations that have inspired much of Buddhist art ever since. Many of them traveled, carrying the teachings to neighboring communities and lands. In this way, Buddhism migrated eastward to Ceylon (Sri Lanka), Burma, Thailand, and Cambodia. Another strain of Buddhism migrated northward through northern India and into China from the northwest via the trading routes across the great deserts of central Asia. In the process, Buddhism divided into two major types: Theravada, "the doctrine of the elders," which is the southeast Asian type, and Mahayana Buddhism, the "greater vehicle," which is the type found in China, Korea, and Japan.

Both Theravada and Mahayana Buddhism teach that all people are equal under the Buddhist law, making Buddhism a "universal" religion like Christianity and Islam, one that can be practiced in many different countries. Mahayana Buddhism, the "greater vehicle," developed a tradition that allowed for "relative truth," which made it easier to accept different kinds of people who held widely varying beliefs, on the theory that they were simply at different stages on their paths toward enlightenment. People at points along the "path" needed to emphasize and draw comfort from different manifestations of the Buddha. People who were sick might want to emphasize the "healing Buddha" while those confronted with death might draw comfort from Amida, the manifestation of the Buddha that comes to carry dying souls to paradise. Others might pay homage to Maitreya, the "Buddha of the Future." Highly educated people might draw satisfaction from the "meditating Buddha" while the uneducated might learn from the "teaching Buddha." The images in various temples were meant to represent these different manifestations of the Buddha, enabling believers to concentrate on different aspects of Buddha-nature.

A key belief of the Mahayana Buddhist tradition was in the existence of bodhisattvas, a new kind of deity that was already "enlightened" enough to be a Buddha but out of mercy toward lesser humans chose to stay behind and help them reach enlightenment too. Bodhisattvas were the embodiment of unselfishness toward others and were respected and even worshipped by many Buddhist believers. The commonest bodhisattva in Korean Buddhism is *Kwanŭm*, the Bodhisattva of Mercy (sometimes called the "Goddess of Mercy," though the deity is not necessarily female). This image is often shown to be all-powerful, with extra arms and sometimes even extra heads, to indicate the ability to solve complicated problems and get people out of trouble. Images of bodhisattvas are important in Buddhist art. They are sometimes depicted as rich and jolly and generous, like Kwanŭm, but at other times they are depicted as emaciated and suffering, having given up everything to benefit other members of the human race.

Buddhism entered China in A.D. 64, Korea in A.D. 372, and Japan in A.D. 552. The first evidence of Buddhism in Korea is in the northern kingdom of Koguryŏ, which straddled the Yalu River, but it is the two southern Korean kingdoms of Paekche and Silla that welcomed the new religion most warmly and wove it into their national cultures. In the southeast, the people of Silla gave their country the nickname of "Buddha-Land." Their kings aspired to the ideal of compassionate Buddhist rulers and sponsored Buddhist monasteries and temples. The greatest Silla temple remains are those outside the ancient capital city of Kyŏngju at Pulguksa, which means "Temple of Buddha-Land." Silla aristocrats became Buddhists as did many of the common people. An elite corps of young Buddhist men became Korea's first organized martial artists, known as *hwarang*, or "Braves in the Flower of Youth." Their physical discipline was derived from the Buddhist idea that sacrifice and service were a noble calling, and they were some of Korea's best fighters.

Stone image of Maitreya, the "Buddha of the Future,"
at Kwanch'ok Temple near Nonsan, in South Korea
(Koryŏ period).

Buddhism flourished in Korea throughout the Three Kingdoms period
(57 B.C.–A.D. 668), being an important part of the culture of Koguryŏ as
well, in far northern Korea. From Paekche, in southwestern Korea, Buddhism
flowed still farther east, toward Japan, and many of Japan's earliest Buddhist
sites are thought to have been designed and influenced by Korean Buddhist
advisors. Hōryūji Temple, near the city of Nara in central Japan, is an example. Paekche was conquered by Silla and Koguryŏ in 668 and much of its
cultural legacy was destroyed, but there are still important Buddhist artworks
to be found in its royal tombs and the stone remnants of its temples.

Throughout the ensuing United Silla period (A.D. 668–918), during
which Silla ruled most of the peninsula from its capital at Kyŏngju, Korean
Buddhism continued to spread and develop. A Chinese visitor once reported

that Kyŏngju was so full of Buddhist temples and pagodas that they seemed like "clouds in the sky." At the same time, however, Korean culture was also absorbing and adjusting to Confucian social norms. An interesting example of the fusion of Buddhism and Confucianism in Silla-period Korea was the monk Wŏn'gwang's "Five Precepts for Laypeople," which included basic Confucian ideas and actually sounds like some of the Confucian "five relationships": (1) Serve your king with loyalty, (2) Serve your parents with filial piety, (3) Treat your friends with trust and faith, (4) Do not retreat from combat, and (5) Do not take life carelessly.

This merging of Buddhist compassion and Confucian social ethics is an important aspect of Korean intellectual history, for as Koreans were adapting Chinese ways of government they also sought religious satisfaction. By the Koryŏ period (918–1392), when Korea had a new united government headquartered in Kaesŏng in west-central Korea, Buddhism was the state religion and Buddhist monks and leaders were important figures at court. In fact, the founder of the Koryŏ kingdom, Wang Gŏn (also known as King T'aejo), gave credit for his achievement by proclaiming that "Founding our dynasty is entirely owing to the protective powers of the many Buddhas." Eventually there were more than seventy Buddhist temples in the capital city alone.

By this time a debate was in progress about the "right" way to be a Buddhist. Scholars of the "doctrinal sect" believed that people should seek enlightenment outside themselves by studying external things like the Buddhist scriptures. Scholars of the "meditative sect" thought that enlightenment, or "Buddha-nature," was part of every person from birth and was waiting for discovery in a flash of enlightenment from within the mind, something like Buddha's own experience. Though there were more than ten Buddhist denominations in the Koryŏ period, these two—the doctrinal and the meditative—were the main ones.

During the Koryŏ period, the kings kept Buddhist advisors close by their thrones and the country celebrated religious piety by building large temples. Noble people donated fortunes to monasteries and the Buddhist church grew rich. Common people, burdened by heavy taxes, often "commended" themselves to temples as "temple slaves" because they could live better under the generous protection of the monks than they could as free taxpayers. Temples acquired so much property, in fact, that certain groups of monks had to be trained in military arts to protect the property, an idea that seems a far cry from the self-denial so prevalent in earlier Buddhism.

One of the most spectacular achievements of Korean Buddhism was the carving of wooden printing blocks for the entire collection of Buddhist scriptures known as the *Tripitaka* in the eleventh century. The *Tripitaka* includes "discourses" or basic teachings, explanations of the discourses, and rules for the priesthood, and it runs to many hundreds of volumes. Devout Korean Buddhists had craftsmen carve everything in the *Tripitaka* onto 84,000 printing blocks (each block could print four pages), a massive project that took many years, partly as a pious response to the fact that Korea was under attack from northern Khitan invaders. By the time it was finished the Khitan actually had been defeated by the Jurchen. It is ironic to note that the entire *Tripitaka* printing-block collection was burned by the invading Mongols in the thirteenth century, following which Korean Buddhists set about carving it all over again. Today, the second set of 84,000 printing blocks can be seen in a large storage facility in the mountainside temple of Hae'insa.

The unreasonable wealth and political power of the Buddhist establishment by the late 1300s was one reason for the fall of Koryŏ and the founding of a new dynasty in 1392. The founders of the new Chosŏn kingdom attacked Buddhism and other folk religions as corruptions that only served to mislead the people. The founders of Chosŏn were Confucianists who wanted to redirect attention to state and society in the present instead of toward prayers to Buddha. The Confucianists were reformers who wanted to root out all kinds of evil that had flourished under the former dynasty. In their view, the wealth that was flowing to Buddhist temples would better be used by the state for education, defense, and public welfare. They believed that Buddhist monks and nuns were wrong to be celibate, never marrying or having children to carry on their ancestors' family lines. They thought that there were too many monks and nuns, in any case, and the new government ordered that these religious professionals, who had previously been honored as a kind of nobility, be treated like members of the lowest social class. And because they thought there were too many temples, they ruled that only temples in the mountains could remain standing. They pulled down many temples in towns and cities and when they built their new capital at what is now Seoul, they ordered that no temples be built within the city limits.

The Confucian attack on Buddhism at the beginning of the Chosŏn dynasty was ironic since the dynasty's founder and his family, along with many of their associates, continued personally to revere the Buddha and to maintain their personal Buddhist faith. Indeed, the purge was more institutional than religious, breaking the political power of the Buddhist church. However, over the course of the dynasty it did succeed in diminishing the visibility of Buddhism in Korea and in relegating it to the status of folk religion. Buddhist believers continued to hike into the mountains to visit temples and pray. Women continued to practice Buddhism in greater numbers than men, and educated men with social ambition actively shunned any association with

Buddhism so that it became a religion for the lower classes. Institutional Buddhism suffered a long period of repression that did not end until the twentieth century. Its eventual revival and resurgence is a major development in modern Korean history.

When Japan began to exert influence on Korea in the late 1800s, Buddhism became a channel for interaction between the Japanese and Koreans. In Japan, unlike India, China, and Korea, Buddhism had never undergone a period of political repression and flourished in many forms in temples that remain all over Japan to this day. In true Mahayana style, Buddhism in Japan accommodated many kinds of beliefs, and many sects permitted their monks to marry and raise families. The Japanese Honganji sect, for example, with a professional clergy that had families, was run in a congregational way with large-group worship services, hymn singing, and community collections for projects including charitable work. When Japanese officials and businessmen began moving to Korea at the turn of the twentieth century, they brought their forms of Buddhism with them and established temples. Korean Buddhists were encouraged to join in and follow Japanese modes of worship. Korean priests were told that it was not an abandonment of their promises to Buddha to marry and live more like the people in their communities. Some Korean clergy did so, and this touched off a bitter division within Korean Buddhism between the Chogye order, which remained celibate, and the T'aego order, which allowed monks to marry.

The Buddhist revival in late twentieth-century Korea has come after several difficult passages. During the Japanese colonial occupation of Korea (1910–45), Japanese residents tended to dominate Buddhism in Korea. After Japan's defeat in 1945, a Communist regime was established in North Korea that did not permit religious freedom at all, renewing its suppression and reducing it, in effect, to a cultural memory. In South Korea, American influence and a Christian president from 1948 to 1960 also did little to help Buddhism recover as younger people and people who wanted to be "modern" and "Western" joined Christian churches instead. In the 1960s and 1970s, however, the South Korean government devoted substantial funds and efforts to reconstructing Korea's historic sites including many Buddhist temples. Buddhism went from seeming "old-fashioned" to being "traditional," something to honor and reclaim as part of modern Korea's identity. As a result, membership in Buddhist congregations has grown. The dispute between married and celibate monks has been settled (both types are permitted in their respective T'aego and Chogye sects). Buddha's birthday (the eighth day of the fourth lunar month in the spring) is a national holiday with elaborate parades, rituals, and lantern festivals. Korean Buddhism, therefore, has succeeded in recovering much of its lost vitality and ranks just about equal with Christianity in terms of membership. Buddhist congregations organize the efforts of numerous laypeople in charitable activities, education, and even missionary work, cementing the commitment of individual Buddhists to each other and their religious communities through daily activities called "practical Buddhism."

The modernization of Korean Buddhism has not obscured the rich artistic and intellectual heritage of earlier periods. Temples are still maintained in traditional forms on campuses that honor traditional principles of design, architecture, and iconography. The greatest Korean temples are still as they were 100 years ago—though better maintained and with incomparably more visitors. Their rectangular compounds house a main hall, in which there are usually three large statues of different types of Buddhas and bodhisattvas. Other buildings include memorial halls to former congregational members who have died, gates and buildings that guard and protect the temple and its believers from demons and other enemies, and living quarters for the resident clergy.

A temple feature that is found in Korea and nowhere else in the Buddhist world is a shrine to the mountain god (*sanshin*) on the hillside above the temple. It usually contains a painting of a kindly old man with a white beard (the mountain spirit), a tiger (a mountain animal), and a pine tree (a symbol of long life). The shrine of the mountain god has nothing to do with Buddhism but more likely refers to the long period when Buddhist temples in Korea had to be hidden away in the mountains at the mercy of mountain forces including the fearsome tiger. Its presence at nearly every Buddhist temple suggests the continuing harmony between Korean Buddhism and other signs and symbols in Korean tradition.

SHAMANISM: THE "ORIGINAL" KOREAN RELIGION

The term "shaman" refers to a person who has extraordinary, even supernatural, powers and can communicate with the spirits that are thought to fill the world in order to persuade, enlist, and even defeat them. Shamans were common in the ancient cultures of Siberia and northern Asia, and Korean shamanism almost certainly was introduced by people migrating southward from the forests of Manchuria and farther north beyond the Amur River. The shamanic tradition is very old, and shamanism almost certainly was flourishing among the ancestors of the Korean people before they first learned of Buddhism or Confucianism.

Shamanism is an extremely simple belief system, though its rich variations make it seem more complex. It has no churches, no scriptures, and not much religious art or music, but it does have a rich oral tradition and certain core beliefs that have been passed down through countless generations.

The spirit world of shamanism is very well populated. Some spirits are related to natural phenomena like wind and water. Others are related to particular places, recalling events or people who are associated with the places; others are the ghosts of important people who are worthy of worship; others are more dangerous death spirits of people who have died tragically and are swirling around in the spirit world waiting for revenge. And others are disease spirits that make people sick.

All these spirits interact with living human beings, affecting their destinies and sometimes punishing them or causing them pain. Happy spirits such as the ghosts of heroes can be enlisted to bring good fortune. Troubled spirits like the ghosts of people killed in accidents or murder victims are extremely dangerous and must be calmed and diverted from harming those deemed responsible for their deaths. Sometimes living people suffer events or diseases and are unable to figure out which spirit is causing the misfortune. At such times a shaman may be useful, for shamans are thought to be able to determine which spirits are responsible for ill-fortune, what the spirits want, and how to satisfy them so they will go away and leave the worried person in peace.

Over the centuries, Korean spirit beliefs have developed and become very elaborate, and influences other than Siberian shamanism have entered the peninsula to introduce new kinds of deities and ghosts and further complicate the Korean spirit world. In China there are many similar traditions that have become a part of Korean spirit belief. One is the ghost of Guanyu, the Chinese God of War, who is thought to have helped Korea fend off the Japanese invasion in the 1590s. Another is the family of Chinese house gods that bless the kitchen, watch over the house, and ensure the success of its occupants. The involvement of house gods in family life is especially visible during important events such as childbirth, when a straw rope is hung across the gateway to the yard to keep out spirits that might harm the baby, and new parents practice rituals honoring Samshin, the god of childbirth. Villages also have collective expressions of spirit belief, as in the reverence paid to a particularly large old tree that has shaded generations of ancestors.

It is difficult to draw the line between folk customs and religious practices in Korean shamanism. Many folkways have nothing to do with religion and are simply Korean society's way of handling routine occasions. These include celebrations of planting and harvest in the countryside, of raising new buildings, opening new businesses, and celebrating the beginning of the New Year.

Others include vestiges of superstition such as the stacking of piles of stones by the roadside to protect a village from spirits coming down a mountain path. But others clearly are religious practices in the sense that they connect with the supernatural.

At the dawn of the modern age in Korea, shamanism accounted for the whole rich tradition of Korean spirit belief. Though the rich variety of folk deities still is part of Korean conversation and consciousness, "shamanism" as such has come to mean something more limited: the practice, invariably by female shamans called *mudang*, or *manshin*, of spirit propitiation on behalf of people who hire them to perform ceremonies called *kut*s. In these ceremonies the shaman interviews the troubled client to determine the nature of the trouble and other details of the case. Then at an appointed time the shaman gathers with the client and her neighbors in the house or the courtyard of the house, usually without men present, and begins the *kut*. For the *kut* the shaman is dressed in special clothing, wears a special hat, and is armed with tools, usually a sword or a trident. She holds a collection of small bells and shakes them while a nearby drummer beats a rhythm. She calls the spirit that is thought to be causing the trouble and tries to start a conversation with it.

As the shaman performs the *kut* she works herself into a semihysterical state that suggests that her powers are fully engaged. She dances energetically, jumping and twirling. She chants, shouts, and sings. She wields her weapons and shakes her bells. At times she may try to show that she has reached the supernatural state by doing supernatural things, such as walking barefoot on the upturned blade of her sword. If a sacrificial animal (usually a pig) is involved in the *kut*, she may balance the dead pig on the vertical sword without using any other means of support. These things heighten the sense of dread and magic in the *kut* and demonstrate the shaman's power over the spirit world.

There are many different kinds of *kut* and not all of them involve such unusual displays. The word *kut* is used to denote a village ritual honoring a benign god just as often as it is meant to denote the energetic summoning of an angry ghost. But all *kut* include a phase where people meet spirits and somehow resolve the conflict between them, whether it is an agreement to protect a new business or an agreement to stop torturing a client with nightmares.

Not everyone is cut out to be a shaman, or *mudang*. The shamans who carry on *kut*s today are regarded with fear and mixed feelings by their neighbors and clients and they do not lead normal lives. They are unmarried (usually widows) when they act as shamans, and they have no other profession so they are not wealthy. They are not particularly well educated, though they are walking storehouses of stories and cultural lore. And by their own accounts, they are not shamans by choice. That is, they have undergone an emotional ordeal that has left them devastated emotionally and specially open to the world of spirits. This ordeal, called *shinbyŏng*, or "spirit sickness," may have followed the death of a husband or child or some other dreadful event that precipitated what amounted to a nervous breakdown. Out of this desperate state they emerged feeling a certain tie to the supernatural world of spirits and they sense a compulsion to engage in the restless life of the *mudang*, drawn to the spirits but at the same time troubled and even terrified by them. This strange state of mind is what makes others wary of them.

However, the religious state that is felt by shamans is not to be misunderstood as mental illness or insanity. Korean shamans often associate with each other and train younger shamans in the various *kut* rituals. In Seoul, at a mountainside shrine called the Kuksadang, they gather often and practice their music, percussion, and chanting. The Kuksadang is the closest thing to a "headquarters" that exists for Korean shamanism. Otherwise shamans look like other Korean women on the street and are only known as *mudang* by their families, close friends, and clients.

Because of its obvious occult nature, shamanism has been an embarrassment to many educated Koreans. Until the 1980s the South Korean government dismissed shamanism as a vestige of the benighted past and discouraged *mudang*s from becoming shamans and practicing their *kut*s. Nevertheless, when the chips are down, shamans are common at *kut*s in neighborhoods throughout Korea, and not only in the courtyards of ignorant or uneducated people. Even formally educated men are familiar with the rituals and beliefs surrounding shamanism, no matter how much they may shun them in public as unmodern and superstitious. And in the 1980s and 1990s, during a time when young Koreans were searching for their own "authentic" national identity, certain shamanist trappings were popular as emblems of true "Koreanness." On university campuses day after day students practiced the percussion typical of *kut*s, began their college festivals with rituals that were strongly shamanist, and often talked about forsaking foreign ideologies such as Christianity and Buddhism in favor of the genuine Korean religion of shamanism.

In these ways, shamanism has survived the colonialism, war, and modernization of the twentieth century to emerge as an important part of Korean consciousness. One cannot really know Korea without understanding something of its appeal.

CHRISTIANITY IN KOREA

Koreans distinguish between Catholicism and Protestantism in Christianity, calling Catholicism "ch'ŏnjukyo" (religion of the Lord of Heaven) and Protestantism "kaeshinkyo" (the Reformed religion). They also use the word "kristokyo" (Christian) to mean "Protestant."

These distinctions reflect the way Christianity came to Korea. Catholic Christianity first entered Korea via China, when Korean travelers there made contact with Jesuit missionaries from the West and Chinese Catholics and returned home with some of their ideas to found the first Catholic congregation in Seoul. That was in 1784. Protestant Christianity took root many decades later, first with believers who had met Scottish Presbyterian missionaries in Manchuria, to the north, and then in the 1880s with the arrival of numbers of Protestant missionaries mainly from the United States.

Until the 1880s, Christianity was outlawed in Korea. This was because Christians were known to disapprove of the most important Confucian family ritual, namely the *chesa*. The argument over whether Chinese Christians should be allowed to continue their ancestral rituals had raged for more than 100 years in the 1600s and 1700s until the pope decided that the Chinese had to stop what he regarded as heathen spirit worship. The Chinese authorities were incensed that the pope, who knew nothing about China and the benefits of Confucian morality, would dare to label Chinese civilization as heathen. They were already uncomfortable about a foreign doctrine that taught about the divinity of Jesus, virgin birth, and original sin. In 1722 the Chinese empire began suppressing Christianity. Only a few Western missionaries were allowed to remain in Peking, because they were regarded as well-educated representatives of Western learning and were useful as a window on Europe.

This episode is known as the "rites controversy," referring to the question of whether Christians could engage in Confucian ancestor rites. The reaction of the Korean government was to go a step further and outlaw Christianity completely, threatening to execute any Korean who adopted the faith. Thus the Korean travelers who started the first Catholic congregation in Seoul in the 1780s were risking their lives to do so.

Periodically the Korean government discovered cells of the secret church in Korea and persecuted its members, executing many. The first executions came in 1801 and were followed by others in 1839, 1846, and 1866. In the persecution of 1866, more than 2,000 Korean Catholics are said to have lost their lives along with 9 French missionaries. From the roster of martyrs during this bloody history came the names of 103 Korean and French Catholics who were canonized by Pope John Paul II when he visited Seoul for the bicentennial of Korean Catholicism in 1984.

Why did Koreans keep risking their lives to join the Catholic church? One answer seems to lie in the tight family and community ties that bound the earliest members of the church to each other in such a way that they could maintain secrecy. Another lies in the fact that some of them were very well educated Confucians who were concerned that Korea was falling behind the times and wanted to investigate new ways of looking at natural and spiritual phenomena. And another reason might be that many of the early Catholics were members of middle and lower classes, intelligent enough to know that as long as the Confucian system prevailed in Korea they would never be allowed to rise in society or realize their potential as human beings.

The forced "opening" of Korea by Japan in the 1870s set in motion a series of radical changes in Korea. The United States, England, Russia, and other Western countries were allowed to set up diplomatic missions and open relations with Korea in the 1880s. Western missionaries soon followed, with Americans setting up Presbyterian and Methodist missions in Seoul in 1885.

Although most Koreans saw Christianity as a strange and unwelcome creed, there were those who responded with active interest and became Korea's first Protestant Christians. One reason for this interest was the spiritual appeal of Christianity, which had also attracted Koreans to Catholicism early in the century. But another reason was Christianity's association with the West and modern things, particularly as a Western alternative to the pressure they were feeling from their aggressive neighbor, Japan. As the Korean royal court fell to Japanese domination and Korea desperately sought foreign alliances that might help them resist colonization, Koreans hoped that the United States in particular would help preserve Korean independence.

In the end, though the Americans did nothing to help Korea resist Japan, Christian organizations including churches and schools continued to be an attractive modern alternative to Japanese domination and the bankrupt Korean monarchial system that had failed prior to 1910. Students and graduates of missionary-run Christian schools were a leading group in the independence uprising against Japan that broke out in Korea in 1919, further associating Christianity and independence in the minds of many Koreans. Christian schools continued to offer modern education in subjects such as philosophy, science, history, and Western languages in addition to required religion courses. In addition, it seemed that Christian churches and organizations, though they existed under the colonial regime and had to obey Japanese rules, nonetheless had a certain amount of protection through their links to foreign churches. The Japanese were reluctant to persecute Christians too openly for fear of attracting the notice and condemnation of the international community. Although it is important not to discount the authentic spiritual experience of Korean Christians under Japanese rule, it must also be assumed that the number of Christians grew to a significant level—a tenth of the peninsula's population in the mid-1930s—because of all these various factors.

This changed in the years leading up to World War II. As militarism overtook Japanese politics and the imperial government set its course for war, first in China and then against the West, the Japanese stopped caring about public opinion in the West and began to assert much more oppressive control over the Korean people. They embarked on a campaign to turn all Koreans into good and loyal subjects of the Japanese emperor, forcing them to speak Japanese as their "national language," for example, and eventually attacking their family identities by assigning Japanese names to the Koreans.

One of Japan's steps in this campaign of cultural genocide was to force Koreans to worship the gods of imperial Japan, including dead emperors and the spirits of war heroes who had helped them conquer Korea earlier in the century. They claimed that the Koreans and Japanese were "one people" and should worship the same deities under the Japanese Shintō religion. They did this even while making Korea into a police state, drafting thousands of Koreans to do forced labor in Japan, and turning Korea into a staging area for their war with China, which they began in 1937. Koreans, of course, resented this bitterly but were powerless before the modern weapons of the Imperial Japanese Army.

For Korean Christians, the requirement to worship at Japanese shrines was more than an insult: it seemed like a violation of their own Ten Commandments to worship any god other than the Christian God. Thus Christian religion and Korean national consciousness merged, and many Christians who refused shrine worship were sent to prison as disloyal subjects. As war came to the Pacific in 1941, Korea subsided into a sullen obedience.

When the United States and the Soviet Union divided Korea into occupation zones in 1945, North Korea was the part with the most Christians. These, however, were regarded with suspicion by the new Communist regime. The Christians were organized, and they did not always obey the new government. Communist youth organizations attacked Christian meetings and Christians organized to fight back. North Korea dealt with its troublesome Christians by creating a state church—a Christian League that it decreed would be the new owner of all church property, all schools, and to which all Christians must belong or face accusations of disloyalty. A trusted Christian member of the new Communist elite in North Korea was appointed chief of the Christian League and other Christian pastors and leaders were forced out of their jobs. Christians soon joined other "class enemies" of the North Korean state—big landlords, businessmen, those who had served the hated Japanese—in their escape to the friendlier atmosphere of the South. Many of them had suffered fierce persecution twice at that point, first under the Japanese and then under the Communists.

After the Korean War that lasted from 1950 to 1953, Korea remained divided and Christians had to stay in the South even though they were natives of the North. Whether Catholic or Protestant, they looked back on a history of suffering and martyrdom and clung fiercely to the faith for which they had given so much. However, not all Korean Christians thought alike, and the controversies and disputes that broke out among them were signs of two things. The first was their commitment to being "right" in their religion and the criticism of others who were seen to be "wrong," and the second was their restless energy and passion for preaching and converting others to become members of the church. Both these factors—commitment and aggressive recruiting—helped the church to swell in astonishing numbers in the quarter century between 1960 and 1985.

Several other circumstances contributed to the rapid growth of Christianity in South Korea. One was the urbanization that accompanied Korea's industrial revolution. The tide of farm people who migrated to the cities meant blocks and blocks of tiny apartments among strangers and the need to discover new communities to belong to. Churches were ready-made communities for Korea's new urban working class, and they welcomed the incoming workers and provided them with emotional, and even economic, support along with the religious.

Another circumstance was the Catholic and Protestant commitment to human rights at a time when South Korea was suffering under a strict military dictatorship. When the South Korean army took power in 1961, it set the country on a path toward modernization, often forcing people to cooperate when they did not want to do so. For example, factory wages were kept low so Korea could make things that could be sold cheaply overseas. This was good for Korea as a country but bad for industrial workers who needed better wages and working conditions in order to survive. South Korea also enforced the National Security Law that gave stiff prison sentences to people suspected of sympathizing with North Korea. People who criticized the military government in the South were accused of helping the enemy in the North, and so even democratic dissent in South Korea violated the National Security Law. Christians actively supported people who were persecuted under this law, demanding not only democratic reforms that would permit free speech,

Yŏngnak Presbyterian Church, Seoul, begun by North Korean refugee Christians, now with a membership exceeding 40,000.

freedom of religion, and human rights but also demanding that Korean workers be treated more fairly with better wages. Christians took these stands because of their religion's respect for individuals in the sight of God. The state harassed and even imprisoned them as disloyal South Koreans. Thus many Catholic and Protestant Christians suffered government persecution again, some of them for a third time.

Today, one in four South Koreans is identified as a Christian, almost exactly as many as call themselves Buddhists. Eighty percent of the Christians are Protestants, and three-quarters of the Protestants are Presbyterians. This makes South Korea the "most Christian" country in Asia, apart from the Philippines which was ruled for 300 years by Catholic Spain and then by the United States. People often ask for an explanation for Christian "success" in South Korea when only 2 percent of Chinese and only 2.5 percent of Japanese are Christians. The answer lies in history: in the suffering and sacrifice of Korean Christians and the circumstances of modern Korea that made Christianity a refuge and force for reform.

"NEWLY RISING RELIGIONS"

Ch'ŏndokyo

Modern Korea has seen its share of what are called "newly rising religions," movements that are a mixture of Korean and foreign ideas and are forged into a religious ideology by charismatic leaders. The best-established of these is called "Ch'ŏndokyo," the "Religion of the Heavenly Way." Ch'ŏndokyo began in the 1860s as a peasant rebellion opposing a variety of policies of the Korean government. The founder, Ch'oe Che'u, found his way to advancement blocked by the fact that he was an illegitimate son, since the sons of parents who were not properly married were not allowed to take the all-important examinations that qualified men to be members of the *yangban* ruling class and to hold government office. He busied himself studying religion and philosophy and in 1860 he had a vision in which God ordered him to "save mankind."

Ch'oe Che'u's religious ideas were an interesting mix of Chinese Daoism, Confucianism, and a smattering of shamanism and Christianity. As his movement developed it became known as *Tonghak*, or "Eastern Learning," to distinguish it from Catholicism, or "Western Learning" (*Sŏhak*), which at the time was seen as a threatening heresy. A basic belief of Tonghak was that common people have rights and should be their own rulers, a belief expressed in the slogan "Innaech'ŏn," which means "People are Heaven," or, more accurately, "People are their own gods."

Korea's Confucian rulers were offended not only by Ch'oe Che'u's audacious claim that people should rule themselves but also by his refutation of the Confucian idea of hierarchy and the whole system of social inequality that prevailed in traditional Korea. Government authorities hunted Ch'oe down and put an end to his teaching by arresting him and having him put to death in 1864.

Thirty years later, the Tonghak movement rose again, this time demanding posthumous forgiveness of the founder Ch'oe Che'u and continuing his demands that peasants be given equal rights and justice under the law. The Tonghak Rebellion of the 1890s grew quickly in the southwestern provinces of Korea and the central government in Seoul was hard-pressed to control it. In addition to the grievances passed down from the earlier suppression in the 1860s, the peasants from southwestern Korea who flocked to join the Tonghak Rebellion included many small-time merchants and peddlers who were angry that the Korean government was allowing Japanese competitors into the market, creating too much competition. Ultimately the government found itself unable to put down the uprising and appealed for Chinese military assistance. This touched off the Sino-Japanese War of 1894–95, a war over control of Korea that ended with Japan's forcing China to renounce all interest in the peninsula and left the Koreans open, in effect, to Japanese imperialism. The Tonghak Rebellion, though not exactly forgotten in the process, thus touched off a much more fateful episode in Korean history.

After the turn of the twentieth century, the Tonghak movement settled down into the Religion of the Heavenly Way, or "Ch'ŏndokyo." It became associated with Korean nationalism, and Tonghak leaders were significant in the Korean independence movement against Japan. Though Ch'ŏndokyo has never gathered enough adherents to rival Buddhism or Christianity, it has continued to be recognized in both North and South Korea as an authentic Korean religious tradition.

The Unification Church

In the West, the best-known Korean newly rising religion is the Unification Church founded by the Reverend Sun Myung Moon. The term "unification" in Korean is the same word that is used for national reunification, giving the name of the church a special meaning for Koreans that it lacks in English. "Unification" has become an almost mystic goal in the Korean mind, something like a perfect future world. In the religious context it is faintly suggestive of the Buddhist Nirvana or the Christian Heaven. The wholeness that is such an important part of Reverend Moon's message is expressed by glorifying marriage, particularly the holy marriage between himself as the holy father, and his wife as the holy mother. Most people are familiar with the scene of a stadium full of brides and grooms having a mass wedding. The Unification Church organizes these mass weddings as part of their celebration of wholeness in marriage.

The Unification Church projects this ideal of wholeness onto the world, envisioning a great unifying trend among the world's peoples and religions under the guidance of Reverend Moon. This is not a new idea in East Asia. Confucius himself once envisioned the world's history in phases leading to an ultimate peace of great unity or *Datong* ("Taedong" in Korean) when peace and unity would reign everywhere. This idea came back in the late nineteenth century when the scholar Kang Youwei proposed a unification of Eastern and Western cultures in much the same vision of the future. In the twentieth century unity has been further from reality than ever, and perhaps that is why so many people in different countries have been attracted to Reverend Moon's teachings.

Sun Myung Moon (Korean name: Mun Sŏnmyŏng) was born in North Korea before the national division and like many North Korean refugees dreams of going back someday to the place of his birth. However, given the hostility of Korean Communism to all religion, he was unable to do so until the 1980s when North Korean president Kim Il-sung welcomed him as a possible ally in the campaign to unite the two parts of the country. For most of his life Sun Myung Moon has existed on the fringes of Korean Christianity, shunned by most Christians and regarded as a strange individual by most South Koreans. But he has drifted in and out of respectability. Well before his visit to Kim Il-sung, he established himself as an implacable anti-Communist and as such was useful to the military regime in South Korea. To support his church he turned to commerce, setting up factories that made weapons as well as gift packages of the medicinal root ginseng. He also performed valuable social services by sending church members as volunteers to poorer areas of the country to run kindergartens and help with farming. And for a time he seemed like a good overseas ambassador for Korea, sending an adorable children's choir called the "Little Angels" abroad on concert tours.

In the United States during the 1970s, he recruited large numbers of young people and sent them to camps where they learned about the Unification idea. Many of these recruits appeared on American street corners selling flowers and turning the proceeds over to the Moon organization, which grew quite rich. He also got involved in American politics, firmly backing President Richard Nixon through the worst of his Watergate troubles and helping finance his defense. He also attempted to found a media empire with the acquisition of the *Washington Times*, which he still owns. These activities were hardly the traditional religious endeavors expected of church leaders, and when American tax authorities closed in on Sun Myung Moon and convicted him of tax evasion, they found him living comfortably in a New York mansion more like a king than a minister of the gospel. After serving time in a federal penitentiary, he returned to South Korea; and although his profile is much lower, he still appears at mass weddings around the world and preaches about a day when there will be unity and harmony around the globe. Now that he is in his old age it seems unlikely that a movement so dependent on a single leader-founder will long survive his passing.

Taejong-kyo, the Cult of Tan'gun

If the Unification Church seems like a response to the particular circumstances of Korean life in the late twentieth century, many other small religious traditions in Korea have longer histories and promise to have more staying power. One of these harkens back to the legendary founder of the Korean race, the god-man Tan'gun who was born of the union of a she-bear and the son of the Creator. The story of Tan'gun, who was in effect the grandson of God and whose story is Korea's foundation myth, was first written down by the Buddhist monk Ilyŏn in the thirteenth century. However, it was not taken seriously or given much importance until the early twentieth century, when an anti-Japanese activist named Hong'an Nach'ŏl had a shattering vision in which he felt himself appointed by the spirit of Tan'gun to found a religion honoring the Great Founder. The religion, at first known as Tan'gun-kyo and then as Taejong-kyo, is at the heart of a nationalist religious movement that has lasted almost a century. Faced with persecution by the Japanese during the colonial period, the followers of Taejong-kyo exiled themselves to Manchuria for safety. Under pressure from Japanese authorities who resolved to annihilate Taejong-kyo as a threat to the Japanese emperor cult, Hong'an Nach'ŏl finally committed suicide. After Japan's defeat in 1945, the surviving members of Taejong-kyo returned to South Korea and eventually established a simple shrine in Seoul that contains a portrait of Tan'gun and is the site of commemorative events on Korean Foundation Day, October 3, which refers to Tan'gun's mystical birth in the year 2333 B.C.

The importance of Taejong-kyo as the religion honoring Tan'gun has been outrun by the cult of Tan'gun that has developed in North Korea under the leadership of the late President Kim Il-sung and his son and successor Chairman Kim Jong-il. In the early 1990s the North Koreans announced that they had discovered the tomb of Tan'gun near the capital city of P'yŏngyang and had unearthed the bones of the god-man *and* his wife. The government then moved the grave to a more auspicious location and built an elaborate mausoleum for the remains of Tan'gun and his wife, apparently appropriating the authority and tradition of Tan'gun for the North Korean regime itself. There are even some who believe that Kim Il-sung's body will eventually be reburied in Tan'gun's new tomb, thereby merging the two Great Leaders (see below, under "Kimilsungism").

"KIMILSUNGISM": THE CIVIL RELIGION OF NORTH KOREA

The Democratic People's Republic of Korea was born in 1948 as a Communist state backed by the ideas of Karl Marx and V. I. Lenin as adapted to the Korean environment by Marshal Kim Il-sung and his Soviet advisors. Adaptation to the Korean scene meant grafting Communist theory to the recent experience of the people in North Korea, which consisted of life under the Korean monarchy (until 1910) and then Japanese colonialism (until 1945). Since 1948, North Korea has drawn on this history and not on the history that is familiar to people in the West. When we think of the "lessons of history" we think about the ordeals of the industrial revolution, the evolution of political systems in the direction of freedom and democracy, and the difficult, often bloody, struggle against dictatorship.

But North Korea's "lessons of history" are quite different. This is because since 1945, North Korea has been a very isolated country. Its leaders have traveled only rarely beyond their own borders. Information has always been tightly controlled, and people spend their entire lives without ever being exposed to the ideas that shaped the West or the "lessons" that have shaped the way Westerners, and even their neighbors in South Korea and Japan, think. Looking back on their own experience, their traditional "reference points" are the Confucian ethics that respect authority, foster loyalty and obedience, and put the community ahead of the individual. Their concepts of modernity were shaped under Japanese colonial rule. This is ironic, since the North Koreans profess to hate the Japanese for what they did to Korea between 1910 and 1945. However, the leaders who ruled North Korea from the 1940s until the 1990s all went to school under the Japanese, learned their childhood ethics in the Japanese system, and learned about politics under Imperial Japan, when the emperor was a god and his subjects were said to owe him everything. In the 1930s, Koreans, like all Japanese subjects, were trained to think of themselves as part of the Japanese "body" or *kokutai*. They were literally taught to think of themselves as the body's hands and feet, unable to exist apart from the body and only having a purpose as part of the body.

To understand the political culture of North Korea it is useful to think about how North Koreans came to see the world after being liberated from Japan in 1945. As they still see it, the southern half of their country was occupied by the United States, which was building a military alliance with the new, postwar Japanese government to dominate all of Asia. They believe that the Americans turned the temporary division of Korea into a permanent split by creating a puppet government for South Korea under Syngman Rhee. When North Korea tried to reunite the peninsula by force as a last resort, the Americans organized an international effort to frustrate the reunification. In the North Koreans' view, the result was that 2 million Koreans died and the DPRK's cities and factories were bombed into rubble, but the Americans and their anti-Communist friends in South Korea succeeded in keeping the nation divided for more than half a century.

After the war, North Korea had to rebuild from the ground up. The North Koreans were most fortunate to receive a great deal of help from China, the U.S.S.R., and the socialist countries of Eastern Europe. But mostly it was the Koreans themselves who reconstructed their country with their own back-breaking labor. And as they worked, the North Koreans vowed never again to be hurt as they had been in the war and earlier, by foreign imperialism.

Out of this bitter experience, Kim Il-sung invented a set of national ideas for North Korea that were to be taught, almost like a religion, to the people from childhood up. Many adults, of course, agreed with him and appreciated his leadership. Others, as class enemies, were silenced, purged, and sometimes even "liquidated," or murdered. However, by the late 1950s, the strong Confucian and antiforeign mind-set of the North Korean people had created a powerful community that was able to put itself back together and march grimly toward a better life.

To understand North Korea it is also important to think about what the North Koreans *didn't* experience. In their closed society they never experienced the postwar economic boom that created the rich material culture of the West. In their information-controlled society they never read the books or saw the movies or heard the music that shaped the contemporary Western world. Since few North Koreans learn foreign languages and few foreigners speak Korean, there was very little discussion or exchanging of ideas with anyone but the Chinese Communists and a few Russian advisors. For fifty years, in fact, the North Koreans have had a chance to create a society and culture with a variant vocabulary, their own version of history, their own standards of right and wrong, and their own national goals.

A good example of this difference is the fact that when Kim Il-sung grew old, he appointed his oldest son Kim Jong-il to succeed him as leader of the ruling political party in North Korea and tagged him to become president later on. Even the North Koreans' best friends, the Chinese, thought this bizarre, since Communists elect their leaders from within the party. To have Kim Il-sung act like a king and anoint his son crown prince was a violation of basic Communist (and modern) ideas. However, if one recalls that the

North Koreans learned their lessons about politics from traditions that reach back to the Korean monarchy and the Japanese imperial system, it suddenly seems less strange.

In the process of reaching for supreme power in North Korea, Kim Il-sung had to defeat a number of rival Communist challengers. This struggle took many years, and during that time Kim gathered around him a tightly knit group of supporters and relatives who were committed to his success. As they protected him, they helped create a system in which loyalty to Kim Il-sung became the main qualification for advancement in government and business. For more than thirty years, the loyalty-to-Kim qualification remained in effect, leading to a system in the 1980s in which virtually everyone in any high position was there because of loyalty, first, and ability, second.

To disguise this, the Kim group began with the idea of *Juch'e* ("Joó-chey"), which means "self-reliance." Kim Il-sung proclaimed *Juch'e* as a unique Korean formula for independence, not only from Japan, America, and the West, but also from the Soviet Union and China, which were challenging each other for leadership of the worldwide Communist movement at the time. *Juch'e* means growing your own food, making your own tools and machines, and learning to do miraculous new things with what you already have. It also means having pride and not being jealous of others and other countries.

North Koreans were ordered to study the *Juch'e* idea and to think of ways to put it into practice. Kim Il-sung's son Kim Jong-il began to write and teach about his father's *Juch'e* idea, and by the early 1980s he was making it part of a larger concept of what he called "Kimilsungism." Kimilsungism is the Great Leader's name run together, of course, but it is not so strange when one recalls that North Korea is full of things named Kim Il-sung, such as Kim Il-sung University. Kimilsungism is the reason for putting up huge statues of the Great Leader, for building great museums full of his possessions, for building palaces and mansions for him to visit, and, in short, for treating him like more than a human being, almost like a god. The reason is to glorify Kim Il-sung, of course, but it is also to give the North Korean people a figure on whom to pin their faith, almost in a religious sense. When times are hard, don't worry: Kim Il-sung is in charge. When failure looms, don't worry: Kim Il-sung will make it come out all right.

Kim Il-sung was well aware of the burden that was put on him when he allowed himself to be spoken of as a god. In the late 1940s he once said that the goal of his regime in North Korea was to make it possible for his people to "wear silk clothes, eat meat every day, and live in houses with tiled roofs" (only aristocrats could afford tiled roofs in Korea under the monarchy). But progress was slow and in the early 1990s, just before he died, he once again said that North Korea was looking forward to the day when the people could "wear silk clothes, eat meat every day, and live in houses with tiled roofs." Saying that was an admission of failure, but it was also an admission of faith. At a time when the North Korean economy was shrinking following the collapse of Communism in Europe and North Koreans were being asked to cut back to two meals a day, he was telling his people to keep the faith. They should still believe in their own efforts and the ultimate triumph of the *Juch'e* idea.

When Kim Il-sung died in 1994, his son Kim Jong-il was expected to take his place not only as head of the Party and commander of the army, but also as president of the Democratic People's Republic of Korea. In the West, certainly, a new leader would have emerged quickly because no one would have wanted the state to be without direction. In North Korea, however, Kim Jong-il stayed out of sight. He gave almost no public speeches and appeared very rarely. Though he kept his job as army commander, which his father had given him in 1991, he waited three years before taking his father's position as head of the Korean Workers Party and even after that the presidency remained vacant. In the West, people wondered if Kim Jong-il was sick or whether there was a power struggle going on. However, in North Korea there was a Confucian-style explanation. A proper son should mourn his father for three years, avoiding celebrations or any outright actions that call attention to himself and away from his dead parent. The explanation made sense only in terms of North Korea's special political culture. Many observers think that the best way to understand North Korea in general—as long as the present system continues there—is to think in terms of Kimilsungism.

CONCLUSION

It may be said that Korea today is saturated with ideas and ideologies. Certainly there are many competing beliefs that divide Koreans from each other and fuel their disagreements. However, certain core beliefs remain constant, even in circumstances as different as those in capitalist South Korea and the Kimilsungist North. Confucianism, the bonds between family members and friends, the respect for authority, the willingness to work hard, the passionate desire to learn and improve one's position—all these have remained through generations of revolutionary change.

3

Arts and Literature

KOREA'S ARTISTIC TRADITION reaches back before recorded history to the people who inhabited northeast Asia in the New Stone Age. These people were part of a mosaic of tribal civilizations that settled in the area, and the things they made have been found in many parts of northeastern China, Siberia, and even Japan. The desire to decorate things and express an aesthetic appreciation even in prehistoric times can be seen in the simple designs cut into the clay of pottery items that lay buried for thousands of years until being discovered by archaeologists in modern times.

The people who are descended from those early artisans today enjoy a vibrant artistic life. In Korea, painters, sculptors, musicians, actors, architects, dancers, and street artists abound. The capital city boasts a number of excellent museums. The Seoul Arts Complex contains theaters, studios, classrooms for advanced studies in the arts, and exhibit space for shows. Several separate theater districts offer original plays and dramatic productions from all over the world. Several universities specialize in the fine arts and there are special schools and classes to train artists. Children in school spend a considerable amount of their time learning traditional arts, such as calligraphy and classical painting styles along with Western painting, which has a different perspective and different techniques. In these ways the Korean art scene is truly international in scope and traditional as well as modern at the same time.

Korea's appreciation for different kinds of art comes naturally. It began with the work of the prehistoric potters and matured during the Korean Three Kingdoms period (57 B.C.–A.D. 668). The Three Kingdoms, together with the later kingdoms of Koryŏ and Chosŏn, balanced local styles of art with much-revered Chinese examples, creating a dual tradition that blends both into something that is uniquely Korean. It is comparable to, but different from, what is found in China and Japan.

Korea's oldest surviving paintings, for example, are hunting scenes on the walls of tombs in the territory once occupied by the state of Koguryŏ. Koguryŏ men were hunters, skilled horsemen who shot deer and other wild animals from the saddle with a bow and arrow. The leaders' tombs were decorated with scenes of their hunting prowess. Elements of the paintings such as mountains and trees are just like similar elements in Chinese paintings of that time. The hunting theme, however, is something that belongs to Koguryŏ, along with the deer and tigers in the paintings that were not typical of China but were part of life in Manchuria and northern Korea.

The Three Kingdoms offer many examples of the dual tradition in Korean art. The southeastern kingdom of Silla, for example, crowned its kings with headdresses of beaten gold whose shapes were reminiscent not only of antlers but also of tree branches, one of the "tools" of Korean shamans who were ancient religious leaders in the forests of Manchuria. Another feature of the Silla crowns is the small, comma-shaped *magatama* jewels, looking like jade teardrops, that hang from delicate gold threads all around the crown. *Magatama* are found throughout northeastern Asia but they are not so common in China. Along with the crowns are numerous other iron and gold objects: belt buckles, harnesses, necklaces and pendants, bowls, and figurines. These hint at combinations of Korean and Chinese ideas of nobility, of nomadic and agricultural ways of life, and of the coming of Buddhism to Korea.

No Korean buildings survive as such from the Three Kingdoms period, though there are many remains. Stone pagodas still stand on former temple sites, some of them with their carvings and decorative inscriptions still readable. Many of them suggest the care and skill of the stonemasons who created them. Hwangnyongsa, the biggest Silla temple, was destroyed long ago but its site was uncovered in 1976 and archaeologists were able to find traces of some of the remarkable buildings described in Kim Pusik's twelfth-century *History of the Three Kingdoms* (*Samguk Sagi*), including a 250-foot-high nine-story pagoda.

Silla's second biggest temple, Pulguksa (Temple of the Buddha-Land), has been preserved and reconstructed many times on its hillside location outside the ancient capital of Kyŏngju. Much of Pulguksa was made of stone, and while its wooden buildings have been replaced many times, much of the stonework on the front of the temple and around the staircases is from the eighth century. Inside the front courtyard of the temple stand two of Korea's finest stone pagodas. The first, known as the Tabo Pagoda, is an intricate assembly of stone roofs, columns, railings, and steps. Its companion, the Sŏkt'ap Pagoda, also nicknamed "The Pagoda that Casts No Shadow," is of a simpler type, made of solid sections of stone.

The crown jewel of Kyŏngju is the eighth-century granite image of Buddha that sits majestically in the Sŏkkuram Cave near the top of Mount T'oham. Built during the reign of King Kyŏngdŏk (r. 742–65), the image is about eleven feet high and sits on a pedestal facing the entrance and is surrounded by images of guardians, disciples, and bodhisattvas carved into the granite panels that line the cave. At certain times of the year the rising sun shines in through the entrance and lights the Buddha, who seems to be serenely watching over the valley and seacoast beyond.

The Sŏkkuram Cave is on the opposite side of Mount T'oham from Pulguksa Temple. It is generally assumed that there was a relationship between the two, and that probably the cave temple was a religious retreat for monks or possibly Silla kings. It is not even clear exactly which manifestation of the Buddha the statue is intended to represent, whether the historical Buddha (Sakyamuni) or the Buddha "of life and light," as a nearby inscription suggests. A further dimension was added to the mystery when marine archaeologists discovered the stone structure of the tomb of King Munmu (r. 661–81) in the water off the seacoast. The structure was located in a line with the gaze of the overlooking cave Buddha, suggesting that the image was intended to watch over the dead king's grave. However, no one can be sure, since there is no surviving documentation to bear out the relationship. In fact, the cave was almost forgotten over the intervening centuries. Under the Chosŏn dynasty and its policy of suppressing Buddhism, Pulguksa Temple and the Sŏkkuram Cave fell into decay. The cave itself was overgrown with weeds and trees and virtually lost to memory until it was accidentally discovered in 1909 by a man seeking shelter from a storm. The cave has now been repaired and sealed from the elements to spare the interior carvings within from further damage from erosion and the effects of industrial air pollution. The Sŏkkuram Cave now ranks as a Korean National Treasure and a UNESCO World Heritage Cultural Treasure.

After Silla, Buddhist art further distinguished the Koryŏ period (918–1392), as the state and the wealthy estate owners patronized temples and contributed funds to build elaborate buildings and beautiful Buddhist images and objects of worship. Chief among these were the main images in the temples, which sat, usually in threes, on a high platform in the center of the main temple hall. Various materials were used to make these images: wood, iron, and bronze. The larger wood images are now gone, but some of the

Stone-carved images of Maitreya on a cliff near P'aju (Koryŏ period).

metal ones have survived. Most are painted, but some are gilt. As with present-day Buddhist images in temples from the later Chosŏn period, the images from the Koryŏ period represent the various manifestations of the Buddha. One is the historical Buddha who actually lived. Another is the Buddha of the present age (Amida). Others are the Buddha of power and light (Vairocana), the meditating Buddha (a favorite of the Zen sect, shown with his hands folded in a position of meditation), and Maitreya, the Buddha (or more properly, bodhisattva) of the future. When images of the Buddha are flanked by a pair of smaller figures, the other two are bodhisattvas, images of saints who have reached the stage of Buddha-hood but have elected to remain in the temporal world to help other sinners find the way.

Koryŏ Buddhism is also remarkable for the paintings that are found on walls of temples, both inside and out. One type illustrated famous stories from the life of Buddha. Another depicted the moral universe, showing heaven at the top and hell at the bottom. Heaven was full of light and beauty and signs of the Buddha welcoming souls to paradise. Hell was dark, filled with demons, and showed horrible suffering. In between was the plane of temporal existence, with people living ordinary lives but subject to temptation and corruption. All three planes were densely filled with fascinating details of daily life and scenery.

But it is celadon pottery that has done the most to make Koryŏ famous in the world of art. The techniques and basic design inspiration are clearly from China and some of the Koryŏ potters themselves were Chinese. However, Korean glazes and shapes evolved away from the Chinese style. The blue-green celadon hue was the result of careful calculation when the potters mixed the glazes. Korean shapes were more natural, with references to bamboo, flowers, the lotus, and gourds and melons. The Koreans made celadon headrests ("pillows"), water bottles, and vases. Some of these were decorated with painted designs under the glaze. But Koryŏ potters also excelled at a new kind of inlaid decoration. They cut designs such as cranes and pine trees into the wet clay and then filled the cuts with clay of a different color, usually black or white, to bring out the design. The pot with its inlaid design was then baked, taken out and covered with glaze, and then baked again. The most highly prized Koryŏ celadons are pots with elaborate designs of this inlaid type, a celadon color that is exactly the right combination of green and blue, and a pattern of hairline heat cracks in the glaze over the entire surface of the vessel.

Koryŏ celadon pottery is a good example of the way Korean artisans adapted ideas that originated in China. This blending of the Chinese "great tradition" with the Korean local tradition occurred in many forms of art. Korean Buddhist temples, for example, include elements of Korean shamanism such as the Shrine of the Mountain Spirit that is always found in a special shrine building up on the hillside behind a Korean temple.

KOREAN PAINTING

Throughout Korean history, the common people have produced a variety of folk paintings known as *minhwa*, or "people's paintings." Favorite *minhwa* themes include tigers, birds (especially magpie), symbols of longevity such as pine trees, and the Mountain Spirit. *Minhwa* are often humorous, or satirical, as in the case of the magpie chattering at the tiger, a little bird harassing the fearsome predator. This is a major motif of Korean folk art: the weaker common people getting the best of the powerful ruling class.

Minhwa are illustrations of stories; such painted decorative pictures typically include paintings of ordinary people doing everyday things, and of this type, the most famous are the genre paintings of the eighteenth-century painters Kim Hongdo and Shin Yunbok. Kim Hongdo's paintings showed boys in school, children playing, and workmen working, often in situations that were humorous. Shin Yunbok liked to paint many of the same things but his most famous scenes are of women. His paintings give us a good idea of what the fashions of the day in clothing and hair styles were like. Some of his paintings depict flirtations and courtship, or parties in which *kisaeng* entertainers are dancing, singing, or otherwise performing for male patrons in *yangban* costumes.

Kim Hongdo was a more formal painter than Shin Yunbok and started out with classical themes that included plums, orchids, lotus flowers, and Chinese-style landscapes. His painting *Ui-i Sailing Home* is full of references to Chinese styles. The components of his painting *Picnic*, though less formal, are still Chinese. *Spring Journey* offers a typical Chinese theme—stopping to watch a swallow in a willow tree—but adapts it to Korea by showing the people in Korean clothes. *The Falcon Hunt* does much the same thing, including two women as part of the hunting party. But Kim also loved to paint scenes of ordinary life and injected humor into his works.

Koreans appreciate Shin Yunbok and Kim Hongdo because they painted their "home culture." But they also appreciate uncompromisingly classical artists such as the mid-fifteenth-century court painter named An Kyŏn. An Kyŏn is most famous for his monumental Chinese-style landscape entitled *Traveling to the Peach Groves in a Dream*, which was painted to illustrate the dream of Crown Prince Yangp'yŏng. Dao Jian, a famous Chinese writer of the third century, wrote a story about a man who found a narrow opening in some rocks and, when he passed through, found himself in a kind of paradise where everything was peaceful and the people had everything they wanted. (The story has undergone many retellings in many countries and is even known in the West as the inspiration for the legend of Shangri-la.) However, after the man went home to tell his friends about his wonderful discovery, he spent the rest of his life trying to find his way back without ever finding the opening in the rocks.

In his dream, Prince Yangp'yŏng dreamed that he was in the peach groves of Dao Jian's story, and when he woke up he summoned the court painter An Kyŏn to listen to his description and paint what he had seen. The result is a most beautiful landscape, full of the mystery and magic of the story. An Kyŏn used mists and rocks and pale colors on the trees to convey the feeling that the prince described to him. The painting is a panorama of the valley in sections that show both the peach grove and the rocks, chasms, and natural obstacles that make it so hard to find. An Kyŏn's *Traveling to the Peach Groves in a Dream* is still one of Korea's most accomplished works of classical East Asian landscape painting. Ironically, at one point it was acquired by a Japanese collector who took it out of Korea, and today it hangs in the Tenri Central Library south of Nara, Japan.

East Asian artists traditionally studied painting by learning how to depict common components in classical paintings such as rocks, flowing water, trees, mountains, various kinds of surfaces, and people and animals. There were handbooks of examples that budding artists were supposed to copy until they had mastered the models of each thing. Chinese painters learned how to paint in this way and so did the Koreans, and the skill of the mature artist lay in his ability to combine the familiar elements and present pleasing variations on the work of the masters. *Traveling to the Peach Groves in a Dream*, for example, contains many elements common to Chinese landscapes of the eleventh century, most notably *Early Spring*, by Guo Xi, now in the Palace Museum on Taiwan.

In the eighteenth century, the most refined Korean artists were scholar-painters who worked in a time they considered to be one of crisis. The much-admired Chinese civilization had been taken over by Manchu invaders and the imperial throne was occupied by emperors who were technically "barbarians." Koreans saw China groaning under a yoke of illegitimate foreign rule, its values trampled and its culture humiliated. Koreans saw themselves as guardians of the light of civilization in East Asia, custodians of the ethical and artistic traditions that the Chinese had shared with them. The long-reigning Korean kings Yŏngjo and Chŏngjo (from 1724 to 1800) sponsored court artists who were commissioned to paint things that inspired a sense of order, reason, respect, and discipline. These two great monarchs themselves led austere and proper lives, and the art they sponsored through the Royal Painting Academy (the *Tohwawŏn*) was often meant to inspire similar qualities in the viewers. They admired portraits of great and moral men. They ordered paintings of rituals and festivals being performed in a correct and orderly manner. They commissioned works that extolled virtuous and unselfish acts, as in stories of obedient children sacrificing their own comfort in order to make their parents' lives easier. Indeed, solemn portraits, multi-paneled screens showing processions and royal audiences and state occasions, and depictions of King Chŏngjo loyally visiting his father's grave are all major themes within this eighteenth-century Korean style.

In the modern era, Korean art has been influenced by world trends. Today's Koreans enjoy modern art and are well versed in the recent phases of painting in the West. In the early twentieth century, Koreans adapted certain methods and perspectives from Japan. Leading artists like Yi Chŏng'u and Yi Insŏng went abroad to study, first in Japan and then in Europe, returning to paint in styles adapted from the French impressionists. In the 1930s and 1940s, Koreans experimented with constructivism and produced works with rigid, metallic shapes that were suggestive of masculine and military feelings.

The war years interrupted the flow of Korea's artistic productivity. During

the Second World War, whatever art there was had to be patriotic and supportive of the imperial cause. After Korea's liberation in 1945, the national
division threw the arts community into turmoil and the Korean War (1950–
53) reduced everyone, including artists, to the level of battling to survive.
There was little time for contemplation and artistic expression, and people
were too busy to visit and enjoy museums and galleries. The prosperity that
came with economic development in South Korea, at least, during the 1970s
and 1980s created a demand for new and more sophisticated art. Art de-
partments in colleges were filled with students trying their hands at painting,
ceramics, and sculpture. Artists' associations encouraged various forms of
modern art, while individuals experimented with materials, perspectives, and
compositions to try to blend traditional and "modern" art into something
uniquely Korean. In the 1980s, during the worst of the South Korean military
dictatorship under strongman Chun Doo-hwan, "people's art" (*minjung
misul*) became a powerful method of social and political protest. "People's"
artists presented scenes of struggle against injustice, depicting politicians and
industrialists as rich and cruel abusers of workers and ordinary people. Their
works pointed to the unfair distribution of the benefits of modernization and
encouraged the struggle for democracy that eventually ended the long years
of harsh military rule.

Probably the Korean artist who is best known overseas is Nam-June Paik
(Paek Namjun), the founder of "video art" and a major figure in avant-garde
art. Paik's creations at first appear radical, technological, and full of wires
and screens and pieces of machines, a far cry from the muddy fields and
thatched roofs of traditional Korea. However, he is part of a generation of
artists who began life very close to these agricultural roots.

KOREAN LITERATURE

The earliest form of literature in Korea was probably a type of ritual poem
or song that was used in worship, and probably was related to ritual dance
and music. The absence of a writing system meant that these expressions
were passed down the generations in oral form and there is no way to recover
them. Koreans started writing with Chinese characters sometime in the early
Three Kingdoms era, probably in the first or second century A.D. when
Chinese influence came through Lolang, a Chinese colony that existed in
northwestern Korea between 108 B.C. and A.D. 313. Though they spoke to
each other in their own Korean language, they wrote things down in Chinese.
Mastery of written Chinese was an expensive luxury and helped draw a line

between educated Koreans, who were an elite minority, and the masses, who remained illiterate. An attempt to adapt Chinese characters to the Korean language was made during the Silla period, when the *idu* system was created. The *idu* system used certain Chinese characters possessing the range of Korean sounds to write things in Korean pronunciation. This made it possible to write down Korean words and expressions, though literacy remained an asset exclusively for the upper class.

Documentary Literature

Korea is rich in government records and documents that tell the country's history from the point of view of the royal court and ruling class. When the historian Kim Pusik and the monk Ilyŏn wrote their separate accounts of the Three Kingdoms era (the *Samguk Sagi* and *Samguk Yusa*) they wrote in classical Chinese, and formal history thereafter always followed Chinese models, which included "annals" that told the story of what happened more or less chronologically, followed by "biographies" of the most important people in the government and leading families, and additional sections that rearranged the material in the annals to tell the stories of individual provinces and counties. The *Chosŏn Wangjo Sillok*, or "Veritable Records of the Chosŏn Dynasty," was a compilation many thousands of pages long that was at once a historical narrative and an encyclopedia of the dynasty with sections covering agriculture, the economy, defense, music, and fiscal matters. In addition, census documents recorded the names and functions of everyone at intervals during the dynasty. Gazetteers served as records of particular locales, including geography, famous people, leading families, and important events. And the government kept meticulous records of who passed the civil and military service examinations and thereby won access to the two compartments of the ruling *yangban* class.

It was therefore necessary for anyone concerned with the public business to be adept at classical Chinese, and for anyone aspiring to become an official at any level to study Chinese and learn the conventions associated with it. This of course was the reason for Korean education to be Chinese-style education stressing mastery of the Confucian canon. The Confucian classics were models for Korean students, full of stories and examples drawn from Chinese, and not Korean, history. The letters and essays that they wrote in the course of their lifetimes were collected into personal anthologies called *munjip* that together constitute an essential part of Korea's literary heritage.

Korean Poetry

While the Koreans were using only Chinese, they developed "Chinese poetry," or *hansi*, a rigid though beautiful literary form that used characters in lines of five or seven characters arranged into rhymed poems of four or eight lines. This poetic form reached its height during the Tang dynasty in China, and Silla intellectuals adopted it along with much else because of their admiration of Tang culture.

Idu literature is much rarer than *hansi* poetry, and only twenty-five *idu* poems survive in the genre called *hyangga*, which did not have to conform to the rigid prescriptions of Chinese poetry. In the Koryŏ period, Koreans began to tell longer stories through their poems and songs. They devised a "long poem" form called *changga*, some of which was in pure Chinese and therefore regarded as cultured and elegant, and some of which was in pure Korean, which was less well regarded.

During the Koryŏ period, Koreans also invented *sijo*, a poem-song format that used the Chinese words that had become part of the Korean language but put them in the context of Korean grammar. *Sijo* were "personal" poems, emotional expressions that communicated feelings of love, regret, grief, and even anger. The first *sijo* poem-songs were probably recorded in the mixed *idu* writing and rewritten later in pure Korean after the invention of the *han'gŭl* alphabet in 1446. *Han'gŭl* was ideally suited for any kind of writing that stressed exact use of Korean, such as poetry, and for that reason it was used for songs and poems even after the ruling *yangban* rejected the alphabet and continued to use classical Chinese for documentary and literary writing. *Sijo* therefore is the literary form most closely associated with *han'gul* and is regarded as a unique Korean style.

A *sijo* poem consists of three lines with an average of fifteen syllables to a line with the total never exceeding forty-five. The love songs of Hwang Chini (ca. 1506–44), an acclaimed woman poet, are among the most beautiful examples of the genre, at times tender and at times petulant and even angry. Her special talent was romantic emotion, but the *sijo* style of poetry was highly adaptable to other themes as well, such as the political and the satirical. The most skilled *sijo* poets employed symbols and allusions to get their points across. As the Koryŏ kingdom was tottering on the verge of ruin, about to be overthrown by General Yi Sŏnggye, the general's son Yi Pangwŏn (1367–1422) invited Chŏng Mongju, one of the crumbling kingdom's most important statesmen, to dinner to try to win him over to the revolutionaries' cause. He put his proposition in the form of a *sijo*, which he is said to have sung to the older man at the table using "the rank weeds of Mansu-san," a mountain on the outskirts of the Koryŏ capital, to refer to Chŏng's loyalty to the dying Koryŏ dynasty.

> What about going this way? What about going that way?
>> Tangled in the rank weeds of Mansu-san, how can you thrive?
> Ah, but if we were entwined together, we could last a thousand years!

Chŏng Mongju (1337–92) is said to have responded with a *sijo* of his own. It endures as one of the best expressions of the cardinal virtue of loyalty to one's lord in all Korean literature:

> Though this frame should die and die, though I die a hundred times,
>> My bleached bones all turn to dust, my very soul exist or not
> What could change the undivided heart that glows with faith toward my lord?

History records that after refusing to join the general's son, Chŏng Mongju left the dinner and was assassinated on the way home, presumably by Yi Pangwŏn's men, as he was crossing a bridge over a stream. And according to legend, Heaven still honors the old statesman's sacrificial loyalty by causing his bloodstains to show on the stone bridge whenever it rains.

One of the Chosŏn kingdom's most famous *sijo* writers was Chŏng Ch'ŏl (1536–93), who himself lived in troubled times and several times suffered dismissal and exile from high office. Near the end of his life he used this metaphor for the feeling of growing old too soon:

> Well within the palace gate in the office of the guard,
>> I hear the twenty-three strokes telling the last watch of the night.
> Time passes and is already gone. Maybe it was all a dream.

Yun Sŏndo (1587–1671) is generally regarded as the greatest of *sijo* poets, ranked with Chŏng Ch'ŏl and Kim Sujang (1690–1769). Yun's fame derives from the volume of his output, crowned by a forty-stanza epic about the seasons, entitled *The Fisherman's Calendar*. Kim Sujang is famous for the whimsical humor in his *sijo*. He wrote this verse about making up his mind for himself:

What is black, they say is white
   what is white they say is black.
Be it white, be it black
   nobody says that I am right.
I had best stop my ears, close my eyes
   and refuse to judge things.

P'ansori Epics

Both Yun Sŏndo and Kim Sujang took liberties with the syllable-count rules of *sijo*, extending the line and inventing a variant form. In time, many *sijo* writers did likewise, and many *sijo* were really drinking songs, sung by revelers around a table, vying with each other for the best rendition, using chopsticks as percussion tools on the table's edge. Their poems (or songs) verged toward another great genre of Chosŏn-era poetry-singing called *p'ansori*, a narrative form that seemed to have no length constraints at all. *P'ansori* folk opera, as it developed in the form of a literary genre, was an epic performance by a single singer called a *kwangdae*, with no props other than a handkerchief and a fan to wield as disguises, tools, weapons, or whatever the moment called for. Accompanied by a percussionist keeping rhythm on a drum and punctuating the singer's points with contrapuntal sounds of agreement, shock, encouragement, and disapproval, the *p'ansori* performer would enthrall audiences for hours with operatic versions of much-loved folktales. *P'ansori* singing required a formidable vocal range, since the performer not only had to sing but also had to express the gamut of emotions in the voices of all the different characters in the story. The performance typically took many hours and usually left the performer (and the audience) exhausted.

A good example of the *p'ansori* genre is the story of the girl named Ch'unhyang, meaning "Spring Fragrance," known in Korean as *Ch'unhyang-jŏn*. Ch'unhyang was the daughter of a *kisaeng* entertainer, a common girl living in the country town of Namwŏn who had a love affair with Yi Mongnyong, the son of a powerful *yangban* in the district. Because of the social difference between them they had to keep their affair a secret and were secretly married. Not long after the marriage, Yi Mongnyong's father ordered him to travel to Seoul, the capital, to advance his career as a budding government official. Mongnyong had to leave his bride behind, and because everyone thought she was still single, when a new governor came to town he ordered Ch'unhyang to become his concubine and threatened to imprison her if she refused. Ch'unhyang could have avoided trouble with the magistrate if she had revealed that she was already married to Yi Mongnyong, but knowing that her husband's chances of success would have been hurt by the news that he was married to a *kisaeng*'s daughter, she kept her silence. She tried to defend herself on moral grounds, arguing that she was a pure young woman who should not be forced to become a concubine to anyone against her will. When her argument failed and she still refused to obey the governor, she was thrown in prison where she suffered terrible torture and other miseries.

Meanwhile, Yi Mongnyong did succeed in Seoul, passing the civil service examinations and being appointed to important positions. He rose to the position of secret inspector, a type of government official who traveled around the country in disguise to spy on other officials who might be abusing their power and exploiting the people. Disguised as a beggar he returned to his hometown of Namwŏn, only to learn that his beloved Ch'unhyang had been insulted and imprisoned by the evil governor. He immediately had the governor fired and then, because he was now in a position to marry anyone he wanted, he openly acknowledged his marriage to the still-beautiful Ch'unhyang and they lived happily ever after.

The Ch'unhyang story was ideally suited for *p'ansori*. The young lovers' dilemma, their tragic separation, the arrival of the evil governor and his abuse of the innocent heroine, Ch'unhyang's faithfulness, the suspense about whether Yi Mongnyong would ever find out what had happened to his wife, and his miraculous return to liberate her and punish the evildoer all were themes that made for a highly emotional presentation, using action, comedy, satire, many kinds of voices, and long expositions on morality and on the arrogance of the ruling *yangban* as they abused common people. The story was popular enough to be sung and told in forms other than *p'ansori*, and in modern times there have been several opera and movie versions.

Han'gŭl Novels

The first Korean vernacular novel was *The Story of Hong Kiltong* by Hŏ Kyun (1569–1618). Like the story of Ch'unhyang it is a satire in which commoners outdo the upper class. The hero, named Hong Kiltong, is the leader of a band of thieves who set up a classless community on an isolated island and succeed in getting along without the *yangban* and their laws and privileges. Nearly a century later, the novelist Kim Manjung (1637–92) wrote *The Cloud Dream of the Nine* (*Ku'unmong*), based on the Buddhist idea of dreams and clouds that hide reality. It too concerned the conflict between pretense and reality in the lives of the ruling class.

Women wrote fictional works, including historical novels, in the seventeenth and eighteenth centuries using the *han'gŭl* script that most educated male writers tried to avoid. The authors were court ladies; that is, wives and mothers of powerful men who had to keep their silence while observing the cruelties and injustices of court politics. Since they were not writing for publication at the time and were in effect keeping secret diaries for their own use, they were not bound by the rigid forms and conventions that stripped so much of the men's writing of emotion and color. As a result, in modern times their *han'gŭl* writings have reappeared as popular novels about court life, full of characters and judgments about right and wrong. Like the Ch'unhyang story these have made good screenplays, and television series based on them have been wildly popular. *The Tale of Queen Inhyŏn (Inhyŏn wanghujŏn)* is one that concerns a manipulative royal concubine who tries to remove the reigning queen in order to get her own son in line for the throne and has to commit multiple murders in the process. Eventually the king realizes the evil of the concubine and has the queen restored to her rightful place.

The most famous court novel by a woman is *The Memoirs of Lady Hyegyŏng* (the *Hanjung-nok*). The writer, Princess Hyegyŏng (1735–1815), tells the story of the court of King Yŏngjo (r. 1724–76) and the tragic fate of her husband, Crown Prince Sado. Written in diary form, the *Hanjung-nok* tells about the plots against Princess Hyegyŏng's husband, Prince Sado, how the plotters convinced King Yŏngjo that the prince was a criminal and deserved to die, and how the king had him locked in a box to starve to death. Like many other Korean classics the theme of the novel is one of miscarried justice—of unfair and arbitrary treatment and the abuse of power. King Yŏngjo was a great ruler but his blindness in the affair of his own son and heir was a great national tragedy. Princess Hyegyŏng's written record not only kept the historical event in the minds of the Korean people but also contributed a work of literature that is a Korean equivalent of a Shakespearean epic in the West.

Modern Literature

Han'gŭl writing came into its own at the beginning of the twentieth century, when Western science and literature entered Korea and the traditions of Korea's past were under attack from every direction. Korea's ancient relationship with China ended in 1895 and Korean intellectuals renewed their search for authentic Korean avenues of expression. The idea of writing novels was new in Korea and the first "modern" novel, entitled *Tears of Blood (Hyŏl-*

ŭi nu) by Yi Injik (1862–1916), was a blend of romantic Chinese-style storytelling and modern ideas, told in themes of modernization, the thirst for modern knowledge, and the quest for individual and national liberation.

A decade later, the novelist Yi Kwangsu (1892–?) took Korean fiction to a new level with his *The Heartless* (*Mujŏng*), a romantic story about the clash between traditional and modern lifestyles, the generational conflict of true love versus arranged marriage, the experience of studying abroad, and the need to sacrifice patriotically for the Korean nation. Yi Kwangsu was a "nationalist," one whose work inspired resistance against Japanese colonial rule and contributed to the March 1, 1919, Independence Movement in Korea.

The failure of the uprising against Japan in 1919 left Korean intellectuals in a quandary about whether to accept Japanese rule or continue what appeared to be a hopeless resistance. Many writers became "cultural nationalists," looking for ways to preserve "Koreanness" and the consciousness of Korean culture through study and "self-strengthening." In the 1920s, Korean intellectuals founded a variety of literary journals, trading ideas through short stories and novellas that were influenced by comparable movements in China, Russia, and the West. Translators introduced Korean readers to the works of Western writers from Dostoevsky to Tolstoy to Zola, creating a niche for criticism and pessimism, things that seemed to belong in any view of Korean society at the time. This form of "realism" helped writers like Kim Tong'in (1900–51) and Yŏm Sangsŏp (1897–1963) write about Korea as they saw it, with all the cruelties that came from Japanese colonialism and the mass ignorance that afflicted their own people. Yi Sang (1910–37) wrote about the inner mind of Koreans, plumbing the depths of psychology and self-absorption. In the 1937 novel *Peace under Heaven* (*T'aep'yŏng Ch'ŏnha*), Ch'ae Mansik (1902–50) uses humor to present a selfish protagonist named Master Yun who is constantly scheming to get ahead but is constantly undone by his own flaws, bad choice of friends, and people who take advantage of him. In a manner reminiscent of the Chinese writer Lu Xun's character Ah Q, Ch'ae makes Master Yun a metaphor for the hapless Korean people under Japanese colonialism.

These works welled up out of a national soul that had been shattered by the death of the monarchy and the Japanese conquest. The overriding theme of most Korean literature in the twentieth century has been the search for national wholeness, first under foreign rule and then, after 1945, in a divided country with two bitterly hostile regimes poised on the verge of civil war. When government censors blocked most avenues of expression, writers continued to discuss the human cost of Korea's political plight. Simply by writing literature in Korean between 1910 and 1945 they performed acts of resistance, since Korea's "national language" officially was Japanese, and the speaking and writing of Korean was, in effect, an act of rejection and even subversion against Japan. Korean children were being taught in schools where Japanese was the language of instruction, and "literature" classes were about Japanese, not Korean, writers. As the war years approached and Japan's grip on Korea tightened, it took more and more courage to preserve the Korean language at the heart of Korean national consciousness. Writers such as Ch'ae Mansik and Yi Kwangsu were risking a great deal to keep Korean literature alive.

When the Allies liberated and divided Korea in 1945, there was a brief moment when Korean writers thought they might be free to establish their own literature in their own land. But very soon it became clear that certain kinds of writing would be illegal, depending upon whether the writer resided in North or South Korea. Korean literature, which had been shaped and distorted by Japanese rule, now was distorted further by the needs of the two Korean regimes. In North Korea, literature had to glorify socialism and the myths of Kimilsungism. In the south, left-wing writers were blacklisted. Both sides insisted on government-approved interpretations on all portrayals of the nation's central ordeal, the Korean War of 1950–53. As a result, in both North and South Korea, Korean literature continued to be a literature that was estranged from reality. Writers felt it whenever they dared not say certain things. Readers knew it when they read stories that whitewashed events and situations of which they had personal knowledge.

Literature in a Divided Korea

Between 1945 and 1950, the Korean literary world was thrown into turmoil by the reckoning that followed "liberation" from Japan. Intellectuals in general were subjected to charges and countercharges of collaboration. Being educated, they were elite people with privileges that had come from cooperating with the Japanese. Opposed to them were writers who had risked their careers and freedom by joining left-wing groups. More than 100 of Korea's best-known writers migrated to North Korea during this period, with some, like Han Sŏrya, becoming committed supporters of the Communist regime. South Korean writers who were associated with those who had moved north were themselves subjected to severe political persecution, partly because of their left-wing views and partly because of their record of friendship with the turncoats. The names of those who went north were expunged from public discourse. Their works were suppressed as the anti-Communist South Korean government organized a national forgetting of what they had written before they went, and nothing they wrote afterwards was allowed into South Korea.

It took many years for the literary community in South Korea to recover from the events surrounding the Korean War. Not being able to write about the central conflict between North and South Korea, writers in the south instead wrote about earlier times under the late monarchy and the Japanese, a genre that became known as Modern Fiction (*kundae munhak*). Mature writers like Oh Yŏngsu who had already established reputations in the 1930s led with stories about the goodness of common farmers. Kim Tongni (1913–) wrote about the "soul" of Koreans, a kind of "humanistic nationalism" expressed largely through religious undercurrents and critiques of modern materialism. Hwang Sunwŏn (1915–) is Korea's most-translated novelist, with several anthologies of his own in English. Hwang is a more romantic writer, concerned with the beauty of the human world and the expression of human feeling.

Contemporary Korean fiction (*hyŏndae munhak*) is the work of writers who were born too late to experience life under the Japanese or even to remember the Korean War and who received their educations in the Korean language. Their writing used more *han'gŭl* and fewer Chinese characters and referred to life in the divided Korea of their own experience. They were the first to tackle the subject of the Korean War, albeit within limits imposed by the South Korean government. Thus they wrote about suffering and victimization, painting the North Koreans as the villains, and later broadening their criticism to assign responsibility to the United States and the distortions that had been forced on Korea by the international Cold War. Social and political criticism landed certain especially outspoken writers in trouble with the military governments that followed the 1961 coup d'état. Under Presidents Park Chung-hee and Chun Doo-hwan the government closed down literary magazines and blacklisted writers regarded as unfriendly to the regime. Some writers became known for underground writings that were passed around campus and read by members of literary societies.

When the pressure eased in the late 1980s and South Korea underwent "democratization," there was a trickle and then a torrent of contemporary literature reviewing and revising the national consciousness of what had happened in the 1940s and 1950s. Cho Chŏngnae's epic *The T'aebaek Mountains* (*T'aebaek sanmaek*) renewed the discussion of the Korean War as a struggle between common people and privileged elites. Set in southwestern Korea in the late 1940s, it revolved around attempts by patriotic left-wing Koreans to resist the division of the country through separate elections for governments in Seoul and P'yŏngyang. That period in that area of the country had been a time of endemic violence and brutality, and Cho's novel was a popular starting point for a reassessment of the horrors of the Korean War era.

Modern Korean Poetry

When it came to literary protest, no figure stood out more than the poet Kim Chiha, who flourished in the 1960s and 1970s. Kim Chiha fell into disfavor as a protester against the government of President Park Chung-hee in the 1960s. As a writer, he became known for the way he mocked the greed of Korea's emerging business class as well as for criticizing the government. His first attack was in the form of a poem called "The Five Bandits," representing the ruling elites of Korea at the time: a rich businessman, a congressman, a top-ranking bureaucrat, an army general, and a cabinet minister. There is also a government prosecutor who is supposed to arrest the "bandits" but instead acts like their faithful servant. They play golf and drink and keep mistresses, raking in money while talking in government slogans meant to make other people do all the work. In other poems such as "Groundless Rumor" and "Gold-Crowned Jesus" he scorned the injustice and materialism that accompanied the government's policies of dictatorship in the name of national security, materialism in the name of economic development, and accommodation with Korea's former colonial master Japan in the name of progress. For his pains Kim Chiha was accused of associating with Communists, then of actually being a Communist, and for engaging in antistate propaganda. He was virtually silenced by a very long term in prison—but not before becoming a hero of the Korean democratization movement.

Modern Korea has produced many other poets. Kim Sowŏl, born in 1903, experienced the life of a typical Korean intellectual during the years of Japanese colonial rule. After being educated in Korea and Japan, he went to live in a remote corner of northern Korea and wrote poems that demonstrated the beauty and imagination that was possible in modern Korean poetry compared with the stilted, formal Chinese-style poetry that was customary at the time. Unfortunately, he could hardly make a living, tried various lines of work, and finally committed suicide in 1934.

Kim Sowŏl is seen as the first Korean poet to break out of the traditional mold. He used ordinary speech and slang in his work, attracting much appreciation from ordinary readers. "Azaleas" is one of his most famous works, a romantic poem that refers to a flower that blooms all over Korea in springtime. In the poem, "Yaksan" is the name of a mountain near the town of Yŏngbyŏn.

If you tire of me and want to go,
    I'll not resist but let you leave without a word.
On Yaksan, Yŏngbyŏn, I'll pick an armful of azaleas
    And toss them in your path.
Walk lightly on these flowers that adorn your parting steps.
    Then if you grow so tired of me that you would want to go,
I might die but I'll weep no tears.

Korea's best twentieth-century poets are remarkable for their range and passion, combining themes of Korean experience and identity with a love of nature and empathy for other human beings. In his anthology entitled *Unforgettable Things*, Sŏ Chŏngju (1915–), a native of Korea's southwest, presents an autobiography in poetic form that is useful not only as a moving literary collection but also as a historical document, taking the reader through the wrenching changes that Koreans have undergone in the space of two or three generations. The poems in *Unforgettable Things* are unabashedly nostalgic and sentimental, as in the case of this one, entitled "Grandmother":

My grandmother worked every day
of every year, in the fields
or in the house.
Without once going
for a visit in the town,
she worked till she wore away
her finger tips.
Village women from time to time
would stop by for a chat.
Her response was
"Chatterbox!"
Nighttimes too,
until the rooster crowed
she would be spinning
her yarn in the corner
of the room by my bed.
Grandmother: she lost
the tips of her little fingers
giving blood for her husband
when he was once deathly ill.

The court dress she brought
in marriage was kept
stored away in a closet,
never worn.
For occasions like Ch'usŏk,
the Autumn Night festival,
Mother would take it out
and just think
what would it be like
to wear this?

Literature in all its forms is one of the most vital expressions of any culture. Korea's national literature offers an especially good opportunity to see into the hearts of the people and to derive a sense of what it means to be a Korean, whether in the classical or folk traditions or in the bruising ordeals of modern times. Until recently, Korean literature was virtually inaccessible in the West. However, the growth of Korean studies as a field of study in the major universities of North America and Europe has produced a new generation of translators, scholars, and teachers who are presenting Korea's songs, stories, novels, and poems to the world in Western languages. Though some of this literature refers to the specific experience of the Korean people, much of it is based on universal themes of love, longing, and the difficult choices of life, things that people everywhere experiences and find easy to understand. With the emergence of so many new works in translation, Korea's best writers are beginning to find their proper place in the international literary conversation, sharing their gifts with readers around the world.

4

Performing Arts

MUSIC OF THE PEOPLE

KOREAN CHILDREN traditionally grew up hearing percussion patterns all around them, from chopsticks being beaten on the wineshop table to the sounds of their mothers "ironing" clothes by pounding them with flat wooden sticks, and the drumming of village musicians. Percussion, in fact, is a major element in Korean music and was an indispensable part of *nong'ak*, or "farmers' music," a form of entertainment and celebration in rural Korea that was performed by touring bands of musicians and has recently been revived as an authentic Korean art form.

The Importance of Rhythm

Nong'ak is a form of folk music, a genre that includes folk songs (*minyo*) that express the joys and sorrows of rural life in traditional Korea. But whereas folk songs stress storytelling and melody (and most of the songs were never written down and are long forgotten), the rhythms of the folk songs have endured in a kind of national subconscious, being repeated and learned over and over again by successive generations. Some of the rhythms had to do with work, for example, cooperative projects like plowing and digging and pounding. Though vestiges of work songs continued into modern times, as in the "Oisha, oisha" chant of men rocking a car to get it free of the mud, for example, the mechanization of work in Korea has made rhythmic singing and chanting less a part of daily life.

One of the most unforgettable styles of rhythm in the countryside was the funeral chant used by pallbearers as they carried the coffin of their friend or loved one to the burial site. These chants differed from village to village, but they normally consisted of verses and a refrain that gave the leader a chance to sing short stanzas about the deceased and for everyone else to join in on the chorus. Villagers learned the community chant in early childhood and grew up hearing and watching the organized grief that accompanied village funerals, with rhythms and singing as essential components. The night before the burial itself the strong men of the village would rehearse their chant by torchlight, sending chills up and down the spines of onlookers. In the morning the body in the coffin would be carried on a bier through the alleyways of the village and out across the fields that the dead man had owned, and finally to a carefully selected site on a hill above the village for burial. The prescribed ritual gave everyone a role to play and impressed upon the participants the importance of family life and community support. Among the important lessons for the children was the inculcation of music as a part of life and death.

Younger generations of Koreans live in cities and have missed out on many of the opportunities their parents had to enjoy and learn the basic rhythms of Korean music through village rituals and celebrations. Recognizing this, university students have struggled to preserve their national musical heritage by forming music clubs and drumming societies that practice folk singing, dancing, and drumming during leisure hours, creating sounds that greatly enrich the atmosphere on Korean campus afternoons. On many afternoons at Seoul's Yonsei University, for example, Korean folk music societies meet in a large grove on one of the campus hills to tap out the rhythms on their gongs and drums. The percussion of the enthusiastic young performers is a pleasing counterpoint to the cacophony of construction equipment, passing trains, buses, and car horns.

University students spontaneously study Korean folk music because they want to make it part of their own lives. The Korean government, for its part, has institutionalized the preservation of *nong'ak* by funding folk music groups, dance troupes, and "living national treasures," musicians and performers whose skills maintain the tradition. Although some argue that government-sponsored preservation means political control of "approved" art forms—and that, in fact, "folk tradition" belongs entirely to the people and should be free to evolve—cultural preservation has saved much of what is left of Korean music.

In 1978, a musician named Kim Tŏksu started a percussion troupe called *SamulNori* (meaning "Four Things Playing") that uses a *kkwaenggwari* (small

University students perform traditional Korean percussion rhythms at Hahoe, a village known for folk arts in southeastern Korea, 1990.

gong), a *ching* (large gong), a *changgo* (hourglass-shaped two-head drum), and a *puk* (barrel drum). *SamulNori* compressed the many players of farm music bands into a four-musician troupe, creating a kind of musical "team." The word *samulnori* quickly became the generic word for this kind of combination, which remains wildly popular across Korea and has toured the world introducing other people to Korea's elegant and intricate rhythms. There are now *samulnori* troupes in Korean communities in the United States, Europe, and even central Asia. Critics say that *samulnori* has "frozen" Korean rhythm into a few set forms, something like cutting down a forest full of thousands of tree species and replacing them all with rows and rows of just one type. This criticism is a natural consequence of trying to preserve what was, after all, a varied tradition springing from isolated villages all across the country. Nevertheless, insofar as *samulnori* has preserved and shared something extraordinary and beautiful, it has been a great contribution to the world's appreciation of Korean culture.

Singing is an essential part of social life in Korea. Like all civilizations, Korea has its own rich store of children's songs, love songs, folk ballads, and chants. These tunes and lyrics are part of the bond that unites Koreans and makes them feel like part of their shared community. There are children's songs about bunnies, Buddhist songs about going to the "Western Paradise" in a boat made of a crescent moon, romantic songs about being away from home, drinking songs, and songs about being in love. Koreans love to sing. Karaoke is only the latest version of informal entertainment that Koreans have always provided for each other, taking turns singing solos for friends at virtually any social occasion. Korean children are often told to sing for their elders and then are praised lavishly for doing so, and they grow up confident in their singing skills and ability to entertain others with their individual repertoires.

Without doubt the most famous Korean folk song is "Arirang," a lyric ostensibly sung by a girl whose lover is about to leave her to head over the mountains via "Arirang Pass":

> Arirang, Arirang, Ara-ri-yo, Heading over Arirang Pass,
>   If you cast me away and leave me,
>   You'll get footsore before you go ten *li*.

The words to "Arirang" are amusing because of their petulance, but it is the haunting melody that enchants Koreans and has inspired variations and elaborations so that there is a special version of the song for many of Korea's different regions and counties. Composers have written adaptations for everything from brass ensembles to full orchestras.

Folk music is related to folk dancing and folk drama, genres that come together in the much-loved dramatic form of mask dance dramas. These are vestiges of village festival entertainment that go back as far as the Silla kingdom. Though it began as a form of court entertainment, it evolved into a distinctly plebeian type of theater that nearly died out before being revived in the national effort at cultural recovery in the late twentieth century. There are only a few types of mask dramas. One, called *sandae*, has an all-male cast who change masks to play the various characters in scenes that detail the misadventures of a typical *yangban* nobleman, his wife, his concubine, and an assortment of villagers and monks who are supposed to be celibate but are actually very interested in women. This combination makes for many running jokes, giving the audience much merriment. Accompanying the action and dialogue is a musical troupe that plays and chants and sings folk songs, Buddhist music, and other religious incantations and shamanist invocations. Like the equally famous mask dance that is performed in the village of Hahoe, near Andong in southeastern Korea, the performance was designed to be a holiday event to amuse rural people taking a rare break from toil in the fields. The dramas, which were long and drawn out and full of jokes and satirical references familiar to the onlookers, were intended to consume an entire afternoon. The plots were rather disjointed but the actors made up for this by their generous use of slapstick and exaggerated dialects and gestures.

A Classic Puppet Play

Kkoktukaksi is the name of Korea's favorite puppet play; it is presented in a form as old as mask drama and shares many of the same origins in Chinese theater. The characters are the hero, Pak Ch'ŏmji, his wife Kkoktukaksi, his concubine, his younger brother, a nephew, a monster, four Buddhist monks, a pair of female shamans, the provincial governor, and the governor's entourage. There are also musicians who act as extras.

In scene 1, Pak Ch'ŏmji goes on a sight-seeing tour and checks into a village inn to spend the night. He is awakened by a loud gambling game going on outside his door and when he gets up he begins singing songs about the wonders he has seen on his trip.

In scene 2, one of the monks is dancing with one of the shamans. Pak starts flirting with the shamans but discovers that they are actually his own nieces. He is very upset and has his nephew come in to break up the scene.

In the third scene, an ugly monster starts gobbling up the birds in a rice paddy and then turns on Pak Ch'ŏmji and tries to eat him. Once again the nephew comes to the rescue and after considerable struggle, punctuated by all kinds of noise from the orchestra, manages to kill the monster.

In the fourth scene Pak Ch'ŏmji goes looking for his missing wife. When he doesn't find her he takes up with the concubine and is caught by his wife who has just returned. The two women start fighting and the hero is forced to give them equal shares of everything he owns in order to get them to stop. However, the concubine gets all the valuable things while the wife only gets

Scene from the famous mask drama of Hahoe Village,
1990. The character in this satirical piece is wearing a
concubine's mask.

the junk. She vents her fury in song and dance and then heads for the
mountains to join a nunnery.

In scene 5, the concubine breaks up with Pak Ch'ŏmji and his neighbors
persuade him to go retrieve his wife.

In scene 6, the provincial governor arrives at the capital and decides to go
pheasant hunting.

Scene 7 is a funeral for the governor's mother, who oddly is not mourned
by her son. Others have to carry the coffin, and one of the carriers drops it.
Pak Ch'ŏmji's nephew reappears to carry the coffin the rest of the way.

At the end of the play is an eighth scene in which a temple is built on the
mountainside to honor the spirit of the governor's dead mother.

KOREAN CINEMA

Kkoktukaksi is very much a traditional Korean folk play with a village theme that belongs to an earlier era. In the postwar era, movies have become a staple of Korean entertainment. The first Korean movie was shown in 1919. Before long, Korean directors were testing the limits of free expression under Japanese rule by presenting movies about beloved Korean stories such as the story of Ch'unhyang, the first sound movie. Though Koreans produced more than 140 movies before 1945, during the war years they were entirely controlled by the Japanese authorities and were mostly propaganda. After World War II, the Korean film industry struggled back to life and the first color movie, *The Diary of a Woman*, came out in 1949. The Korean War then set the industry back again, and it was not until the mid-1950s that Koreans were able to produce major works of cinema art, the first of which, again, was the Cinemascope version of the Ch'unhyang story (1955).

Realism in Korean Cinema

In the decades since then, Korean cinema has overcome its troubled beginnings and has developed into a vibrant and popular medium enjoyed by all Koreans, at least in the south. Facing economic hardships, low budgets, difficulties in importing film and equipment, Korean moviemakers nonetheless were managing to produce numerous films even in the 1950s. They devised their own styles and themes, portraying the experiences of Koreans under wartime conditions, adapting works of literature, and even lightening the mood with comedies. Among the genres of Korean moviemaking was "women's movies," about the powerlessness of womanhood in a militarized society dominated by a system of male privilege. Another genre was the "road movie," about leaving home and somehow finding it again. "Road movies" (*kil yŏnghwa*) were especially appealing in light of the audiences' own twentieth-century experience of being relocated to Japan, or being refugees from North Korea, of being separated during war, of leaving the farms and moving to the cities, and even emigrating to faraway countries to start new lives. Korean moviemakers entered their works in international film festivals, winning awards in the Asian region and then in world competitions such as the Cannes Film Festival.

Sŏp'yŏnje, a Unique Korean Masterpiece

The award-winning 1993 film *Sŏp'yŏnje* ("The Western Style") by Korea's leading director Im Kwŏnt'aek is an example of how mature and proficient Korean film art has become. The title refers to a richly emotional kind of *p'ansori* singing that is typical of southwestern Korea. In the story, three wandering family members—a man, his stepdaughter, and younger stepson—travel the village roads bonding as a *p'ansori* troupe. The man spends much time teaching the two children how to sing in the *p'ansori* style. The method of teaching, together with the man's enjoyment of the music and the children's eagerness to learn, partly to please their stepfather and partly to excel at the music, reminds everyone in the audience of childhood struggles to study hard and learn well. In one scene, for example, they sit on a porch while he drills them on particular phrases of a much-loved Korean song. In another, the three appear in a valley having mastered the song and walk along singing and dancing in a sequence that is simply lyrical.

The girl works especially hard at becoming a good *p'ansori* performer under her stepfather's guidance. All around them, however, are signs that *p'ansori* is out of style among ordinary people who seem to prefer more modern and international kinds of music. The boy resents his stepfather, grows rebellious, and runs away. His sister becomes depressed and loses some of her skill, following which her stepfather, in a shocking act, cold-bloodedly feeds her medicine that he knows will make her blind. He wants to teach her the deep personal suffering that is required to transcend to the level of a truly great *p'ansori* artist, and though what he does is cruel and inhuman, indeed as a blind artist she does become a brilliant performer.

Eventually the stepfather dies. Some time later the runaway stepson returns to his sister, and in an agony of emotion they spend an entire night singing the famous *p'ansori* epic about the girl Simch'ŏng, who through her own virtue and sacrifice finds a way to restore sight to her own blind father. They don't talk about their tragic family life but spend the hours investing all their emotional energy in the music. Together they give a stupendous performance.

Sŏp'yŏnje is essentially a flashback from the standpoint of years after the events. For Koreans, it is an "inside" movie because of the way it probes the depths of the audience's memory through the use of music. In several different episodes of the film the characters find ways to use their art to help them cope with crushing adversity. The movie shows how art can be much more than a means to make a living. It becomes a way for them to regain life itself. This is why the movie created such a sensation in Korea when it came out in 1993. It struck a deep chord in the consciousness of Korean audiences even though few of them, especially younger viewers, could sing any *p'ansori* or had ever wandered village paths or suffered such terrible tragedies. As one critic put it, "the film is not so much about *p'ansori* as about the voice within us all."

Urban Korea

Economic prosperity has enabled Koreans to give more attention to the arts, both as creators and as consumers. In addition to the folk genres that flourish even in hard times, the boom years at the end of the twentieth century gave people opportunities to take music lessons and studio art classes, to sing and act in public, and to attend every kind of performance from Seoul Symphony concerts to traditional mask dramas to avant-garde plays in the tiny experimental theaters that are main components of Seoul's various university districts.

In their spare time, young people and theater connoisseurs in Seoul like to visit Taehangno ("University Street"), the former location of Seoul National University, which contains the city's greatest concentration of cafes, theater stages, galleries, festivals, and music halls. The generation of university students that functioned as the foot soldiers of the democracy movement in the 1980s has grown up to display formidable artistic talents in the 1990s. In Taehangno, the traditional musical arts of *samulnori* and *nong'ak* coexist with rock and roll, heavy metal, and every shade of popular music in between. Hip-hop and rap have taken their place in Taehangno street performances, while in quiet moments people like to stop and listen to the elderly saxophonist who has become something of a neighborhood institution over the last ten years.

In the theaters of Taehangno, Korean playwrights present their works of social and political protest, their adaptations of Western plots, and their translations of world classics. In the 1980s they were famous for their resourcefulness in finding ways to express illegal criticism of the military dictatorship of Chun Doo-hwan. Nowadays the political protest is more muted and the themes are more likely to be romantic. The social criticism is aimed more at the material world than the ruling classes, since the audiences seem reasonably well-off. Indeed, in the open-air plazas, on the sidewalks, and in the street itself, which is closed to traffic on many weekends, the atmosphere is one of festival and pure enjoyment. Indoors, certain places seem reserved for members of the "386 Generation," the group that is now in their thirties, went to college in the 1980s when the air was thick with protest, and was born in the 1960s, before the economic takeoff.

Some denizens of Taehangno complain that the area is getting too commercial, the theater space is so expensive that struggling new playwrights can't afford to stage their productions there, and there are too many young people bent on having a good time instead of appreciating art. While Taehangno is unlikely to be replaced anytime soon as Seoul's premier performance area, the action is slowly shifting to the Shinch'on area on the west side of town where Yonsei, Ewha, Hong'ik, and Sŏgang Universities are all concentrated with their combined populations of more than 60,000 students. Hong'ik University is famous as a school for artists and the area has a tradition of harboring underground art and music. The clubs and music halls continue to reverberate with the sounds of underground bands while up and down the streets and alleyways students choose to spend their leisure time in computer cafes, experimental movie theaters, and clubs that offer jazz, rock and roll, and specialized genres such as feminist rock.

Much of the action in Taehangno and Seoul's other performing arts areas is representative of international urban culture, the universal style that is so heavily influenced by American and European trends. Visitors are constantly being surprised by the original touches that Korean artists and performers apply to things that seem at first glance to be familiar. In the 1980s there was a strongly nationalist flavor to the arts in Korea, one that drew on the Korean *minjok*, or "race" or "tribe," and referred to the Koreans' shared history of suffering and oppression. The art was meant to challenge and disturb the status quo and criticize the national obsession with economic development. Today the arts have mellowed and the mood is less angry, but the convergence of Korean rhythms and musical forms continues to surprise and enrich, as in the discovery of a traditional farmers' dance being performed across the plaza from the old man playing cool jazz on his saxophone.

5

Daily Life and Folkways

KOREAN FAMILY LIFE

FATHERS AND GRANDFATHERS are the main authority figures in Korean families. This has been true since the official adoption of neo-Confucianism as the state philosophy at the beginning of the Chosŏn period, around A.D. 1400, and it reflects the historic pattern of patriarchy in East Asian culture. The famous "five relationships" of Confucianism—ruler/subject, father/son, older/younger, husband/wife, friend/friend—make husbands responsible for wives and fathers responsible for children. Children, in return, are required to practice "filial piety." Filial piety (Korean: *hyo*) begins with the fact that people are eternally indebted to the parents who give them life, nourish them as helpless infants, protect and provide for them in childhood, and show them how to become good human beings. During childhood people acquire an appreciation for the family heritage that is being handed down to them from previous generations through their parents. They learn that as adults they will be responsible for maintaining and preserving the family heritage and for passing it along to their own future children. They understand that they are part of a network of relatives, with duties and obligations to everyone else in the family. They also realize that they can call upon their family for support throughout their lives. The obligations are mutual and operate as an important source of identity and emotional security.

The idea of filial piety is so pervasive in Korean culture that the language itself is structured to reflect the junior-senior relationship of the parties in any given conversation. A younger person will attach "honorific" elements to sentences to show his or her respect to a parent, teacher, or boss. Throughout every day, people are constantly figuring their relative positions and adjusting the way they speak accordingly. Filial piety is thus the model for almost all social relationships in Korea.

Koreans accept filial obligations as part of life. The obligations set the patterns for getting along with other people and make it easier to know how to act in daily situations. Everyone agrees that parents have a duty to their own ancestors to be wise and benevolent toward their children. Everyone also agrees that it is the children's duty to obey their parents and to repay them with loyalty and sincere effort. In relationships outside the family, people also understand how to behave toward others who are above or below them on the social scale. The idea of filial piety is a model for all these relationships as well.

The obligations that are so important to Korean families are expressed in many aspects of daily life. They determine the tasks that are "women's work" in the household, beginning with early rising to cook the morning rice for the family and the plethora of domestic chores and duties that occupy mothers and female relatives throughout the day. They determine the disciplines and duties of children going to school and doing their best to excel at schoolwork and to be helpful and obedient around the house later in the day. They also determine men's duties to represent the family honorably outside the household, to strive for success and productivity in their work, and to be good guides and providers.

Today, when most Koreans live in cities, there is much nostalgia for the days when farming households often consisted of grandparents, parents, and children—three (and sometimes even four) generations under one roof. There was no old age insurance or social security system, so different generations of a family took care of each other. Grandparents took care of infant grandchildren and it was common to see an old woman with a blanket tied around her containing a baby or even a toddler. The grandmother would go around the village on errands or visiting neighbors with the child strapped to her back, each contentedly keeping company with the other. The grandfather would go out and make his own rounds of visits with other elderly men of the village, sometimes sitting to play a board game or dropping in to the wineshop for a drink. This went on while the middle generation—the parents—were busy working and the school-age children were in classes or helping in the fields. There was a place for everyone and considerable freedom to move around and enjoy friends.

City life has changed that, and in today's high-rise apartment buildings there is little to compare with the social interaction that was so much a part of Korean village life. Nor is there the space. Korean farmhouses were never roomy, but it was easy enough to step outside onto the porch, or into the yard, or out into the village pathways to encounter neighbors. Elderly people nowadays find it boring to be cooped up in apartments with elevators that can only take them down to traffic-choked streets where there is nothing to do but shop. The neighbors are rarely old friends, and there is a feeling that much has been lost in the rush to "progress" from traditional to modern life. Now that there is medical insurance and a certain amount of old age pension support, older Koreans often opt for their own apartments and live apart from their adult children for as long as they can. In this respect modern urban life in Korea resembles life in the United States.

KOREAN HOUSES

The basic layout of the Korean house is still to be found in the countryside and in urban areas where the residents have enough money to own the land that is required to preserve the characteristics of the traditional home. The house is built above ground level in an L-shape, with rooms placed side by side along the inside of the wall that surrounds the family courtyard. People therefore step up and into the rooms, and they always remove their shoes before entering.

Some of the rooms are connected to each other but all of them open on the inner courtyard, either directly or via a porch that runs in front of several of the rooms. Since the rooms open inward toward the central courtyard and their back walls actually make up part of the outer wall of the enclosure, the perimeter of a Korean house can present a rather plain face to the passerby in the street. The back walls of the rooms may have small windows that look directly out onto the street, but a person can walk all around the outside of the house and learn very little about who or what is inside. This assures privacy and security. The women of the household are supposed to be safe from prying eyes and casual encounters with men on the outside, and the wealth of the household is not supposed to be obvious to thieves.

The two parts of the L-shape are the rooms of the living quarters, normally with the kitchen at one end. The other two walls of the enclosure have the gates—normally there is a grand entrance called a *taemun*, which is big enough for a vehicle, and usually there is a smaller pedestrian gate cut in one side so people can pass to and fro without having to open the entire *taemun*— and, if the compound is big enough to warrant it, there is a smaller back gate that is only for people. In olden times—and still in many farmhouses— there is the privy, or outhouse, inside the wall a few paces from the living quarters. In the country there may also be a pen in one corner of the courtyard for an ox or other animal. There may also be a pigpen. In the center of the courtyard there may be a well, sometimes with a pump. In the city, of course, there is running water from the central system.

Koreans have a unique system for heating their homes in the winter. The kitchen is built lower than the other rooms. Cooking is done over a fire whose smoke and hot air are fed through a system of channels underneath the floors of the rooms that lead to chimneys at the other end of the house. Since the floors in these rooms are solid rock, mud, and mortar, they retain the heat that is channeled through them, keeping the occupants warm throughout the day and night. Koreans call these *ŏndol* floors, and they are so fond of the system that even in modern apartments they build copper pipes in the floors to carry warm water and achieve the same effect.

The *ŏndol* heating system is one reason why Koreans sit on the floor, sleep on the floor, and work and eat at low tables instead of raised tables with chairs. At night, the few pieces of furniture are pushed to the side and pads and quilts are brought from the closet and unrolled for sleeping, again on the warm floor. The floor in a Korean house therefore is not really a "floor" at all but a special living surface that is constantly being cleaned and polished. Stepping on this surface with shoes on would be like stepping on the sofa or bed with shoes on in an American house. This is why Koreans always leave their shoes outside the room door or underneath the little porch, if there is one. In fact, it feels so unnatural to enter someone's living space with shoes on that even in modern or "Western-style" homes and apartments there is a little entryway designed for taking shoes off and putting them on.

The basic Korean house is built first by laying the floor with its channels for the *ŏndol* heating system and a covering of flat rocks, mud, and mortar. The structure itself rises on upright beams that support the beams of the roof structure. Doors and windows consist of wood-framed openings with actual door and window panels covered with white rice paper instead of glass. Mud brick walls are constructed between the uprights and covered with plaster, while the roof is covered with straw thatch. Simple wood and earth materials are used for the kitchen and outhouse. The enclosing wall is made of stones laid along layers of earthen bricks and protected from the rain by a "roof" of thatch running along the top of the wall.

Until the second half of the twentieth century, when Koreans began moving into better and more urban kinds of dwellings, this basic farmhouse was part of everyone's experience. Even today, most Koreans share the sensory memories that come from having lived in the basic Korean farmhouse. These include the sight and feel of the wallpaper, the yellow-brown color of the earth and mud, and the sound of rain splashing in courtyard puddles during the summer monsoon. The smells include the wood smoke that emanated from the cooking fire and sometimes seeped up through cracks in the foundation to permeate everything in the house, the musty rolled-up bedding, *kimch'i* pickle in jars and cooking oil in the pan, and dried fish. And their fingertips "remember" the feel of the wood porches worn smooth by generations of sock-clad feet, the comforting warmth that came from underneath the floor, and the holes that were poked in the door paper so people could check on what was happening in the courtyard. These are powerful memories that help make Koreans feel like Koreans.

The wealth and size of a family have dictated variations on the theme of the basic Korean house. All houses, no matter how elaborate, are built around a courtyard. However, a better home would have a *sarangbang*, or visiting room, for the man of the house to entertain his friends and do business. This room usually has its own door to the street as well as a door onto the family courtyard, an *ŏndol* floor of its own, and accoutrements such as books and a low desk. Women and children are generally not welcome in the *sarangbang*, but rather spend the day separately, in women's quarters known as "inner rooms" (*anpang*).

The rooms of a Korean house serve multiple purposes. What might appear to be a living room during the day becomes a bedroom at night, as people take their bedrolls and lay them out on the warm floor. At mealtimes the same room might be a place where food tables are brought in and people gather to eat. The furnishings might include a television, chests or armoires for the rolled-up bedding to be stored in the daytime, and cushions on the floor instead of chairs. These multiple functions mean that fewer rooms are needed, heat is used more efficiently, and families get used to living in much closer proximity than most Americans experience in their family life.

The rooms can be transformed into dining rooms at mealtimes because food is dished up in the kitchen and served on small eating tables that resemble short-legged trays. Nowadays many families eat together, but in traditional times the men of the household were served first and ate separately. Women ate in their own rooms and children ate at their own table, either with the women or last of all. The work of cooking and cleaning up was entirely the responsibility of the women of the household or, in some cases, the cook or housemaid.

A wealthier family's house might be distinguished most readily by the fact that it had a roof of tile instead of straw thatch. Tile roofs on the rooms, *sarangbang*, gates, and even along the walls indicated real status in a village and were proof of a family's prosperity. Members of the *yangban* class lived in tile-roofed houses and as recently as the 1960s there was a stigma of poverty associated with living in a thatch-roofed house. In the late 1960s when South Korea began building the first Seoul-Pusan expressway, officials noticed many thatch-roofed houses within sight of the road. Seeing these as an embarrassment for a modern country, they ordered the owners to get rid of the thatch and install tin roofs if they couldn't afford tile. Similarly, in North Korea, one of the Communist government's goals, not yet realized, has always been to enable its people to "wear silk clothes, eat meat three times a day, and live in tile-roofed houses."

Today there are many Korean mansions with tile roofs that have both *ŏndol* rooms and carpeted Western-style rooms with furniture. In the wealthier neighborhoods of the big cities the comfort and style of these dwellings are the equal of fine homes anywhere in the world. In some cases they have gardens planted with lawns and carefully manicured trees, shrubs, and flowerbeds. Westerners would call these "Japanese" or "Chinese" gardens since they are more familiar with gardens in those countries, but in fact they contain the elements that are common to gardens throughout the region. These include trees that are often cut in topiary fashion, hedges, dwarf trees and shrubs, running water and small ponds that sometimes contain fish, decorative rocks, and man-made items such as stone lanterns, statues, and short sections of decorative wall.

LIFETIME EVENTS

According to the Confucian tradition in pre-modern Korea, there were four ceremonial milestones in a man's life: "capping," wedding, the funeral, and ancestral rituals. "Capping" was the coming-of-age ceremony for a young man, when his hair was put up in a topknot and he was officially given his responsibilities as a male adult in the family. Marriage marked the beginning of his own household, even if the newlywed couple continued to live with the man's parents. Funerals, of course, marked a man's becoming an ancestor, and the rituals in his memory that were performed by his descendants composed the fourth type of "life" ceremony.

Because of the stress on lineage in Korean culture, the ancestral ritual known as the *chesa* has attracted much attention as a key element of family life. The "standard" *chesa* is a family ceremony that remembers one or two, or sometimes three, generations of ancestors in the father's lineage. Families honor their ancestors in *chesa* ceremonies on Lunar New Year's Day and Ch'usŏk, the Harvest Festival. They also honor specific ancestors on the anniversaries of their deaths, particularly if the person being honored has died within the past three years. The ceremony is simple yet elegant and respectful. The men of the family gather in a hall or main room of the house of the eldest living male descendant, into which has been placed the "ancestral tablet" (*shinju*) of the deceased. The tablet is the object that symbolizes the spirit of the ancestor and, if the family has the means, is usually stored in a special shrine called a *sadang*. When it is brought into the house for the *chesa*, the tablet is treated like an extremely valuable and even holy object. Written on it is the name of the ancestor and his titles, if any, and the dates and hours of his birth and death, essential elements for determining his fortune. It is always kept in a polished lacquer case and the case is kept closed except during the actual ceremony, when it is opened enough to expose the tablet to view.

Before the ceremony the women of the household—who until recent years never participated in the ancestral ceremony itself—will have arranged dishes containing assorted grains, meats, fruits, nuts, wine, and pastries or confections along with bowls of rice and soup with chopsticks and spoons as if for a feast. The eldest male relative is the master of ceremonies and leads the men in offering the food to the ancestral spirit. He does this by spooning cooked rice into the soup bowl set before the ancestral tablet. The ceremony varies by region and household but normally the other men take turns symbolically feeding the spirit and then together they do a deep ritual bow, the ultimate sign of respect. They get down on their knees, put their hands on the floor, and then touch their foreheads to their hands. The bow is done slowly and repeatedly, with the participant rising to his feet between each bow.

The complete *chesa* consists of several rounds of this ritual serving and bowing. It may also involve statements addressed to the spirit that resemble prayers to the dead ancestor. It is this feature of the ceremony that has always caused friction between the Confucian tradition and Christianity in Korea, as elsewhere in East Asia, since Christians are supposed to reject spirits and worship only Jehovah, in keeping with the Ten Commandments. However, Christians, like all Koreans, strongly feel the need to memorialize their ancestors in one way or another. They have therefore found ways to turn the traditional ancestral ceremony into a memorial service instead of a feast that connotes communing with the dead.

Birth Customs and Birthdays

Much folk tradition exists to guide the preparation of a Korean mother-to-be. There are food taboos and strict cleanliness practices. As the time for birth approaches, household members do various things to signify "openness" and free passage to ease the delivery. They wear loose clothes and leave things untied. They postpone repairs of holes in the roof and windows. They leave the doors open during the day. The expectant mother borrows clothes from a neighbor who had an easy childbirth. If she dreams of horses and tigers she may expect a boy. If she dreams of flowers she may expect a girl. There is much speculation about the gender of the child and guesswork based on parental characteristics. Most of the time there is a decided preference for a son, but if several sons have already been born to perpetuate the family name, the family may sincerely wish for a daughter.

When the birth occurs it is customary to string a straw rope called a *kŭmjul* across the gate of the family's yard. This is to keep evil spirits away and to request privacy until the mother and family are ready to receive well-wishers. Various items are woven into the straw rope to indicate the baby's gender. In most places red peppers indicate a son and charcoal indicates a daughter. Additional items might include pieces of paper, seaweed, pine branches, and stones.

Inside, family members concern themselves with the recovery of the mother, who traditionally eats soup made from boiled seaweed, a rich source of iron, and rice. Of equal concern is the survival of the baby, since Korea traditionally has suffered a high rate of infant mortality. The family tries not to tempt fate by bragging too soon about the baby or making the baby seem attractive to predatory spirits. A humorous variation on this theme is to give the child a baby name that will repel spirits, such as "Dog Dung" or "Silly One," at least for the first few weeks.

The baby's survival is "official" at the age of 100 days, when a ceremony called the *paegil* takes place. The *paegil* ceremony for a healthy infant is an occasion for friends and neighbors to gather to offer thanks to the Samshin Halmŏni, or "grandmother spirit," who is said to watch over mothers and infants, to offer felicitations and admire the child, and to share in a feast that betokens a long life. An even more important occasion is the *tol*, or first birthday, when the baby again is the center of attention and engages in a little ceremony that indicates his or her future. At the *tol* ceremony the baby is dressed up in a full Korean child's costume, boys wearing miniature officials' caps and girls wearing makeup. The child is then seated in front of a table bearing various kinds of foods and objects such as money, notebooks, brushes, pens, thread, and toys and urged to make a selection. If the child picks up the money, it is said that he or she will be rich. If the child chooses a book, he or she will be good at school. Choosing food means a career in government. Choosing something that can be used as a weapon indicates a

A one-year-old girl and her parents dress up to celebrate her first major milestone in life, Seoul, 1987 (courtesy of Lee Hyesok).

future in the military. Thread indicates a long life. The choice ceremony is full of fun and laughter and is followed by feasting and the presentation of gifts to the child and envelopes of money to the parents, who no doubt face elaborate expenses not only for the party but for the upbringing and education of the child being honored.

Koreans calculate their ages by saying that a person is in the first year at birth. Therefore, a newborn girl is already said to be "one," though what is really meant is that she is in her first year. And she becomes "two" not on her next birthday but on the very next New Year's Day, so that a child born in December (being "one") can actually turn "two" the next month. A better way to express it is by thinking of how many years the person has "known." A person born in the year 2000 has known that year as "one" and 2001 as "two," regardless of the time elapsed since conception or birth. It comes down to recognizing that when a Korean states his or her age in years, it is at least one year more than it would be in the West.

Though Koreans traditionally shared the experience of becoming a year older at the same time on New Year's, modern Korean families regularly celebrate birthdays in the Western style with parties and dinners and congratulatory exchanges of gifts. There is even a Korean version of the song

"Happy Birthday." But there is one birthday that has always been climactic in Korean tradition—the sixtieth. Before the adoption of the Western calendar with its characteristic decades and centuries, Koreans used a system for counting time that ran in sixty-year cycles instead of hundred-year centuries and the years had sequential names, not numbers. The year corresponding to A.D. 1924 was the first year of one cycle and was therefore called the *kapcha* year. The following year, 1925, had the second name in the cycle, which was *ŭlch'uk*. The third year, 1926, had the third name, *pyŏng'in*. A man could be born at any point in the sixty-year cycle but the name of his birth year would not come around again until he turned sixty. A person born in 1943, a *kyemi* year, will turn sixty in the next *kyemi* year, which is 2003. Since this is well beyond the traditional life expectancy in Korea, though many more Koreans live far beyond the age of sixty today, it remains an occasion for considerable celebration. The sixtieth birthday ceremony is called the *hwan'gap* (literally "returning to the *kap* year" or "first year") and is a time for friends and family to gather, feast, and offer deep bows and fine gifts.

Death Customs

Korean funeral customs are a mixture of filial piety, reverence for ancestors, and the rural environment of traditional Korea, all influenced by instructions on family rituals that are contained in classical texts from the Confucian tradition of East Asia. The ideal response to the death of an aged male relative involves a gathering of the family to witness the individual's last hours (though women were not supposed to witness the death of a man, and vice versa). When the man dies, a quilt is used to cover the body and the relatives commence formal mourning, beginning with a loud wail to announce to the villagers that the death has occurred. A relative is sent up onto the roof of the house with a coat belonging to the deceased, to wave it toward the sky in a gesture that symbolizes inviting the spirit not to leave but to return to the body. After this the body is bathed and prepared for burial, a process that may take a day or more while relatives are notified and mourners arrive from other places. After being washed and dressed the corpse is bound tightly with cotton bands tied at seven places from head to ankles. If it has not been prepared in advance, a coffin is constructed. Then the wake begins. The process usually lasts three days: the day of death, the day following, and the third day, which is the day of burial. During this period the family members wear full mourning costumes made of loose-woven hemp cloth, tan in color, made into pantaloons, jackets, and a special kind of peaked hat.

The chief mourner is the eldest son, and it is his duty to grieve visibly,

Mourners (women in white cotton, men in hemp cloth).

wailing and even collapsing and needing to be upheld by his brothers while he cries for his father. Other relatives also wail and cry out loud, venting their feelings and joining in the survivors' bonding ritual. Meanwhile, neighbors and friends from surrounding villages arrive to offer condolences, being received by the eldest son and making contributions toward the expense of the funeral ritual. The visitors' names are recorded in a condolence book and they are invited to stay as long as they want, to join in meals and funeral preparations.

Most villages keep an elaborate wooden bier, the equivalent of the American hearse, in which to transport the coffin from the home to the gravesite. This is a frame, or platform, that is carried by pallbearers, onto which is placed the coffin. The decorations vary with the age and social position of the deceased, but they always include streamers and paper flowers that can be burned at the gravesite as a kind of prayer offering to heaven. The night before the actual burial, the pallbearers bring the bier to the family's courtyard and spend several hours rehearsing their chants. The next morning the coffin is loaded onto the bier and the procession begins its rhythmic journey to the gravesite, which has been carefully chosen on a hillside overlooking the man's fields and perhaps the village itself. The procession makes its way to the grave by a circuitous route that permits the deceased one last visit to his fields.

Leading the procession is a person bearing a funeral banner, a musician or two, someone carrying a black-draped photograph of the deceased, and a funeral director singing the verses to the village's traditional funeral chant, which is chorused by the pallbearers as they carry the bier. Behind the bier comes the eldest son in tan hemp mourning clothes, holding himself up on a staff and venting his grief in crying and wailing. The other relatives and mourners follow in a small parade until the entire company reaches the gravesite on the hill. There the mourners will have prepared a grave. In some villages the coffin is lowered into the grave. In others, the body, still tightly bound from head to toe in mourning cloth, is taken out of the coffin and placed in a specially dug trench in the bottom of the grave. Boards from the coffin are laid to cover the trench, and earth is then shoveled in to cover the boards and fill in the grave. The remaining boards are placed into the graveside fire along with the paper decorations from the bier. All these processes are accompanied by the singing and chanting of the village's funeral song.

A proper village funeral always features a tent beside the gravesite where mourners are invited once again to express their condolences to the family and to make contributions. Wine flows freely and everyone is invited back to the family home in the village to partake of a post-funeral feast. After the funeral the family fashions an ancestral tablet for the spirit of the deceased, carving it of fine wood and inscribing it with essential data. Mourners who arrive too late for the funeral may still express their sorrow in front of this tablet. Later it is placed with the tablets of other family ancestors.

The spirit was thought to remain in the tablet for several months or even years following the funeral. Thus it was very important to offer reverence to the spirit in regular *chesa* ceremonies. The *sosang* ceremony on the first anniversary of death was very important. The *taesang* ceremony on the second anniversary officially ended the mourning period, and only then, theoretically at least, were the family members supposed to stop wearing the hemp mourning clothes. All through the two-year mourning period the children of the deceased were supposed to live subdued lives, refraining from celebrations of any kind and refusing alcohol and other indulgences.

Modern urban Korea, of course, cannot accommodate the traditional village funeral. Instead of a bier there is often a truck. The dead are buried with much less of a wake. The graves are in burying grounds that are confined to zones outside the city limits, and the mourners have to get there by chartered bus. The government officially frowns on the expense involved in traditional funerals and urges families to stick to simpler observances. Nevertheless it is only natural for Korean families, like families everywhere, to express their respect and anguish at the death of a loved one by gathering their friends and staging an impressive ceremony. Though the environment has changed, the impulses and feelings are much as they have always been.[1]

KOREA'S CULINARY TRADITION

Korean food is still thought of as exotic in the West and non-Koreans still consider it an adventure to visit a Korean restaurant. The pungent aromas and tremendous variety of things served with a Korean meal raise many questions and heighten the mystery that surrounds Korean cuisine. Best known is the tangy *kimch'i* dish of pickled vegetables that challenges the palate with a hot and sour taste that takes a few tries to get used to.

Rice is the central element of the main course in any Korean meal, whether breakfast, lunch, or dinner. A simple meal can be made of a bowl of rice and just a few side dishes for flavor. *Kimch'i* would be one of these. Others would be cooked vegetables and perhaps some fish along with sauces such as *toenjang* soybean paste or *kochujang* red pepper paste. There is also a cup of tea.

Soup is the second element of a meal and usually comes in a bowl to the left of the rice bowl. It ranges from the bland vegetable soups, one of which, the seaweed soup called *miyŏk-kuk*, is often eaten for breakfast, to the fiery *tubu chige*, a stew made of tofu ("*tubu*" in Korean) and red pepper paste with the possible addition of boiled clams. *Mae'unt'ang* is a popular fish soup containing white fish (cod, snapper, or pollock), scallions and other chopped vegetables, *tubu*, *kochujang*, and sometimes egg. The variety is very broad.

Arranged around the rice and soup are the *panchan*, or side dishes. Koreans do not use knives and forks, though they use spoons for mixing and stirring things as well as for eating soup. The main utensil is a pair of chopsticks for the rice and side dishes. The lack of a knife is not usually a problem since the cooking process involves cutting things into bits that can easily be managed with chopsticks. One of the few things that is eaten with the fingers is a lettuce-leaf rollup of rice, *kochujang* pepper paste, and samples from the side dishes, that is popped into the mouth.

Koreans do not normally eat desserts such as ice cream or cake. Pastries and sweets are part of their diet but they tend to be consumed in bakeries and tearooms and not generally after ordinary meals. Instead, there is something that is intended to cleanse the palate at the end of the meal. One typical "after-meal" is *sungyung*, a broth made from water boiled in the bottom of the rice pot. Another is a selection of whatever fruit is in season, often together with tea.

The famous *kimch'i* pickle, which could be called Korea's national dish, has many variations, but the main one is made with Chinese cabbage, garlic, ginger, salt, and red chili pepper and occasional other vegetables. The cabbage is cut and packed into a brine containing the other ingredients where it soaks up the flavors and ferments in special crock pots for more or less time depending on the season. Winter *kimch'i* is made during a kind of national festival known as *kimjang*, which follows the cabbage harvest in the fall. The food markets receive truckloads of Chinese cabbage and the average family will buy as many as 100 heads, with all the accompanying necessities including the ingredients for the alternate forms of *kimch'i* that are made with radishes, turnips, and cucumbers. At home the women of the household will trim and wash the vegetables, prepare the brine, and pack the raw *kimch'i* away in big jars (called *tok*) to sit for several weeks before it can be doled out in small side dishes at the table. *Kimjang* is a major social occasion, a kind of national pastime where people socialize in the markets and in helping each other prepare the food. The process is the same at other times of the year but involves smaller quantities and different combinations of ingredients, and the fermentation period varies. In the summer it may be just a day or two.

If *kimch'i* is Korea's most famous vegetable, its best-known meat dish is undoubtedly *pulkogi*, composed of thin strips of marinated lean beef that are barbecued over hot coals. Barbecued beef ribs called *kalbi* are also popular. Pork and poultry are also common meat dishes along with fish. Meats are cooked according to a wide variety of recipes: ground, sliced, roasted, fried, or broiled, always with appropriate seasonings.

Being surrounded on three sides by the ocean means that Korea enjoys abundant seafood. The coastline is dotted with fishing villages and communities that make their living from the sea. The inlets and bays of the southern coast are full of oyster beds. The deep cold waters of the East Sea (Sea of Japan) are rich in migrating schools of fish. Shrimp boats light up the surface of the sea at night, attracting shrimp to the fishermen's nets. Mechanization of the fishing fleet has enabled Korean fishermen to go farther out in larger boats and bring back bigger catches: some go as far as the South Pacific and the Gulf of Alaska in search of salmon, tuna, and even whales.

Along the west coast, where the water is more shallow, fishing is sometimes done with traps that take advantage of the high fluctuation in tides to catch mullet, shad, and corvenia. Boats go out to catch ray, eel, and croaker. Cuttlefish and squid are favorites, and a favorite snack in Korea is the dried squid jerky called *ŏjingŏ* that is sold in every roadside shop and grocery and convenience store in the country. Since no place is very far from the sea and transportation is excellent, South Korea's fish markets are lively places full of fresh delicacies for the table.

Seasonal Foods

Koreans look forward to each of the year's four seasons for the different kinds of foods that are typical of each one. The spring brings strawberries. Summer brings peaches, melons, and tomatoes, which Koreans count as fruit. Fall brings apples and pears and other delicacies of the harvest season such as persimmons. During the winter, people warm up with tea and roast chestnuts. People delight in the variety.

The wide-scale adoption of greenhouse farming has also made it possible to extend the growing season. Sheltering fields under vinyl "tents" makes it possible to harvest Korea's succulent strawberries much earlier in the year. Bananas, which used to be imported, can now be grown in heated greenhouses on Cheju Island off the southern coast. And although Korea has always had mandarin oranges, Koreans now grow their own Florida-style oranges in the southernmost part of the country.

Chinese, Japanese, and Western Food

Koreans do not normally entertain guests in their own homes, which are set up as private domiciles. Nor, for the most part, do couples entertain other couples. Instead, women have their own friendships that are confined mainly to the household and to aspects of women's work outside the home, such as communal *kimch'i* making. Social life—that is, interaction with those who are not related but are associates in the "public" sphere—is more typically a male prerogative, and it takes place away from the house. Though the household head may have a *sarangbang* visitors' room at home in which to receive and entertain friends, he normally prefers to go out to a restaurant, coffee shop, or tearoom to meet his friends and associates. So much interaction goes on in restaurants, in fact, that even the smallest Korean village has an establishment where one can order food and get together outside the home. The menu in the village restaurant may be wholly Korean, but in any larger town there will invariably be one or more Chinese restaurants. In a small city there will also be at least one Japanese restaurant. In a medium-sized city such as Taejŏn or Taegu there will be Western restaurants also, and in the largest cities such as Seoul, Inch'ŏn, and Pusan there are world-class international restaurants, many of them in international hotels. The capital city features not only French, Italian, and American cuisine but restaurants that feature Mexican, Indian, Thai, and Pakistani menus in addition to thousands of Chinese, Japanese, and Korean restaurants.

Koreans are also shifting their dietary patterns at home. Though rice is still the staple at any meal, there is an increasing emphasis on wheat products such as bread and noodles. Korean food takes a lot of time to prepare and Western convenience foods are continually gaining popularity as family members spend less and less time in the home because of outside obligations. This change in the pace of life accounts for the popularity of fast-food chain restaurants including the ubiquitous McDonald's, Wendy's, and Burger King.

Wines and Liquors

No important occasion is complete without a celebratory meal or feast, and no feast is complete without wine. Korea now makes very good Western-style wine from grapes, but traditional wines and liquors have always been made from grains, chief among them rice. The lowliest wine for everyday consumption in village wineshops all over Korea is a coarse, milky-white brew called *makkŏli*, sour to the taste and with a consistency like soup. The commonest types of *makkŏli* ("quick-brew") are made from a rice mash that ferments in ten days to two weeks and is stored in whatever tub, vat, jar, bottle, plastic or metal container is handy. It is usually dispensed from a metal teapot and drunk from a bowl. *Makkŏli* quality varies by age and place; however, there are standard recipes and the taste is so basic to life in the village that it stirs a great homesickness among soldiers at camp and students away in the city where vast quantities of *makkŏli* are consumed in university districts.

Moving up the scale from lowly *makkŏli*, the common types of wine are *t'akju, yakju,* and *soju. T'akju* is a wheat-based wine made from grain husks that are left in moist cakes to ferment for several weeks and then made into a mash that is eventually strained, fermented further, and served up as a light beverage with about 10 percent alcohol content. As with *makkŏli*, the making of *t'akju* is completely unregulated at the village level and varies widely in quality, taste, and alcohol content. *Yakju* is made the same way as *t'akju* but it is strained better and has a higher alcohol content, often exceeding 15 percent. Both *t'akju* and *yakju* can be served warm, which tends to increase their effect.

Soju, the most potent of village drinks, is made from rice mash and is thoroughly strained and allowed to ferment until it is something like vodka, with an alcohol content of 25 percent. *Soju* is brewed commercially by liquor companies that make it under strict controls and sell it in bottles under brand names. Accordingly, it is more expensive than the coarser kinds of village wine.

A lazy afternoon in a country wineshop.

Variations on these liquors include *chŏngjong*, a rice wine that is served warm and corresponds to the better-known Japanese *sake*, and ginseng wine, called *insamju*, which consists of a glass decanter of *soju* with a ginseng root in it. Ginseng, which is prized for its restorative qualities and medicinal value, is best when it occurs in a root that resembles a human body with limbs. A decanter of *insamju* that contains a finely shaped ginseng root can be very expensive and makes an excellent gift.

Under Japanese rule (1910–45) the colonial authorities took over the liquor industry in order to establish standards and collect taxes. They also imported new alcoholic beverages such as beer. Korea thus has acquired much experience making Western-style beer in modern breweries that are now licensed to bottle American and European brands such as Budweiser and Heineken. Korean distillers also make their own Western-style whiskies.

Drinking as a Social Event

Drinking is an important part of Korean social interaction, especially among men. In the village there is always at least one wineshop where the farmers gather after hours to trade stories and drink from *makkŏli* bowls or small (one-ounce) glasses. Drinking etiquette involves rounds of drinks that are traded. When a person's glass is empty he is never supposed to fill it himself. Instead, the host or someone else at the table will make sure the glass is refilled or will pass him his own glass to share. An honored guest is supposed to drink from all the glasses that are presented to him and to return the compliments by refilling the glasses of others. The result is that people at the table quickly become drunk. There are endless kinds of drinking games and there is often much merriment. There are famous occasions when the drinkers challenge each other to compose couplets of poetry within a time limit or be forced to consume another glass of wine. Drinking is almost always accompanied by singing, both individually and in the group. In the uppermost strata of society, the drinking establishments are mansions with luxurious rooms where fine food is served and the merrymakers are waited on hand and foot by beautiful young women in traditional Korean *hanbok* dresses. Since all these activities revolve around the consumption of alcohol, there is naturally a considerable amount of alcohol abuse, and Korea is no stranger to the social and familial consequences of alcoholism.

It is considered inappropriate for Korean women to drink alcohol until after their children are grown up. Then it is common on social occasions such as picnics for women to get together in groups of their own. These outings are often accompanied by considerable alcohol consumption, with resulting high spirits, singing, dancing, and occasional mishaps and hang-overs.

KOREAN COSTUMES AND FASHIONS

The traditional Korean costume is a loose-fitting ensemble called *hanbok* ("Korean clothes"). The woman's *hanbok* consists of a short jacket called a *chogŏri* that covers the bodice that serves as the top part of a long flowing skirt called a *chima*. The *chogŏri* jacket has sleeves and is fastened together in the front by a wide flowing ribbon that is tied with an elegant bow, creating the effect of a willowy figure with long graceful lines. The man's *hanbok* is composed of roomy pantaloons (*paji*) tied at the ankles and belted with lengths of wide cloth tape, and a jacket with pockets that reaches below the waist and is fastened with buttons or small ribbon ties.

These women's and men's costumes are subject to many variations depending on weather, season, and the wealth of the wearer. The simplest and commonest *hanbok* are white cotton ensembles worn by farm women in their daily work. City women invariably wear Western clothes for daily use but resort to *hanbok* when they want to dress up. Men wear *hanbok* less, both in the countryside and city, because their costume is less well suited to modern industrial and office environments. But all Koreans, whether women, men,

Village newlyweds, the bride in her traditional *hanbok.*

or children, own *hanbok* for family occasions such as the New Year's Day bowing before grandparents. And on national holidays in parks and recreation areas families prefer to appear in *hanbok* as an affirmation of the tradition being remembered on the occasion.

The design of the women's *hanbok* especially appears to have been influenced by Chinese court costumes of the Tang period (A.D. 618–907) and earlier. Paintings of Chinese palace women and dancers at the imperial court in Changan (today's Xi'an) indicate the same willowy ideal for the style of women's clothing. Koreans, however, have adapted the components of the design over the intervening centuries and the *hanbok* is now instantly recognizable as authentically Korean. Variations on the design include the bright colors that are typical of children's *hanbok,* the elegant red and blue brocades that are often seen in evening wear, and the calf-length short *hanbok* skirt that was stylish in South Korea in the 1950s and remains the style in North Korea.

A hundred years ago, most Koreans wore shoes made of elemental materials, mainly straw, by-products of the rice harvest. The twentieth century brought leather shoes and sandals for city wear and rubber *komushin* shoes in the country villages. Because Koreans remove their shoes whenever they are indoors at home and in many other places as well (e.g., temples, restaurants), it is best if the shoes can easily be slipped on and off. *Komushin* were slip-ons with wide mouths, the women's style being gondola-shaped with an upturned toe as a decorative touch and the men's version being wider and simply foot-shaped. *Komushin* are still worn by women when they dress up in *hanbok*. Their socks, called *posŏn*, also have an upturned toe and are made like little boots, tight around the foot with a wide ankle. Koreans have never practiced the foot-binding that was common in China at the end of the nineteenth century.

Decorations and accessories for both men and women include small coin purses tied with cords that have beads, amber drops, or miniature wood or ivory carvings on the end. Korean women traditionally wore their hair in braids in childhood and then gathered it in a bun at the nape of the neck after marriage. Males also braided their hair when they were children but put it up in a topknot when married, enclosing the topknot in a cap that served as the lining for an elegant tall hat of woven horsehair, called a *kat*. The *kat* was a proud badge of adult manhood, connoting nobility though it was increasingly worn by all men by the turn of the twentieth century. Today, the *kat* is seen only in festivals where the intention is to re-create life in the olden style. Even then, the topknot that used to be visible through the open weave of the hat is never to be seen, since virtually all Korean men wear their hair short in modern fashion.

HANYAK: KOREAN FOLK MEDICINE

South Korea today has a plan to cover all citizens with medical insurance and roughly half of the population at present is enrolled in some part of the national health plan. This finances access to Korea's many hospitals and medical centers and helps with the cost of drugs.

Western "scientific" medicine was first introduced into Korea by missionary physicians in the late nineteenth century, and the large medical complex at Yonsei University traces its history back to the first missionary clinic in Korea that was founded in 1885. The Japanese colonial authorities introduced national medical standards and regulations, administered tests for doctors and nurses, and established the first government-run medical center as a branch of what is now Seoul National University. Today, most of Korea's

Country gentleman in full *yangban*-style dress.

top universities have research and teaching hospitals, even small towns have clinics and hospitals with trained medical professionals, and the tiniest villages have pharmacies that sell daily doses of medicines ranging from antibiotics to birth control pills. In addition, the South Korean government's Ministry of Health and Social Affairs maintains public health programs that assist in controlling epidemics and eradicating health menaces such as tuberculosis and malaria.

Although Western medicine is firmly established, Koreans use it in combination with an older, more traditional approach to wellness that is called *hanyak* ("Chinese medicine"). *Hanyak*, which is sometimes referred to as "herbal medicine," has its roots in ancient Chinese texts about the body, updated in Korean texts that were compiled during the Chosŏn dynasty (1392–1910). *Hanyak* practice consists of diagnosing imbalances in the body that are causing illness and prescribing appropriate natural remedies. These are usually in the form of drugs derived from herbs that are intended to restore the body's ability to keep itself in chemical balance.

The theory of balances in the body is an ancient concept related to Daoism and the theory of *yang* and *yin* (Korean: *yang* and *ŭm*); that is, the way opposites complement each other. Light complements dark; day complements night; male complements female; rain complements drought; good complements evil, and so on. The Chinese devised theories about the body that described it as being made of the world's five basic elements: fire, water, wood, metal, and earth that likewise had to be kept in proper proportion. They associated bodily organs with these elements. Kidneys, for instance, were associated with water. The liver was associated with wood. The heart was associated with fire. A diagnosis of heart disease (fire), might therefore be treated with something that strengthened the kidneys (increasing water to control the fire). The *hanyak* practitioner's job was to assess the balances in the body through examination: by looking at the tongue, the brow, and the skin, by taking the pulse and palpating the organs, and by listening carefully to the patient's voice and complaints. This would lead to a judgment about what organs or forces in the body had to be controlled.

Hanyak rarely involves surgery. However, it includes a sophisticated theory of nerve connections within the body that explains the body's shifting balances. Twelve main lines of force carry impulses from every part of the body to the major organs, affecting the balance. The practitioner affects these impulses and transfers by inserting a needle at carefully selected points along the nerve track. The insertion of long sharp needles at these points can interrupt pain impulses, cramps, muscle tension, and even, it is said, certain kinds of internal injury. The pain-blocking effect of acupuncture is so effective that doctors and patients often choose it over anaesthesia for use in Western-style surgery such as appendectomies and caesarian section births.

Once the practitioner has arrived at a diagnosis about the body chemicals that are out of balance, he prescribes from the richly varied *hanyak* pharmacopoeia. The drugs are taken from roots, wild flowers, leaves, and vines, the same sources of many of the drugs that are prescribed in Western-style medicine. (Quinine, for example, is an ancient Eastern drug that has been adopted by the West to treat malaria.) Other *hanyak* drugs come from animals such as bear and deer. Deer horn, for example, is prized as a restorative for the flagging sexual powers of middle-aged men, one of many tools in the fight against the effects of aging. Building on ideas in the *hanyak* tradition, Koreans each year consume millions of tiny bottles of tonics and elixirs that are meant to keep up feelings of well-being. Ginseng is another prime restorative, one that is successful as a national export and has found its way into health food stores all over the world.

KOREAN FESTIVALS AND HOLIDAYS

Koreans have two kinds of holidays: national holidays that fall on prescribed dates of the solar calendar and commemorate aspects of national life, and lunar holidays that coincide with phases of the moon and belong to the older agricultural tradition. Many of Korea's holidays are versions of holidays celebrated in other countries, while other observances are uniquely Korean. The official holidays in South Korea are as follows:

New Year's Day (January 1). On this day schools and offices are closed. People visit each other and sometimes exchange gifts in the Western style.

Lunar New Year's (Sŏllal, the last day of the lunar year and first two days of the lunar new year, see below under lunar holidays). This new year celebration is more elaborate than the "official" New Year's on January 1. For Lunar New Year's young people call on their elders and offer their formal bows.

Independence Movement Day (Samil Day, March 1) commemorates the uprising against Japanese colonial rule that took place on March 1, 1919. There are commemorative ceremonies at locations associated with the Independence Movement, such as the park in downtown Seoul where the Declaration of Independence from Japan was read in 1919.

Arbor Day (April 5) is an environment holiday that commemorates the campaign to restore forests to the mountains of the Korean peninsula. During the reforestation campaign, teachers and parents led groups of children into the hill to plant tree seedlings. Since the success of the reforestation program, it has become an occasion for family and group picnics.

Buddha's Birthday (eighth day of the fourth lunar month; see below under lunar holidays). Buddhist temples are decorated with lanterns. The faithful visit temple to worship and in the evening there are lantern parades.

Children's Day (May 5). A school holiday during which families typically visit parks and playgrounds and enjoy the clean air and warm temperatures of spring.

Memorial Day (June 6). An official occasion for mourning the dead, particularly those who died in the Korean War, 1950–53.

Constitution Day (July 17) commemorates the promulgation of the South Korean constitution on July 17, 1948. It is a holiday that celebrates South Korea's democracy. Government offices and many businesses are closed, and people leave the city for the clean air of the mountains.

Liberation Day (August 15) is the anniversary of the liberation of Korea from Japanese colonial rule on August 15, 1945. There are parades and speeches that recall the struggle against Japan and the importance of Korean nationhood.

Ch'usŏk holidays (Fourteenth–sixteenth of the eighth lunar month; see below under lunar holidays). This is the most important holiday of the year for visiting and tending ancestors' graves and affirming family ties.

National Foundation Day (October 3), commemorates the origin of the Korean people in the legendary story of Tan'gun (see Chapter 2). On this holiday government officials host receptions and there are congratulatory messages from foreign dignitaries and heads of state. People who belong to the Tan'gun sect visit his shrine in Seoul and pay their respects to his spirit.

Han'gŭl **Day** (October 9), commemorates the invention of the Korean alphabet called *han'gŭl*, in the year 1446. This holiday is a break from work and school routines. In the old royal palaces there are calligraphy contests where experts with brush and ink display their fine technique.

Christmas (December 25). This is a special holiday for Korea's many Christians, but it is also celebrated by non-Christians who enjoy it as a midwinter festival and a chance to trade cards and gifts.

LUNAR CALENDAR SPECIAL DAYS AND FESTIVALS THROUGH THE YEAR

Before the advent of the Western twelve-month solar calendar, Koreans (like other East Asians) marked time by following the phases of the moon. Festivals and holidays came to be associated with certain seasonal cycles of the moon and the agriculture that was typical of those seasons. The lunar calendar is an agricultural calendar; however, since most Koreans are only one or two generations removed from farm life, its rhythms are still an integral part of Korean consciousness.

The shortest day of the year—the winter solstice that falls on December 21 in the solar calendar—is the reference point for the lunar calendar. The lunar year begins on the second new moon after the winter solstice. The calendar then follows the phases of the moon, with a new month beginning on the first day of each lunar cycle. Lunar months are therefore one or two days shorter than months in the solar calendar and begin and end on different days. A lunar year of twelve lunar months therefore is shorter than a solar year. This means that "New Year's" keeps getting earlier every year until it is necessary to insert an extra "intercalary" month (*yundal* in Korean) to "recalibrate" the calendar so that the seasons fall more or less where they are supposed to.

It was the duty of astronomers in the court of the Chinese emperor to decide calendrical matters, fixing dates for the seasons and determining when to insert intercalary months. In practice, roughly every third lunar year has an extra month inserted, usually in the spring or summer. As a result, many of the observances in the lunar calendar fall on different dates depending on whether or not the year has an intercalary month. The best way to understand the lunar calendar is to keep in mind the longest and shortest days of the year and the intervening equinoxes. Important days of the lunar year include the following:

Sŏllal, **the Lunar New Year's holiday**. The government, schools, businesses, and all other modern enterprises use the international solar calendar and the business year begins with a New Year's holiday on January 1. But a few weeks later there comes a three-day holiday for *Sŏllal,* the lunar New Year's holiday.

On *Sŏllal,* even in the cities, people dress up in flowing *hanbok* Korean clothing and visit older relatives and seniors to pay respects and participate in ceremonies memorializing ancestors. The lunar New Year's holiday is everyone's birthday, in effect, since people say they are a year older after the turn of the year. Families feast on *Sŏllal* and younger people perform ritual *sebae* in front of their elders, bowing low to the floor to show respect and receiving praise and affection in return. They enjoy playing *yut,* a kind of board game where the players throw four half-round sticks and move pieces around the board according to how many of the sticks fall flat side up.

Taeporŭm, **the Moon Festival**. The fifteenth day of the first lunar month is *Taeporŭm* (or just *porŭm*). Everyone makes a point of enjoying the first full moon of the year. This is the "moon festival" of the lunar calendar, and Koreans sometimes refer to it by its Chinese designation, *Mangwŏl,* which means "Moon Viewing." Girls pray to the moon for a good marriage and women pray for sons. People visit each other's houses and enjoy wine and the foods of the season in honor of the occasion. They set off firecrackers and sometimes hold intervillage competitions such as tugs-of-war and mock battles in the moonlight. The winning village is supposed to have the better harvest later in the year.

On the twenty-sixth day of the first lunar month, animals are supposed to stop hibernating (i.e., Korean Groundhog Day, or *Kyŏngchip*).

Ipch'un **("Spring Begins")**. This is the day for greeting the new growing season by writing fresh slogans and expressions on the gateposts of a person's farmhouse. "Spring Brings Great Joy," is an example. "The Great Sunshine Brings Many Blessings" is another. The phrases often refer to the traits of the zodiac animal that represents the new year. In the year of the turtle, for example, they might mention longevity, since turtles grow very old. In the year of the tiger they might mention safety from thieves and ghosts, since tigers frighten such plagues away.

Ch'unpun, **the Spring Equinox**, is the "sliding" day in the lunar calendar that falls on the solar March 21, when the day and night are exactly the same length.

Ch'ŏngmyŏng. This comes two weeks after *Ch'unpun* and is the day to prepare seedbeds for planting rice. The actual date for this task varies by latitude.

Hansik, **Cold Rice-Eating Day**. This falls in the solar April, 105 days after the winter solstice, and originates in a Chinese story about a nobleman who was so loyal to his fallen sovereign that even fire could not get him to transfer loyalty to the new ruler. A later emperor set aside a day when no one should build a fire or eat hot food, to remember his steadfastness. On *Hansik*, Koreans visit their own ancestors' graves early in the morning and tidy them up, and eat cold food all day.

Kogu. The twelfth day of the third lunar month is *Kogu*, a day when rain is expected to fall and help the crops grow.

Buddha's Birthday (Ch'o P'a'il). This falls on the eighth day of the fourth lunar month. In addition to holding services, Buddhist temples become virtual fairgrounds and are festooned with multicolored lanterns. There are parades in the evening with monks, nuns, and laypeople carrying softly lit lanterns making for a very beautiful effect. Buddha's birthday is a national holiday in South Korea.

The fourteenth day of the fourth lunar month is *Mangjong*, the day for harvesting the winter barley crop and getting the fields ready for rice planting. This is another "sliding" day depending on location.

Tanojŏl (**or just "***Tano***"**). The fifth day of the fifth lunar month. Traditionally *Tanojŏl* has been as big a festival as New Year's, with dressing up and feasts and visits to elders and ancestral tombs. But since the weather is warmer, outdoor sports are also part of *Tanojŏl*, the most "typical" being wrestling for young men and swinging on an extremely tall swing for young women who were normally kept safely sequestered in their homes. The swings traditionally were supposed to enable the cloistered girls to see over the walls and catch a glimpse of the boys outside. In recent times the swings have gotten taller and taller and this is now a kind of acrobatic event with male as well as female athletes.

Haji, **the summer solstice**; the longest day of the year. Lunar date varies but corresponds to June 21 in the solar calendar.

Ipch'u, **the official beginning of autumn**. This occurs about six weeks after the summer solstice.

***Ch'ilsŏk*, the Night of the Spinning Maiden and Herd Boy**. Rain is always expected on the seventh day of the seventh lunar month, an occasion that celebrates the love of two stars called the Spinning Maiden and the Herd Boy. The legend is that long ago their romance interfered with their work and they had to be separated by the Milky Way. They are allowed to meet only once a year, on the seventh of the seventh. Magpies fly up and make a bridge for them across the Milky Way, and the rain is made up of the tears they shed when they have to part.

***Ch'usŏk*, "Autumn Evening."** This falls on the fifteenth day of the eighth lunar month. This is the Korean Thanksgiving Day, a national holiday on which Koreans visit their ancestors' tombs and pay respects wearing traditional Korean *hanbok* clothing. Usually falling in late September or early October by the solar calendar, Ch'usŏk is also a harvest festival involving considerable feasting and celebration. Among the performances are archery contests for older men and weaving exhibitions for women. In far southern Korea, women do a torch-lit circle dance called *kanggang suwŏllae* wearing elegant Korean costumes. Now that most Koreans live in cities, Ch'usŏk has come to mean a spectacular jamming of the country's transportation system as millions of city dwellers try to get to their ancestral villages in the provinces.

***Ch'upun*, the fall equinox**, September 21 by the solar calendar.

***Tongji*, the longest night of the year**, is the winter solstice, December 21 by the solar calendar.

***Sohan*, the "Small Cold" of winter**, occurs about a week after the winter solstice.

***Taehan*, the coldest day of the year**, is about three weeks after the winter solstice.

During the twelfth lunar month, which is called *Sŏttal*, people settle accounts, pay debts, and prepare to welcome the new year. Traditions vary by region. In some places people stay up the whole night before New Year's. In other places there are rituals and ceremonies to exorcise evil and start the new year with a clean slate, and sometimes there are concerts by farmers' bands playing *nong'ak* ("farmers' music").

NOTE

1. For a fuller description of traditional Korean funeral rites see Roger L. Janelli and Dawnhee Yim Janelli, *Ancestor Worship and Korean Society* (Stanford, CA: Stanford University Press, 1982), especially Chapter 3, pp. 58–85.

6

Life in a Korean Village

UNTIL THE LATE TWENTIETH CENTURY, most Koreans lived in rural areas and supported themselves through an economy based on agriculture. Their seasons and holidays were related to the agricultural calendar and their lives were tied to the weather and the success or failure of their crops. Though the proportion of the population living in villages and cities has been reversed in the process of economic modernization, most Koreans still feel closely tied to their ancestral homes in the countryside and many have relatives still living in ancestral villages.

RICE AGRICULTURE

When we speak of the Korean agricultural economy we are speaking of rice agriculture, for rice is the basic food of the Koreans and an essential part of every meal including breakfast. The variety is provided by other foods that are served separately as *panchan*, or "side dishes." The clean white rice that appears on the table is the product of an elaborate process of farming that has always been at the heart of the Korean economy and is still essential to the nation's economic health.

The Koreans' emotional affinity for rice is rooted in memories of mothers and grandmothers who got up before dawn every day to start the day's rice cooking. Rice was in their lunchboxes at school. Water that was boiled in the nearly empty cooking pot made a comforting family drink. Burnt rice made a crunchy snack. Puffed rice was a special treat; it was shot out of metal cannons by peddlers who came through the neighborhood and subjected the raw grains mixed with sugar to intense pressure until they exploded all at once. When the puffed rice was finished, it was eaten like popcorn. There was also rice candy wrapped in "rice paper" that melted in a person's mouth. The grown-ups drank rice wine. Houses were roofed with rice straw thatch. Life was full of things related to rice.

In a way, it is ironic that Koreans should be so attached to rice, since their country is so mountainous. After all, since Korean-style rice has to spend much of the growing season in flooded paddy fields, it takes flat land to maintain rice culture. Yet rice has always been the farmer's crop of choice. In order to grow it, Koreans construct elaborate stair-steps of terraces up the sides of mountains, making different levels of flat land to grow rice even where the land is hilly. There only has to be a mountain stream to provide water. Part of the water can be diverted into the top level of the paddies and then allowed to flow slowly down the valley, step by step, until it reaches the bottom. The carefully controlled flow of water can thus irrigate dozens of paddy fields as it makes its way down the mountainside.

Of course, some land is simply not suited for rice at all and is used for other crops. Alternative grains include barley, millet, corn, and wheat. Other fields contain soybeans, spinach, radish, and the myriad ingredients of Korean cuisine. There are apple orchards, vineyards, tobacco fields, pumpkin and potato patches. Since Koreans started making greenhouses out of vinyl sheeting, it has become possible to grow oranges and bananas and other things that could not ordinarily be grown in Korea's temperate climate. This variety is further enriched by beef, pork, poultry, milk products, and seafood. But snowy white rice remains the country's elemental food.

The "rice cycle" begins in March or early April when rice seeds are spread in seedbeds of very wet earth. There the seeds germinate and develop into rice seedlings, little rice plants that grow to a height of eight to ten inches. The seedlings grow so thickly that they soon resemble a lawn that needs mowing, and they cannot grow to maturity unless they are separated and given more space. In June, therefore, they are transplanted into large flat paddy fields. To prepare the paddies to receive the seedlings the farmers first harvest whatever winter crops might have grown there (e.g., winter wheat or barley). Then they plow the earth, fertilize it, and flood the fields with water, making them look like square ponds. Then the farmers gather bunches of seedlings from the seedbeds and toss them into the irrigated paddies, where the villagers work in groups transplanting the seedlings into the paddies. They stretch a string across the field to guide them as they plant the seedlings a foot apart in row after row, bending over and reaching down into the water to press one plant at a time down several inches into the soft mud. It is

Working terraced rice paddies up a hillside.

backbreaking work, and to help pass the time the villagers sing, gossip, and tell jokes. Men, women, old, and young all do this work together. Students also show up to help, and schools usually cancel classes on this vitally important day in village life.

The schedule for growing and transplanting the seedlings varies with latitude and altitude. Near the southern coast it is warm enough to permit double-cropping, and there are two rice cycles in a year. Farther north, however, rice is a summer crop, and farmers try to grow a barley crop that is harvested in the late spring just as the rice seedlings are getting ready for transplanting. This means that the fields are engaged in growing something nearly all the time and farmers have to worry about using up all the nutrients in the soil. This kind of farming cannot happen without generous applications of chemical fertilizer.

Middle school students transplanting rice seedlings in rows.

Korea's weather pattern is ideal for rice culture. Late in June, just after the transplanting is completed, warm monsoon winds carry humid ocean air across Korea and generate a rainy season that keeps the country wet and enables the seedlings to resume growing in the paddies. By late July when the rainy season ends, the plants are two feet high and ready to make the transition from wet paddy ground to dry field growth. The fields are drained and the villagers spend their time pulling weeds and fighting insects. By September the fields have started turning yellow and heads of grain have appeared, bending the tops of the plants with their weight. In early October comes the harvest. Until recently, when many villages began depending on machines to do the cutting, the farmers themselves would take razor-sharp sickles and squat down in the fields cutting the rice plants one by one as close to the ground as possible. As with the transplanting of seedlings, which is a village project, the harvesting is done by teams of neighbors helping each other, field by field, assisted by hired male laborers. It is exhausting and dangerous work, since the sickles can do serious injury to hands and fingers.

The demands of rice agriculture have played an important part in shaping Korean history and social organization. A farmer cannot grow rice by himself or even with the help of just his own household. The entire village has to cooperate, whether the villagers are all members of the same two or three clans or completely unrelated. They help each other clear the fields. They line up to transplant the rice seedlings in orderly rows. They work in teams to harvest the rice. And they thresh the grain and weave the straw together, when the harvest is done. Agriculture is an intensely social kind of work, and the closeness of the communities is one reason why Confucian social ethics (see Chapter 2), with their emphasis on harmonious social relations, have always been so prevalent.

SOUTH VALLEY HAMLET

Many Korean villages still preserve some of the rich traditions of agricultural society, but modernization has brought fundamental changes in the way rural people live and work. The traditions too are fast disappearing. In order to dramatize the transformations that have overtaken Korean village life in recent generations we will focus on a real place in south central Korea named "Poksu," which can be translated in English as "Blessed Longevity." Poksu is actually the name of a *myŏn*, or district, one of several that make up the country (*kun*) of Kŭmsan in South Ch'ungch'ŏng Province. The village that lies at the heart of Poksu District is Kongnam-ni, or "South Valley Hamlet." It sits at the junction of two steep valleys, and since Korean roads normally follow valleys, South Valley Hamlet exists at the fork where two main roads leading from southwestern Korea diverge to go around opposite sides of a mountain complex to the city of Taejŏn. Under Japanese colonial rule in the early part of the century, South Valley Hamlet became the headquarters of the Poksu District, a territory that stretches for about thirty miles along a system of valleys connected to a central stream that flows northward to the Kŭm River.

South Valley Hamlet contains the Poksu District (*myŏn*) headquarters led by an elected chief (*myŏnjang*) who before democratization was formerly appointed by the government in Seoul with the advice of the provincial governor in Taejŏn City. It also boasts the district's central post office, a place that a generation ago was the district's only communications hub with its only public telephone. At that time, the post office was also the district bank, offering postal savings accounts in a system introduced by the Japanese when they ruled Korea earlier in the century. It had a warehouse for fertilizer and seed that was stocked by the National Association of Agricultural Co-operatives and was dispensed by association agents on periodic swings through the county. And it had an elementary school in a Japanese building left by the colonial authorities in 1945, a drugstore, a wineshop, and a candy and cigarette store at the fork in the road that sold tickets for the buses that

Suyŏng-ni, one of the main villages in Poksu District.

came through Poksu going both directions at three-hour intervals throughout the day.

Until the advent of mass communications, South Valley Hamlet—and indeed, all of Poksu District and Kŭmsan County—was isolated in the mountains growing rice, cotton, tobacco, and its prime specialty crop, the medicinal root ginseng. In fact, Poksu and South Valley Hamlet were so remote that the only entertainment was provided by the villagers themselves. Most evenings in the wineshop the drinkers entertained each other with ballads and jokes. Seasonal festivals were occasions for more organized entertainment in the form of farmers' music (*nong'ak*) that sometimes featured itinerant dancers and musicians. The residents of South Valley Hamlet—the ones who could read—were exposed to mass media only through newspapers that came in the mail a day or two late. Beyond that there were only the movies that came to town in the form of a truck driven by a small crew who would hang a huge white sheet, crank up a generator, and enthrall the entire population of the village with worn prints of second-run films.

The generator was necessary because Poksu District got no electricity at all before 1967. A village up the road from Poksu had managed to squeeze a little current from a generator connected to a waterwheel, but the contraption broke down so often that the people rarely bothered to run it. Needless to say, the lack of electricity meant that there were no appliances that used electric motors. There was no refrigeration and no radio or television, and whatever light there was at night came from candles and kerosene lanterns. The biggest thing that happened to Poksu District in the late 1960s was the arrival of an electric wire that was strung by the government-owned power utility along the road from Kŭmsan town. The electricity was unreliable and often lasted only a few hours a day. The power was expensive and to save money people tried to economize at first by running fluorescent tubes through holes in their walls so that they could cast a dim light in two rooms at once. By the end of 1968, however, the current was steady enough to enable people to make some changes in the way they lived. Once they got used to having electricity in the evening they started staying up past their normal bedtimes reading, talking, eating, drinking, and arguing. They also invested in the cheap transistor radios that were being made by Korea's fledgling electronics firms. The village rang with the sound of competing households blaring music, comedies, and soap operas. One family made it a point to turn up the volume on religious programs from CBS, the country's Christian network.

Every five days South Valley Hamlet hosted the "five-day market," a version of the traditional rural bazaar where villagers from surrounding hamlets brought things to sell and trade. The "market" was an area of mats spread out on the ground with tubs of fruit and vegetables, boxes of nails and simple tools, implements like plowshares and ox yokes, used-clothing, and occasionally a live animal such as a dog, pig, or even a calf. The hardware merchants normally traveled with the market from village to village, while the produce and used clothing sellers were local people. Several people did specialized work on a to-order basis: a carpenter who could make furniture and could also fix tin roofs; a watch repairman who also fixed bicycles and small motors; and a shoemaker. The hamlet had no restaurant as such, but the lady who ran the wineshop would cook a meal if a traveler came by or the drinkers got hungry.

The jobs connected with these aspects of South Valley Hamlet were mostly part-time jobs that supplemented people's incomes from farming the valley's main crops: rice, barley, and tobacco. The people who performed them were from several different extended families, most of whom cheerfully identified themselves as "sangnom," or humble commoners. Their homes had mud walls papered inside with newspapers and posters, and heavy wooden pillars held up the roof structures, which were covered in thatch or, in rare cases, galvanized metal. It was a poor village and the residents had few valuable possessions. Even so, most of the dwellings were surrounded by traditional walls made of mud and stones, topped with long swatches of woven thatch or, more rarely, tiles. The walls were subject to erosion whenever it rained and constantly had to be repaired. Gaps were common and the walls obviously were more symbolic than useful.

The Hamlet's Historic Home

The finest home in South Valley Hamlet—and Poksu's top historical attraction—was the family residence of the Cho family across the stream from the main village square. In the 1960s it bore on its compound gatepost the nameplate of Cho Inse, the thirteenth-generation lineal descendant of the entire county's most famous hero, Cho Hŏn (1544–92), who gave his life in battle during the Japanese invasion of 1592.

Cho Hŏn was an example of a special kind of traditional Korean military defender—a civilian who undertook to rally local village men against invaders when the national army proved unable to stop the enemy. In 1592, when the Japanese invaded Korea as part of their audacious plan to conquer the mainland, they defeated the Korean Royal Army rather easily at first and the king and his court actually had to abandon the capital city of Seoul and flee northward to the Manchurian border for safety. Defense of the peninsula and its communities was left to brave individuals who organized spontaneous citizen militia forces known as "righteous armies" (Korean: ŭibyŏng). The "righteous armies" used whatever weapons they could find to defend their families and property against the invading Japanese. Sometimes they won and sometimes they lost, but the righteous armies of the 1590s have always been revered for their patriotism and sacrifice.

The scholar-turned-commander Cho Hŏn won several important battles before confronting the invaders in the Battle of Kŭmsan together with troops raised by the monk Yŏnggyu Taesa and fellow-yangban Ko Chebong. The battle, in the third week of the eighth lunar month of the year 1592, was very bloody and both sides suffered heavy casualties. In the end, however, the Japanese prevailed. Cho Hŏn and his company were among the so-called Seven Hundred Martyrs who died in the battle and were buried together just north of Kŭmsan town. The site is now a national shrine with a large stone tablet on which the story of the battle is inscribed in elegant script.

Poksu District is about fifteen miles from the shrine, but in the 1960s the residents of South Valley Hamlet were proud to tell their children and grandchildren the story of the Seven Hundred Martyrs. They liked to point out that Cho Hŏn's spirit still resided in the ancestral tablet that was lovingly kept by the Cho family inside the shrine whose tile roof could be seen inside the Cho family compound across the stream. The return of various city-dwelling members of the Cho family to the ancestral home for memorial *chesa* ceremonies was a normal feature of holidays like the Ch'usŏk autumn festival for all of South Valley Hamlet.

Cho Hŏn's descendant Cho Inse himself did not actually live in the compound but was in Seoul, where he had a job with the Korean National Railroad. The household comprised Cho's wife and children and his widowed mother, along with a young cousin from a mountain village who boarded at the house while attending Poksu's elementary school. In the kitchen wing of the house there lived a family of servants who spent their days tending the vegetable garden inside the Cho family compound and doing the cleaning, cooking, and shopping for the household. The head of the servant family was a man descended from generations of Cho family "retainers," permanent household staff who traditionally tended the family fields and did the manual labor necessary to maintain the establishment. The Chos lost most of their land through government-sponsored land reform and other sales, but they continued to maintain a few acres adjacent to the house in South Valley Hamlet. Here they grew barley and tobacco like other Poksu farm families, as well as cotton and fruit in an orchard, which helped the entire operation turn a yearly profit.

The Cho family house itself was typical of a *yangban* home, having been improved and altered over many decades by succeeding generations. Part of the house was in Japanese-style, with sliding glass doors opening onto a polished wood hallway along the south side that was designed to be warmed by the winter sun (but was something of an oven in summer). Inside, however, the rooms were Korean-style with heated floors and elegant wooden cabinets.

One of the cabinets contained the family treasury. One treasure was a quiver that was said to have held the arrows that Cho Hŏn shot at the Japanese during the Battle of Kŭmsan. Another was a commendation certificate written in Cho Hŏn's memory by his students after the battle. Others included a bound treatise by Cho Hŏn himself and several books that were said to have belonged to him, including editions of the ancient *Book of Mencius* and the historical text *Tongguk t'onggam* (*Precious Mirror of the Eastern Land*). There was also the all-important Cho family *chokpo*, the genealogy that documented Cho Hŏn's own lineage and the generations descended from him down to Cho Inse's late father.

South Valley Hamlet and the Regional Economy

The Poksu District headquarters, office, school, post office, bus stop, and market all identified South Valley Hamlet as a center. So did the fact that the county health authorities used part of the district headquarters building as a clinic every two weeks, administering immunizations and seeing patients. The drugstore at the fork in the road was the only other medical facility for the entire district of 10,000 people. The nearest clinic was an hour bus ride away in the county seat, Kŭmsan. If a person got hurt or suddenly ran a fever, it was the job of the drugstore operator—who was self-taught and not licensed as a pharmacist—to diagnose the disease and prescribe the right drugs. If someone was badly injured and needed an ambulance, someone would have to use the post office telephone to call a taxi. This would arrive in about an hour to take the patient away to Taejŏn City or Kŭmsan town, either one of which was more than an hour away. The roads that forked at South Valley Hamlet were unpaved and rough in the best of weather, but in snow or mud they were slippery and occasionally impassable. The one that went straight north to Taejŏn lacked bridges. Even a moderate rain would close it and force a trip on the other road, which had bridges and a tunnel through the mountains but was twelve miles longer.

Though Poksu and South Valley Hamlet were remote in many respects, they were nevertheless part of an integrated market structure. Like the famous Standard Marketing Areas in China described by G. William Skinner,[1] the Korean agricultural economy was organized in levels. The bottom level was a small village surrounded by fields whose inhabitants converged on a place like South Valley Hamlet for their five-day market supplies, cigarettes, medicines, and bus rides to the city. The next level above South Valley was the county seat, in this case Kŭmsan, where there were county offices, a government clinic, a county police headquarters, an area office for the agricultural cooperative, a cultural center, and a middle school as well as an elementary school. Whereas Poksu at the district level might hope for four hours a day of electricity, Kŭmsan had eighteen hours. At the Kŭmsan level there were also stores, a permanent open-air market, barbershops, coffee houses, inns, Chinese as well as Korean restaurants, a bus station, taxi service, an auto repair shop, an electronics store, a bathhouse with hot water two days a week, and a hall that showed movies on weekends.

From the county level a person could travel an hour on a reserved-seat bus to the next level at Taejŏn City, the provincial capital where there was electricity around the clock. Taejŏn had the governor's offices and two train stations that linked the entire province with the main lines to Seoul, Pusan, and the southwest part of the country, luxurious inns, a Western-style hotel with air-conditioning, and a hot springs resort. It had high schools and colleges, two hospitals, department stores, movie theaters, a very large permanent market, car dealerships, Japanese and Western restaurants, commercial banks, and bathhouses that operated every day of the week. And from Taejŏn the railroad went to the highest level of the national economy in Seoul, which was connected through myriad banks, industries, and government agencies to the world beyond Korea's shores. For the people of South Valley Hamlet, a trip to Kŭmsan was a monthly occasion and a trip to Taejŏn might happen twice a year. Most of the adult villagers had been to Seoul or Pusan at least once, but not necessarily by their own free will. Many remembered serving in the army or having to flee the invading North Korean forces. Some of the older residents had worked in Japan during the colonial period and had traveled quite a bit, though often in circumstances they preferred to forget.

The Saemaŭl Movement Comes to South Valley Hamlet

If regular bus service was the biggest improvement in the 1950s and electrification was the most significant change in the 1960s, the most revolutionary influence in the life of South Valley Hamlet in the 1970s was the success of the government's Saemaŭl (or "New Community") Movement. The Saemaŭl Movement was President Park Chung-hee's response to the criticism that his administration was paying too much attention to industrialization at the expense of the farm sector, which was continuing to languish in poverty.

The Saemaŭl Movement therefore was a national push to improve living standards at the village level. Under the slogan "Diligence, Self-Help, and Cooperation" the government targeted many areas at once. For example, after having developed a national cement industry in the 1960s, the Park administration was able to give 300 bags of cement to each of more than 35,000 villages on the condition that it be used for community purposes such as irrigation, sanitation, and construction of buildings for common use. To improve transportation the government built more than 65,000 small bridges to make weather roads out of the tracks that flooded like the one leading from Poksu to Taejŏn. The layers of rice straw that thatched millions of Korean farmhouses were economically replaced with roofs made of cement tiles that did not rot in the rainy season, house innumerable rats and insects, and require laborious re-thatching every autumn.

The movement also augmented the nation's rudimentary public health program by assigning government-paid doctors to small towns and villages, building health centers in places like South Valley Hamlet, extending health education classes to villagers, and increasing the number of family planning and communicable disease control workers. Since much of the countryside was afflicted by waterborne diseases such as typhoid and cholera, the gov-

Plowing the old-fashioned way.

ernment pushed the construction of safe water supplies. The Saemaŭl Movement funded the digging of new wells that were away from the polluted water tables of the villages themselves and ran pipes to communal faucets and, eventually, into individual homes.

Partly as a public health measure but mostly to boost production, the government invested in the production of two kinds of farm chemicals: pesticides and nitrogen fertilizer. Though the pesticides created pollution problems of their own, they cut down on the crop losses that were due to insects and rodents. The fertilizer, which was distributed at subsidized rates through the National Agricultural Cooperative system, replaced the manure that had been used through the 1960s and enabled farmers to continue growing two crops a year safely in many fields without completely depleting the nutrients in the soil.

The country's industrial development also spun off new products that proved essential for rising living standards in the countryside. The new plastics industry made vinyl sheeting available to farmers to use in two ways. They spread the vinyl on fields to hold in moisture and control pests while the plants themselves grew up through holes punched in the plastic, and they built greenhouses to grow high-profit vegetables during the colder weeks of early spring and late autumn. Another type of industrial product was the small gasoline engine that was adapted for use as a "mechanical ox," a gas tractor that could be hooked up to a plow, or hitched to a wagon, or connected to a pump, performing a variety of tasks more cheaply and efficiently than animal power. The mechanization process also led to the spread of more sophisticated machines to harvest and thresh the grain crops. One machine even took trays of new rice seedlings and transplanted them in wet rice paddies row by row, ending the ordeal of having the villagers line up in water up to their calves and bend over to push the seedlings into the mud one by one.

But the most important agricultural innovation of all was the development of a new kind of high-yield rice that dramatically increased the country's annual grain output and enabled the growing population to retain rice as its staple food. Increased production meant rising farm income without a rise in prices in the market. The new rice strain was accompanied by increased efficiency as Saemaŭl Movement workers showed farmers how to share resources through coordinated planning and cooperative work. The government set up training institutes and cycled thousands of farmers through classes on organization and leadership. The central training institute in Suwŏn started training in 1972 with 150 village leaders from across the country and by 1988 was training more than 20,000 a year.

Koreans regard the Saemaŭl Movement as a great success. The cooperative elements of the movement were translated into urban projects as well. Though critics complained that the training institutes were dispensing a kind of government propaganda that limited the vision of Korea's future to one industrial-style model, the exposure of professors, businessmen, judges, and religious leaders to the cooperative ethic of the Saemaŭl Movement seems to have contributed something to an evident national determination to work together to overcome long odds.

Without the government-led development of community spirit, one wonders, for example, if Korea's spectacular success in reforestation would have been possible. On a daily basis one notices improvements in community consideration: respect for people ahead in a line for tickets or taxis, an end to spitting on the sidewalk, less shoving, less littering, and slightly better driving.

High in the mountains of central Korea, the economic modernization of South Korea and the Saemaŭl Movement brought revolutionary changes to South Valley Hamlet. The roads that fork in the center of the hamlet were paved, and more than a few households own private cars, a thing that could not have been imagined in the 1970s. The houses have dependable electricity around the clock and almost all have color televisions, refrigerators, fans to keep them cool in summer, and rice cookers to produce perfect pearly rice for breakfast. No longer do housewives have to get up at 4:30 to start the fire.

South Valley Hamlet has a health center with a doctor and keeps records on the families in the Poksu District to guarantee the continued high child immunization rate, among other things. The Japanese-built wooden school building has been torn down and replaced with a new educational complex that brings a middle school education to the children of Poksu District. The paved roads and frequent bus service make it possible for older children to ride fifty minutes on the old "long" road to high school, and there is a junior college in the county seat of Kŭmsan town. The literacy rate is nearing the national statistical standard of 93 percent.

One of the most significant changes in the Poksu District in the past thirty years has been a steady decline in population. This is due not only to the falling birth rate but to a relentless migration of the people from the farms to the cities. The migration is driven by a quest for better education, because the area's villagers remain convinced that their children must attend school in Seoul, or at least the provincial capital of Taejŏn, in order to get good jobs after graduation. This has always been the case in Korea, but the difference in recent times is that rising farm incomes have enabled even average farmers to send children to the city for schooling. In the city the children live with relatives or rent rooms, and eventually they grow reluctant to return to the life of the village. The efficiencies of the Saemaŭl Movement have enabled farm families to get along with a smaller labor pool, and the better wages available in the cities dictate that families separate. South Korea may be tending in the direction of postwar Japan, where women and older, retired men do the farmwork while the younger men work in industrial or white-collar urban jobs.

In South Valley Hamlet, some of the out-migration has been overseas. The idea of opportunities abroad is not new. During the Japanese colonial period, many Poksu District residents went to Japan to work, more or less voluntarily. A few served in the Japanese army during World War II. In 1969, the district lost its communicable disease control worker when she was recruited to work as a nurse in Germany. She was one of many Koreans who were encouraged by the Seoul government to work overseas, "exporting" their skills in order to earn foreign currency so that Korea could buy much needed imported technology. At the same time, Korea was contributing two army divisions to the American-led effort to defend South Vietnam from a Communist takeover, with the United States paying all the expenses in U.S. dollars. Korean workers helped build support facilities for the war under contracts from the United States to large Korean construction companies. The same companies later won contracts in the Middle East and Korean technicians and workers earned money on those projects as well. Several young men from Poksu served in Vietnam and saved enough money to help their younger siblings go to school in the city.

All across South Korea there are now farm households where family members have worked abroad and may have acquired passing fluency in another language. The Korean companies that have invested in building plants in China have provided a major boost to foreign language learning in Korea, which was formerly limited to English. Most Koreans, even in the remotest villages, have relatives living in the United States, Canada, Brazil, or Europe. Two generations ago, their families might have lived with three or even four generations under one roof. Now there are many older parents whose children have emigrated and who have never seen their grandchildren.

Despite all the changes that have come to South Valley Hamlet, the Cho family still maintains the ancestral home across the stream. The family shrine is intact, maintained with the help of the Poksu District office as a "cultural property." Family members come and go, most reliably on national holidays when memorial services are called for. Cho Inse's aged mother, now deceased, went abroad for the first time in the 1980s. Her trip to California was made possible by the almost hourly flights between Seoul and Los Angeles International Airport. She went to visit her son, Cho Hŏn's thirteenth-generation descendant Cho Inse. He and his wife live in Los Angeles with *their* son, and their grandchildren are normal American teenagers.

NOTE

1. G. William Skinner, "Marketing and Social Structure in Rural China," *The Journal of Asian Studies* 24: 1, 2, 3 (November 1964, February 1965, May 1965).

7

Life in Urban Korea

NORTH AND SOUTH KOREA both became highly urbanized in the second half of the twentieth century. Where 80 percent of the population formerly lived in provincial villages and towns, a comparable proportion of Koreans now live in major urban centers. Some estimates in South Korea put the rural population at lower than 14 percent. Urbanization has been more controlled in North Korea, where people need permits to travel, change jobs, and move. Even so, the capital city of P'yŏngyang now has more than 2.5 million people and several other North Korean cities have populations of around half a million.

It is in South Korea that urbanization has been truly spectacular. Seoul has always been Korea's greatest urban center, a kind of Mecca for anyone wanting to get ahead in politics or commerce. The twentieth century has magnified this tendency to make Seoul the headquarters for every kind of modern enterprise, creating a massive in-migration of people from the countryside. Seoul's population passed the million mark in the 1950s and continued growing until the 1990s when its city limits encompassed 11 million people. The city grew and annexed surrounding communities until it merged with the port of Inch'ŏn on the west coast and Suwŏn to the south, creating a conurbation with a combined population of 15 million—one-third of the entire national population. Eight million more live in four other big cities—Pusan (3.7 million), Taegu (2.2 million), Kwangju (1.1 million), and Taejŏn (1 million)—and millions more live in South Korea's medium-sized provincial centers.

Many things have caused this massive migration. The first is the hardship

City Hall Plaza, Seoul.

of rural life and the desire of many farm families to see their children live better and enjoy more reliable incomes. The second is the development of opportunities of every kind: better schools, entry-level jobs, industrial and professional training, the plethora of government agencies, and thousands and thousands of positions in businesses and organizations of every imaginable kind. More than ever Seoul is where the action is, even if it takes an hour or more by bus and subway within the city to get to work.

The third reason for the urban migration is the way Korea has become an integrated nation with good communication, mass media (both national newspapers and national radio and television networks), and quick transportation making daily existence in every corner of the country seem like part of a unified culture. A hundred years ago Korea's innumerable mountains and valleys were cut off from each other and walking was the main form of transport from one settlement to the next. Country people rarely left home and had a hard time visualizing life in other places. A city the size of Seoul would have seemed a most mysterious and even intimidating place. There were few attractive opportunities for anyone who did not already belong to the ruling class. In fact, there were many reasons not to leave one's native place with its family and acquaintances in search of a life alone in the city. Today, however, people can find jobs, places to live, and networks of people willing to accept them in the cities. City life is also no longer a mystery to country people. They read national newspapers, listen to national radio, watch national television, and think nothing of communicating with people in far corners of the country and even overseas, by portable telephone.

TRANSFORMATIONS AND ADAPTATIONS

The migration of Korea's population from the countryside to the cities has transformed Korean life and revolutionized Korean society in the space of two generations. Or to put it another way, today's young Koreans are the first generation ever to grow up knowing nothing about rural life. Their parents grew up on the farm though they may have gone to middle school in the city and probably were the generation to move to the city for good. Their grandparents, who may still be in the provinces, can remember back beyond the Korean War to the Japanese era, when it was a great rarity to attend school at all, and probably learned their earliest school lessons in Japanese. The adaptations that have been required of the Korean people over the past fifty years may be said to offer a most effective lesson in the resilience and resourcefulness of the human spirit.

The transformations have affected every facet of Korea's national existence. In traditional times, cities themselves had different purposes. Apart from Seoul, Korea's small cities were administrative centers housing magistrates' offices, or they were market towns, or occasionally frontier garrison centers. They were usually surrounded by walls that symbolized the difference between the unruly countryside and the organized town, the primitive life of farming and the more developed life of specialized work.

Today, city walls and gates are still to be seen, even in Seoul, but they are historical curiosities that bear no relation to the dimensions of the city or any of its functions. Modern life has eliminated the fear of danger from the countryside. It has also revolutionized defense, rendering barriers like city walls completely ineffective. The last wall-type defenses in Korea are the tank traps designed to hinder a second North Korean invasion and a road through the mountains north of Seoul that cannot be crossed from the north by any infiltration team without being observed and apprehended by soldiers posted along the road's length. Apart from these rather crude arrangements, Korea's military defense consists of radar, electronic surveillance equipment, aircraft and antiaircraft facilities, and a very large military force armed with the latest weapons of every type. However, the more important truth is that the 15 million people of Seoul and environs cannot be protected from a determined attack by an enemy willing to use chemical, biological, or nuclear weapons.

Where the city once locked its gates at night, it now lies open to attack and must depend on diplomacy and international agreements for whatever security it enjoys.

Though more vulnerable than ever, Seoul is incomparably more intelligent, complicated, and capable than ever before, literally functioning as the brain—or rather the central computer—of the entire South Korean nation of 45 million people. The brain in Seoul "knows" what is going on in every part of the country and can literally "see" what its leaders want to see there. The city's people circulate with packets of the brain's knowledge and supply the organized intelligence and effort necessary to produce the wealth of the country's $500 billion economy. They operate in social hierarchies of white-collar and blue-collar workers in every kind of enterprise, organization, age group, religious affiliation, and allowable political persuasion.

In terms of daily life, perhaps the most obvious transformation has been in the manner of housing. Where today's forty-year-olds can remember playing under trees outside of their own houses in the country, their children today are accustomed to life in tiny apartments, often on the upper floors of tall apartment blocks where the only view is of an identical building across the parking lot. Where the parents may remember living with their own parents and grandparents, city life affords space for only the nuclear family: one set of parents and their children. The addition of even one relative makes things unbearably tight.

Urbanization has created a spectacular housing crunch, and for mile after mile on the south side of the Han River, apartment complexes containing hundreds of identical buildings line up for miles and miles. These cramped living spaces are not cheap: it takes couples many years to save up the money to buy one. Only half of Seoul's residents own their own apartments, but the goal of having a place of their own is a foremost objective of personal work and planning, and when they get their own apartments they are resourceful in finding ways to make them livable. Interiors, while small, are comfortable. They heat them in the traditional *ŏndol* style by circulating warm water through pipes in the floor. Though one or more rooms may be furnished in Western style, with chairs and tables, bedrooms especially are furnished Korean-style with bedding on the floor at night and the room cleared for other uses during the day.

The chronic housing shortage has prompted the Korean government to launch drive after drive to increase the number of available housing units. But with the demolition of older buildings and the pressure for housing within the city itself, the supply never equals the demand in terms of cost or quantity. The winners are the property owners who become rich overnight by selling their old houses for huge sums of money to developers who tear them down and put up multi-story apartment buildings. The losers are the renters who have to move farther out of town and sometimes even end up in shantytowns that are likewise destined to be taken over as soon as the developers are ready to build more apartments.

The housing crunch is only one form of stress that has attended the urban transformation of Korean life. Because the government of South Korea organized the country's economic development along capitalist lines, it was designed to extract the maximum amount of work from Korean workers at the lowest cost while allowing the benefits of economic prosperity to be concentrated in the upper middle class and the privileged few. The results of this design are easy to detect not only in urban housing patterns but also in Korea's markets and sweatshops. As part of the capitalist design, workers in every kind of workplace from sweatshops to modern factories and mills have been discouraged from raising their demands for a better distribution of the wealth.

Over the past fifty years the labor movement in South Korea has experienced a shifting landscape of conditions. It has never been allowed to flourish and there have been times when labor "unions" were entirely shop unions made up of committees that would work with management to do management's bidding in the factory. The government has done everything possible to prevent the creation of trade unions that unite workers in a particular kind of work, such as coal mining, and that have the potential to acquire the power to shut a vital industry down. The rationale has been that South Korea is under such a military threat from the North that wartime conditions exist, in effect, and any such strike by workers would be unpatriotic and subversive of national security. This excuse was used for decades to crush attempts to organize labor in a legitimate quest for better working conditions and fair wages. The beneficiaries of this government stance were the large corporations (the *chaebŏl*), whose owners enjoyed government support, guaranteed financing and access to markets, and exponentially rising incomes. To drive down a street in Seoul or to visit a market and then a department store is to see the results in terms of the disparity between rich and poor.

No economy has ever provided equally for everyone, of course, and the attempts to equalize incomes and privileges under socialism in the twentieth century are almost all failures. Nevertheless, the disparities between rich and poor in Korea are particularly hideous and have created great strains in urban life. These were made even more apparent in 1997–98, when a downturn in the economy threw millions of South Koreans out of work. The first ones

Working men at a streetside peanut stand, Seoul. The man on the left is wearing a *chigye* A-frame that enables him to carry very heavy loads.

to be laid off were often the most vulnerable ones, particularly hourly workers in small factories making things under subcontracting arrangements for the larger corporations. A drop in demand for the products brought on by falling incomes nationally immediately put these workers, a majority of them women, out of work. Often they were earning supplementary incomes to make ends meet in a very expensive city, and a common consequence of their unemployment was the loss of cars, houses, and children's educations. The tragedy therefore multiplied quickly and it was clear that in the South Korean economy, no matter what its recent successes, few workers were very far from the edge of disaster.

Urbanization and the economic development that drives it also led to a number of difficult environmental problems. These include air pollution from the millions of automobiles and buses on city streets, which is bad enough to cause serious health problems for the elderly and others with poor respiration. Taxis are required to burn clean propane gas, but private cars are gasoline-fueled and many of the thousands of diesel buses belch black smoke throughout the day. The traffic itself is a spectacular problem, for as Korea has developed its own automobile industry and incomes have risen to enable Korean consumers to buy autos, possession of a private car has become an essential middle-class status symbol regardless of the shortage of parking space or the lack of freeways or high-speed roads to traverse the vast urban space. The result is that Seoul experiences traffic jams of epic proportions. The worst is on Saturday afternoon when schools and businesses close and Seoulites begin their weekend excursions by attempting to exit the city all at once. The second worst is on Sunday night when they all return. It can take two hours to make the last twenty miles before the toll booth on the main expressway leading into Seoul from the south.

In addition to the air pollution that comes from having so many vehicles on the roads is the air, ground, and water pollution produced by the thousands of factories that discharge every kind of chemical effluent into the environment. The city's sewer system is also inadequate to the task. Meanwhile the city government struggles with the mountains of trash and garbage that the citizens produce, collecting as much of it as possible for deposit in immense suburban landfills. Residents are required to organize trash into recycling categories and to pay special prices for city trash bags, which is the only form of trash the city will pick up. Violators of the strict littering and pollution laws have to pay very heavy fines. Nevertheless, the city's sanitation system is taxed to the breaking point every day of the year.

Littering and environmental pollution have been an unpleasant aspect of urbanization and economic development. A contributing factor has been the way Korean manufacturers package goods, borrowing from Japan the bad habit of wrapping and rewrapping store-bought items as if they were gifts. The result of the overpackaging has been an aggravating increase in the amount of paper, plastic, Styrofoam, and ordinary food and drink containers by the side of the road and in every public place. There are signs, however, that Korean consumers are getting the message about this from regular campaigns to fight litter and to encourage disposal in approved containers. Many manufacturers are using "green" materials in an effort to encourage recycling. Korea thus appears to be passing out of the phase, common to many industrializing economies, in which maintaining environmental quality takes a back seat to industrial growth. Though South Korea is one of the world's top producers of greenhouse gases, the signs point to more environmentally friendly policies in the future.

CIVIL SOCIETY AND URBANIZATION

Amid these forbidding conditions, the millions of Seoul citizens who have recently become city dwellers have been obliged to find ways to join new communities that can help replace the comfort and satisfaction that was part of village life. Their need for social contact and belonging has given rise to the development of the richly articulated civil society that is such a vibrant force in modern Korean life. They have become part of many different kinds of voluntary associations of people who cooperate without government direction for agreed-upon purposes, functioning largely without government interference. The associations include labor unions, religious denominations and organizations, charitable foundations, chambers of commerce, professional societies, the thousands of other clubs and associations that are organized by the members themselves to pursue private interests. These "intermediate organizations," meaning groups that stand between government and the individual and help individuals organize and protect their interests apart from state goals, are essential to the development of democracy, and in South Korea they have served to invigorate and enrich daily life in myriad ways.

Civil society as it is known in South Korea today did not exist under the traditional monarchy or under the Japanese colonial regime, which took an intrusive interest in such innocuous organizations as the YMCA while censoring all activity that could turn into a Korean rebellion against their domination. Civil society also does not exist in North Korea, where everyone is expected to focus on the community and its "Great Leader" Kim Jong-il. Civil society organizations are intended to help people act in freedom and make common cause with like-minded individuals. It is therefore an important contributor to democracy, and it has functioned in that way in South Korea.

Religious organizations are among the most effective components of civil society in South Korea and they have played an important part in the process of urbanization. Korea's smaller towns and villages acquired churches in the early 1900s, largely the result of the Protestant and Catholic missionaries who fanned out on remote tracks "itinerating" in teams to search for villagers who might be attracted to the gospel. One attraction was the invitation to move into town and attend one of the mission schools that were providing modern education in a time when there were few public schools. Students who eventually became Christians were urged to start churches in their home villages and to convert the villagers beginning with their own family members. These nuclei became the building blocks of Korean Christianity as it developed before 1960.

As Christians migrated from the country into the cities, they maintained their connection with their Christian denominations and sought community in urban congregations. Even in places where newcomers were strangers, where people moved to look for factory jobs, they went to church to find friendly people who might welcome them and provide them with a support network. Church members helped each other find housing and jobs. They met together and shared their problems and took up collections for emergencies. Many churches included groups from particular places in the countryside. Foremost among these were the North Korean refugee churches made up of Christians who were forced to move south in the 1940s or came south during the Korean War. Other churches identified themselves as comforting places for people from such-and-such a county or province.

Modern urban Koreans thus have coped with the bewildering cacophony of city life in the midst of strangers by forging their own small support communities. In a typical case a person might belong to a neighborhood association in an apartment complex, a labor union, a Red Cross volunteer disaster watch association, an alumni group, and a Presbyterian church with a strong component of members from his or her ancestral area. Each of these organizations provides the individual with a different network of contacts and advice and offers the individual a chance to make an important social contribution. In this way, the development of civil society has done much to organize and moderate the traumatic transition from farm to city life.

EDUCATION

The Korean passion for education is one reason for the country's rapid economic development and a major element in the process of urbanization. It is rooted in the traditional respect for the educated *yangban* class and the awe with which uneducated Korean commoners used to look upon anyone who could manage the magical process of reading and writing. Under the monarchy, educated men were appointed to office and ruled over others, and education was reserved for the few at the top of the social scale.

Mass education did not begin until after 1910, during the Japanese colonial period. The Japanese installed a system of government schools that began to spread the power of literacy. Foreign missionaries also created a school system that taught secular subjects and welcomed children from all social classes. Despite these major initiatives, however, fewer than 20 percent of the Korean people had ever attended a school of any kind by 1945, when Korea was liberated.

Koreans possessing education were the ones who moved into leadership positions immediately after 1945. This fact was obvious to Koreans in general, who demanded access to education for their children and forced both governments, north and south, to put a high priority on educational development. The Korean War (1950–53) was a serious setback for these efforts.

Many schools were destroyed in the fighting. In some places teachers were forced to meet their classes outdoors, on hillsides and riverbanks, attempting to teach without textbooks or writing paper. The result was a new determination to promote mass education after the war, and in South Korea the government spent more money on education than on anything other than national defense.

Today, the South Korean educational system is based on a 1968 charter that defines the government's mission of educating every Korean child for citizenship and participation in modern life. Educational policy is set by the Ministry of Education, which determines curriculum, commissions and approves textbooks, and enforces uniform standards for all levels of schooling throughout the country. The system consists of elementary schools (six years), middle schools (three years), and high schools (three years). Elementary schooling is free and compulsory. Fees are charged in the middle and high schools, but 90 percent of the children go on to middle school and 88 percent of those continue into high school. The school year begins in March, and to make the 220-day annual requirement, students go to class five and a half days a week, with Saturday afternoons and Sundays off.

South Korea's educational plan sets forth several main purposes for elementary school. The first is literacy—the ability to read and write Korean. Others include scientific knowledge, arithmetic, social studies, physical education, acquisition of an appreciation for art and music, and the development of moral knowledge. "Moral knowledge" includes a sense of social responsibility, the ability to share and seek justice, practicing self-reliance, and respecting the country's laws and institutions.

In middle school, students continue studying the same subjects and add a certain amount of vocational training, including knowledge of simple mechanics and home economics. They study their own Korean heritage but they also study world history and they begin English, which is the required second language for all Korean students. Their teachers watch them and evaluate their aptitudes and play a role in helping them decide whether or not to go on to high school. If they are among the majority of those who do continue, they are steered toward "general" or "vocational" high schools. They also take achievement tests that aid in identifying their aptitudes for the "general" (i.e., college-bound) or "vocational" tracks.

The basic routine of South Korea's high school students involves going to regular classes from 8 A.M. until midafternoon, with time after that devoted to athletics, extracurricular activities, and study sessions. Their subjects include advanced versions of what they studied in middle school including English and mathematics (normally including calculus). They may also study an additional language such as Chinese or German, and in vocational schools they may study agriculture, engineering, and home economics. Many of the boys go into ROTC, hoping to serve as officers when they fulfill their required military service, normally at around age twenty.

Many Korean high school students get up early to study before school. A large number attend after-school "cram classes" to help them master topics for the all-important college entrance examinations that have to be taken in the senior year. Families put a lot of pressure on Korean students to excel, both for the family's reputation and for the students' own future. This pressure drives students to work long hours in the evening at the cram schools and at home doing homework. Few students have outside jobs or much of a social life outside of school, even on the weekends. Nevertheless, during breaks in their daily routine, Korea's high school students manage to squeeze in a little time for fun at fast-food restaurants, video game parlors, and tearooms.

Korea's parents and grandparents used to drive their children to do well in school because they could remember when education by itself was desirable as the guarantee of a successful future. Today, things have changed. Although Korea has plenty of public and private schools and numerous colleges and universities, mass education has created tremendous competition. There are so many college graduates, in fact, that unemployment or underemployment is a serious problem for them. Settling for a high school diploma is sure to limit a student's opportunities but mere possession of a college degree is no guarantee of a bright future, either. Colleges and universities vary in their reputations, and it is important to get into a top school and graduate with others who are similarly educated to move into the society's important professions and positions. High school students therefore bear the heavy burden of competing for freshman class slots at the very best national institutions. Their performance on the entrance exams determines whether or not they will be accepted. The competition provides useful motivation for most students but for some others it is too much and leads to a sense of failure and depression even before they get through secondary school.

University Education in South Korea

Modern postsecondary education in Korea was virtually nonexistent before 1910, and under Japanese colonial rule, Koreans who wanted to attend college either had to go abroad (most often to Japan) or had to attend one of only four institutions in Korea, three of them private and all of them small. Korea's first university was the Japanese-run Keijō (Seoul) Imperial University founded in the 1920s, which turned out to have more Japanese than Korean students. Today its modern version, Seoul National University (SNU), is South Korea's most prestigious institution of higher learning and is seen as being in a class by itself. The second tier of prestige schools includes the most important private universities: Yonsei, Koryŏ, and Ewha Universities. Ewha is the country's top university for women. While these schools are the ones most hotly sought by college-bound high school students, the country has many colleges and universities that are smaller and somewhat more specialized but nonetheless excellent.

About a quarter of South Korea's high school graduates go on to the country's nearly 350 postsecondary institutions. They study to be businessmen, doctors and dentists, teachers, government officials, scientists, engineers, musicians, and many other things. Their choices of major reflect social trends and values. In the 1960s, the top choice at SNU was law and diplomacy, since politics and world affairs seemed like the most important thing in national life. But in the 1980s, as Korea's economy grew and prospered, the preference shifted to business and has remained there ever since.

Until recently, college applicants had to gamble somewhat with their college choices since they were only allowed to apply to one school at a time and even had to pick a major in advance and apply to study in a particular department of the school even before they graduated from high school. For many, this was a de facto career choice. For example, a school with formidable admission standards might have a dental studies department that had somewhat lower standards. A high school senior seeking the prestige of being a student at this top university might choose to major in dentistry simply because it was the easiest department to get into. He or she would therefore choose to follow a career as a dentist without necessarily being interested in teeth or oral surgery. The system, in other words, was subject to abuse.

In the late 1990s this system was relaxed and students were allowed to apply to several schools at once. This made it more like the American system, where high school seniors apply to "reach schools" and "safe schools" hoping to gain admission to their first choice but knowing that they can fall back on their safe choice. The change has made life harder for admissions officers at Korean colleges and universities but it has made things better for applicants by eliminating the worst features of the previous single-choice system.

South Korean college students find that life becomes easier once they have been accepted. Though some maintain the pace and keep striving for high grades, most take the opportunity to relax. Graduation, no matter what their grades, will make them members of the institution's alumni group and their place in the network of graduates is assured. Afternoons on college campuses sometimes resemble festivals with groups of students meeting to pursue their interests in a plethora of clubs and associations, teams practicing on the athletic fields, sophomore boys in ROTC drilling in uniform, music clubs practicing singing and playing instruments, couples strolling on the paths, and constant traffic in and out of the student union building and, to a lesser degree, the campus library. It is a highly social atmosphere and most students enjoy it to the fullest. Many students have part-time jobs on campus and some tutor younger children in their homes near the campus. Altogether it is one of the best times of a person's life.

Students as the "Conscience of Society"

Students play an interesting role in Korea's national life. Centuries ago, new graduates of the royal academy were regarded as moral models by virtue of their years studying the Confucian classics and qualified to rule wisely over the people. In modern Korea, university students have also commanded respect for their hard work and potential as future leaders. In 1960, they were in the forefront of a mass movement protesting a corrupt presidential election and actually forced a change in the government in what is often referred to as the "Student Revolution." The movement involved clashes with police in which 189 demonstrators, most of them high school and university students, were killed, making them martyrs in the cause of democratic development. The martyrdom of students in the cause of democracy was enhanced twenty years later when the South Korean army attacked citizens of the city of Kwangju, in southwestern Korea, who were demonstrating against the illegal seizure of power by General Chun Doo-hwan (see Chapter 2). No one knows how many were killed in the Kwangju massacre of May 1980, but even the government admits that more than 200 citizens died and many of them were students at Kwangju's two universities. The cemetery containing their graves is a now a national shrine, as is the cemetery in Seoul commemorating the Student Revolution of 1960.

Since the 1950s in South Korea it is students who have taken to the streets to articulate grievances against powerful political leaders and unpopular government policies. Although South Korea has always aspired to be a democratic country with freedom of expression, the government has usually been a partial dictatorship that punished dissent and criticism. The ostensible reason for this was the fact that there was an ongoing military confrontation with North Korea and the South could not afford to be disunited in the face of the North Korean threat. As a result of this stance, however, laws were enacted that punished *any* kind of criticism, even when it was legitimate, and denied the people their constitutionally guaranteed freedom to speak, associate, publish, and hold a variety of political opinions.

Students were the one group in society that was in a position to face the government and make public demands for change. This was because they could act as individuals essentially responsible for only themselves and did not have to censor their own actions in order to keep their homes or businesses or to ensure the safety of their families. They were also in a better position than anyone else in society to meet, develop ideas, and plan mass actions in secret. At a time when newspapers were censored, religious leaders were watched and intimidated, and opposition political party members were often put in jail, it was the nation's students who risked their own freedom to gather on campus and march out into the streets bearing signs and slogans criticizing the government. When they did so they broke the law and had to endure police attacks, tear gas, beatings, and even imprisonment, in order to say what everyone in the country was thinking. The government punished the demonstrators by threatening their parents and even drafting young male students into the army where they were sometimes beaten and occasionally killed in basic training.

Rallies by university students were an essential part of the breakthrough that occurred in 1987–88 and that ended decades of military rule and started a series of truly democratic reforms. The rallies were a reaction to the government's decision to appoint another general as president for the next five years. In this instance the students were joined by housewives, workers, shopkeepers, and office workers who poured into the streets to swell the demonstrations. This was a dramatic turn of events because a passive alliance had developed between the Korean government, the business community, and the middle class that was enjoying an unprecedented standard of living even under military rule. During the 1980s, even when the government was at its most dictatorial, Korean citizens in general seemed willing to tolerate curbs on their political freedom in exchange for rising incomes. In addition, the fact that Seoul had been chosen to host the 1988 Summer Olympics put a damper on people's willingness to protest openly. The government made much of the fact that Korea needed to appear to be a safe and congenial place in order to attract athletes and spectators to the 1988 Olympics.

However, the outrageous political abuses of the Chun Doo-hwan regime broke the silence of this majority and inspired crowds exceeding 100,000 people to spill into the streets of Seoul to demand a democratic presidential election. The Chun regime was forced to choose between a bloody crackdown like the one in 1980 and a change in the election procedure. With the world press watching and television crews on the scene to document conditions in

Students beginning an antigovernment "demo" at Yonsei University. Leaders wear traditional clothes to emphasize their loyalty to Korean values. Ordinary students join in. Eventually, when the column is large enough, it will march off campus to confront the police.

Korea, the government backed down. There was a democratic election in December 1987, and over the ensuing five years South Koreans were enabled to enjoy greater freedom than they had ever known. Both of the presidents who were freely elected in 1992 and 1997 were famous former opposition leaders whom successive military rulers had thrown in jail for demanding democracy in the 1970s and 1980s. Though the change came about because of pressure from across Korean society, without students in the forefront between 1960 and 1990 it is unlikely that it would have happened at all.

CHANGES IN KOREA'S YOUTH CULTURE

The political activism of South Korea's students between the 1960s and 1980s gave way in the 1990s to a generational stance that seemed more interested in enjoying the country's unprecedented prosperity and finding opportunities for enjoyment. There is a dramatic contrast to be seen in the successive generations since the Korean War, the first having been driven by the basic need to survive, the second having driven the development of democracy, and the present one seeking economic security together with a higher quality of life. Whether one sees the educated, stylish, urban young people of turn-of-the-century South Korea as entitled to reap the benefits of their elders' hard work or whether they are merely seen as self-absorbed, they are more interesting in many ways and perhaps more full of potential than any preceding generation. For example, they are the first generation to receive the full benefit of Korea's mass education system, uninterrupted by war or hampered by lack of facilities. They are more sophisticated than their elders were at their age, being well aware of the limits of democracy and prosperity. Their sophistication makes them more volatile politically, since they are not committed to any particular vision and must therefore be courted by the political system in an era where their votes can be freely cast.

Today's South Korean youth are also the country's first truly international generation, schooled in the uses of the Internet and better trained in international languages than their elders, with many of them having friends and relatives living in foreign countries. They are the first generation of Koreans to grow up with the freedom to travel, especially to countries that were forbidden and unknown to their elders such as the People's Republic of China or even North Korea. Indeed, theirs is the first generation of South Koreans to grow up with the idea that their part of the Korean peninsula is stronger and better off than the north, that a North Korean invasion does not loom as an everyday deterrent to free speech and expression, and that reunification can wait, if necessary, for the day when their society proves to be the pattern for a united Korea. If older Koreans sometimes express exasperation at the lack of political and historical consciousness among the young and complain that they do not appreciate the lessons of the Korean War or the sacrifices of the workers who built the economy, they also realize that the education, good nutrition and health, and economic and intellectual potential of the younger generation are proof that the earlier struggles were worthwhile.

CULTURE AND SPORTS IN URBAN KOREA

Cities the size of Seoul or Pusan produce limitless opportunities for cultural expression and recreation. Here, as in so much of modern Korean life, traditions mix with newer, often imported, genres. There are plenty of historical sites and artifacts carefully preserved by the government's Cultural Properties Bureau. These range from the collection of the National Museum of Korea, with its rich display of traditional art objects, to private collections such as the Ho'am Museum, many of whose pieces exceed those of the

National Museum in artistic quality and importance, to the modern art galleries of Seoul's university districts and the massive Seoul Arts Complex south of the Han River. Even in the darkest days of the Korean War era, the government struggled to preserve the ancient royal palaces in Seoul. These have now been restored and even expanded to replace buildings removed by the Japanese in the early 1900s and even earlier, by the Korean royal government. There has been an explosion in the publishing of top-quality art books to disseminate an appreciation for Korean art of all kinds. Many of these books have been aimed at foreign consumers in an attempt to win recognition in the world for Korean art, beyond the already-recognized genre of celadon pottery for which the medieval Koryŏ period is known around the world.

Sports

Hosting the 1988 Summer Olympics put Korea on the world sports map. However, physical culture and athletic performance has always been an important part of Korean life. Koreans are very proud of Son Kijŏng, the Korean marathon runner who won the gold at the 1936 Olympics in Berlin. Another perhaps even more famous Korean contribution to the world of sports is *T'aekwŏndo*, a disciplined martial art that pits two people against each other without weapons. "Discipline" is the essential word in *T'aekwŏndo*: mental, physical, and spiritual. The martial artist goes through stages of training and practice under the tutelage of a master who passes him or her onto the next stage. The student masters the discipline of each stage leading up to earning the black belt, which symbolizes the highest skill. The object of a *T'aekwŏndo* match is not to injure but to subdue one's opponent with force and maneuvering skill that could be used to kill an opponent in a real-life attack. Restraint, therefore, is an operative part of *T'aekwŏndo* practice. Other traditional forms of Korean sport include a type of wrestling called *ssirŭm*, which is something like sumo wrestling and involves throwing the opponent out of the ring. *Hwarangdo* is a martial art similar to judo, which was practiced in ancient times by warriors in the Silla kingdom. Koreans also practice archery and horsemanship using traditional bows, arrows, and riding accoutrements.

When it comes to modern sports, Koreans train to compete in all forms. Football (soccer) is a schoolyard sport played by every Korean boy, and Koreans wildly cheer their teams at the World Cup, which Korea and Japan are cohosting in 2002. Baseball is also popular and every Korean high school and college has a baseball team. Women athletes excel at volleyball and table tennis and have won international championships in each. However, no sport is more associated with modern urban life than golf, in part because of the social connotations that accompany it. It takes much skill and practice to play golf well, meaning that the player must have enough leisure time to pursue it. And since land is so expensive in Korea, the value of a golf course is such that access to it is very expensive, making golf club membership in Korea more expensive than joining any but the most exclusive American country clubs. Golf is a prestige sport typically played by business tycoons and top government officials. Yet it is also possible for an ordinary person to find ways to develop golfing skill. In 1998 Koreans were ecstatic to see Park Se-ri, a twenty-year-old woman, advance to the finals of the U.S. Women's Open Golf Tournament and win the championship. The daughter of ordinary workers in the city of Taejŏn, Ms. Park instantly became a national hero.

USING PUBLIC AND RECREATIONAL SPACE

The skills that Park Se-ri developed as a young golfer won her access to open green spaces that are beyond the reach of most Koreans. Most Korean golf courses belong to expensive country clubs and are the preserve of business executives and top politicians. Ordinary citizens have to seek their recreation in public areas and their moments of peace and quiet are precious indeed.

At first glance Seoul, the capital of South Korea with its population of 11 million, seems to be an unrelieved cityscape of apartment blocks and disorganized neighborhoods crammed with shops, restaurants, offices, and residences jumbled together without any rhyme or reason. Many people live in Seoul for years, passing by on the main streets and mass transit lines, without ever exploring the "alleys" that honeycomb the neighborhoods within the huge urban blocks of the city. These winding alleyways are remnants of the old city, narrow walkways with walls on either side that offer few hints of the wealth or leisure that often lies within the houses. But if one passes through one of the roofed wooden "great gates" into a well-to-do family's courtyard, the impression is suddenly different. The finer houses of the city are richly furnished, with rooms of polished wooden *maru* or heated *ŏndol* floors. Many houses have rooms furnished in modern style with sofas and chairs and tables and modern appliances and artifacts of the electronic age. Given the price of land in Seoul, it takes considerable money to maintain a family in a traditional Korean house within the city, yet many families manage to do it and preserve the genteel traditional Korean style.

People who are not fortunate enough themselves to live in these Korean "mansions" still enjoy visiting some of the traditional restaurants that operate in buildings that once were the homes of members of the *yangban* nobility. Some of these are Seoul's famous *kisaeng* houses, places comparable to Japanese geisha houses, where guests are treated to lavish meals and various kinds of entertainment by professional female entertainers known as *kisaeng*. The *kisaeng* house experience draws many of the city's elite, especially when businessmen want to entertain clients or diplomats want to entertain other dignitaries. Korean *kisaeng* houses draw foreigners, also, with Japanese especially enjoying flying over for a weekend or even just an evening.

When Koreans relax, they head for the outdoors even if it means spending hours on a crowded bus in search of the natural environment. Park space is at a premium, but one dividend of the fact that Korea is covered with hills and mountains is that even in the cities there are heights that remain wooded and useful for hiking, picnics, and recreation. In Seoul, for example, there is a mountain in the center of the city that, though heavily built up around its base, remains green, wooded, and beautiful at higher elevations. The massive Pukhan Mountains on the north side of Seoul are easily reached by city bus and on Saturdays there are enthusiastic hikers all along the Pukhan trails. Spurs of the Pukhan Mountains reach down into the city itself, intruding green arms to the very edge of downtown. These urban hills are troublesome to climb and difficult to build on, but they give the city character and beauty and relieve what would otherwise be an unrelieved landscape of concrete, pavement, apartment blocks, and vehicle-generated smog.

Although parks are small and very few in number in the city itself, larger tracts have been set aside in the suburbs. One favorite place to spend a weekend day is the Children's Park in eastern Seoul. Another is the "farmland" park on the southern edge of the city, which also contains the city's zoo.

Superhighways have made it possible for families to pile into the family car or sport utility vehicle and head for a completely different part of the country on the weekends. Destinations include famous temples, historic sights, favorite scenery, ancestral homes, and resorts at the beach or in the mountains. The difficulty is that when everyone goes at once the roads become choked with traffic and there are serious delays. However, once people arrive at their destinations they love to hike, picnic, and simply enjoy the clean air. The mountain complex at Mount Sorak east of Seoul is a favorite destination.

Going to the beach is a relatively new form of recreation in Korea. Traditionally the sea has been a place for fishing, and seaside development has been slow. Certain spots have been famous for their beaches: Hae'undae near

Pusan, Kangnŭng on the east coast, and Taech'ŏn and Mallip'o on the west. Until the 1980s, recreational beach-going was limited to overnight trips and explorations of beach areas in search of shellfish and other marine delicacies. Beach sports were expensive and the equipment was hard to transport without private cars. In the 1980s, however, when the Korean middle class became mobile, families began camping at beaches and playing beach sports. They started waterskiing, windsurfing, and holding beach concerts. Taech'ŏn, for example, which has always been a beautiful beach, had nothing more than a motley row of cheap inns until the 1980s. In the 1990s, however, it suddenly became a family resort with a campground, hotels, restaurants, a boardwalk, an amusement park, and equipment rentals for every kind of beach sport from snorkeling to surfing to parasailing.

Buddhist temples in the mountains attract many leisure visitors whose quest is for cool shade and clean air. The legacy of the Chosŏn-era prohibition against having Buddhist temples in the cities is that the mountain forests now contain temples that function as tourist destinations. Though they are not intended as recreational space and the monks and nuns who inhabit them seem hard-pressed by the crowds of visitors, Korea's mountain temples have been rejuvenated by the new flow of income as they offer opportunities for reflection on the link between past and present.

Buddhist temples typically are compounds that contain a number of buildings, even in the mountains. The compounds are enclosed by walls and are laid out in rectangular fashion, usually facing south like royal palaces. One approaches a temple on a mountain path that leads to a gate structure in which there are large figures of fierce-looking guardians trampling little demons that represent the forces of evil in the world. Beyond the gate is a courtyard that usually contains a pagoda, and beyond that is the main hall containing images of the Buddha and his attendants, who may include bodhisattvas and other figures from the Buddhist pantheon. One removes shoes and enters this building reverently, always facing the Buddha, and kneels on the floor to meditate and pray. A table before the Buddha holds an incense burner, and the worshipper usually donates a little money and burns a stick of incense during the visit. On the wall behind the Buddhist icons is usually a large mural painting or some other kind of backdrop that is meant to inspire reverence and thoughts of Buddha's infinite mercy. On the walls on either side of the building may be paintings of heaven and hell or of Buddha's life, and on the outside walls of the temple building, around the back of the building, is usually a series of "herdboy" paintings that depict a boy looking for an ox. The ox symbolizes enlightenment, and the way the boy perceives the ox is at first by imagining it and then by finding it, but only after an elaborate search.

Up behind the temple on the hill there is almost always a small shrine to the mountain spirit, a non-Buddhist element reminiscent of Korean shamanism that honors the deity of the forest on the mountain. The mountain spirit is portrayed in a painting inside the shrine, as an old man with a long white beard sitting under a pine tree and attended by a friendly tiger and an assistant. In addition to this, if there is a monastery or convent attached to the temple, there are also dormitories and dining halls for the monks or nuns.

Before World War II there were hunting resorts in the Korean mountains. People came from as far away as Europe to look for the famous tigers that were said to menace Korean villages, especially in the northern part of the country. One of the resorts near the sacred Korean mountain of Paektu-san was run by a family of Russians who had fled the Russian Revolution and led expeditions into the mountains to shoot tigers, leopards, deer, and wild boar. However, by 1940 the tiger was virtually gone from Korea's mountains and the other wild animals were becoming ever more rare. In the latter half of the twentieth century hunters have been limited to using air guns and certain kinds of shotguns, and their targets have been mainly birds such as pheasants.

Remarkably enough, there is one area of Korea that has become more wild, not less, since the Korean War. That is the four-kilometer-wide strip across the middle of the country that constitutes the Demilitarized Zone (DMZ) and separates North from South Korea. Though one can hardly regard the strip as "demilitarized," since soldiers regularly patrol it and occasionally fight each other, most of the zone is seeded with land mines and people cannot use it. Migratory birds have found havens in the DMZ and bird-watchers love to go as close as they can to the boundary to spot rare types of cranes and other wild birds.

The wildlife sanctuary that is provided by the DMZ is a glimpse of what Korea's natural environment must have been like before the population growth and modernization of the nineteenth and twentieth centuries. Modern life has brought dramatic changes and improvements in the standard of living. However, it has also meant water pollution, toxic waste, smog, and the health effects of an overtaxed environment. Koreans have embraced the modern style but they have also learned that mountains of discarded plastic and nonbiodegradable trash along with vehicle exhaust and other emissions that increase ozone and threaten respiratory health have created a national emergency. Similarly, the wholesale cutting down of trees all across Korea earlier in the century has led to a realization that the land belongs to everyone and has to be replenished. Koreans therefore have embarked on aggressive environmental protection campaigns and are working to save what is left and restore whatever can be recovered. For fuel they have shifted to coal, oil, and propane gas. This, together with an aggressive reforestation campaign, has restored South Korea's forests and the natural beauty of the hills. Air and water pollution has been harder to control but the entire population is aware of the problem and most people are cooperating in efforts to address it. There has been noticeable progress in air quality, for example, and there are signs of hope that the Korean people can live and prosper together without ruining their natural habitat.

CONSTANTS IN KOREAN LIFE

The process of moving from farm to city has been a major motif in the lives of millions of modern Koreans. The process has been traumatic for many and difficult for most, involving major transformations and adaptations. They have had to learn to depend on new networks of friends to replace rural family networks and to acclimate themselves to a highly competitive economic environment. They have also had to give up the slower pace and simpler style of village life in favor of long hours in traffic jams and straphanging on crowded commuter subways. The different generations have experienced completely different styles of life and today's young people can hardly imagine the things that their parents and grandparents have gone through during the multiple transitions from colonialism to democracy and farm life to urban existence. Yet certain constants are also visible. Koreans continue to place primary importance on family life; they maintain their strong ethical framework and their loyal relationships among their old friends and new ones made through joining new kinds of associations. They put a premium on education and maintain high standards for their children and their own success. In many ways, therefore, the traditional furnishing of their high-rise apartment units is a kind of metaphor, the home appearing on the outside to have been transformed beyond recognition but maintaining its integrity on the inside.

8

Gender, Marriage, and the Lives of Korean Women

BOY PREFERENCE

AT THE BEGINNING of Korea's push for economic modernization, the government launched a nationwide campaign to arrest the postwar population explosion through better family planning. Though funds and resources were severely limited at the time, the Ministry of Health and Social Affairs was able to employ family planning workers in most of the country's districts. In Poksu District of Kŭmsan County, the district headquarters was assigned a worker named Mrs. Kim to persuade the villagers of South Valley Hamlet to limit the number of children they were having through the use of various contraceptive devices and methods. Mrs. Kim's job was to counteract the prevailing assumptions that old people needed children to take care of them, that families needed sons to perpetuate the lineage, that the farm needed many family members to perform the labor, and that diseases and disasters made it necessary to assume that not all children would live to adulthood. While the Seoul government did not try to put over a "one-child policy," as in China in the 1980s, it did train its family planning workers to insist that two children was an ideal number and that the gender of the children didn't matter. Though the campaign's propaganda posters depicted a happy couple with a daughter and a son, the official government line was that it was perfectly fine to have two of the same sex, whether sons or daughters.

Mrs. Kim won prizes for her success in teaching the women of Poksu about birth control. As she toured the district giving talks to "mothers' clubs," she made many friends and won many women over to the government's birth control program. She persuaded them that conditions were healthier and children were more likely to survive to adulthood than before, so that two children would be sufficient. She pointed out that tractors and other new machines would make it easier for fewer people to work the family farm. She had little trouble making the point that with fewer people in the family there would be more money and resources for each one. But she had trouble with women who only had daughters. She was completely unable to convince them that baby girls were just as good as baby boys. Women who had only daughters were invariably hoping to have another child, and if it turned out to be a girl they would simply try again until they finally had a son.

The "boy preference" of the village women frustrated Mrs. Kim. She knew she was fighting an uphill battle against an ancient tradition. Korean parents had always expected their sons to stay near home, or at least to return after getting an education, to carry on the family. A son's success in school was regarded as a success for the whole family. A son was an emblem of the family lineage, a performer of the ancestral rituals, a supporter of parents in their old age, and an object of family pride. Clearly it was worth some sacrifice to provide for his education and give him special advantages. A daughter, on the other hand, was expected to grow up, marry, and move away to become part of her husband's family. It made sense to teach daughters how to cook, sew, and be good mothers, but the best "success" for them would be to marry away into a good family. As a rule, Korean farm families did not educate their daughters. The girls of Poksu District never got any education until the 1950s, when the government built a schoolhouse in the central hamlet. Instead, they had always stayed home helping their mothers with child care for younger siblings, cooking, cleaning, and doing the laundry by pounding clothes on flat rocks beside the village stream. They started practicing these domestic arts when they were only five or six.

The village women greatly respected Mrs. Kim because she had gone as far as high school and held a government job. In addition, she was an attractive woman, friendly and able to tell a good joke, and she had a good memory that enabled her to remember the names of everyone she met. These traits made her an especially good example for the village women. Mrs. Kim was also known as a good wife and mother. She and her husband had two bright and adorable children, and both of them were daughters. Whenever she told people that they should regard girls and boys equally, she gave her own family as an example.

However, as Mrs. Kim passed her own thirtieth birthday she felt trouble brewing in her family. She and her husband lived with Mr. Kim's parents, and the family planning worker's mother-in-law was very disappointed that both of her grandchildren were female. Mr. Kim was her eldest child, and the mother-in-law was upset that he had no son of his own to carry on the family line. She would mention that the Kim family had enjoyed a succession of strong, bright sons for many generations and that only now, with this particular daughter-in-law, had newfangled ideas about family planning been introduced to break this honorable family tradition. She did not approve of family planning and would often tell her daughter-in-law that it was wrong to limit families to two children. She would point to the Korean War and other national tragedies as signs that people should not rely on the government or economic prosperity to guarantee their security in old age. The best insurance was having sons, as always, and the Kim family was most unfortunate to have this stubborn daughter-in-law who thought government policies were more important than the family's needs.

Mrs. Kim sincerely believed in her family planning work and thought it was good for the women of Poksu District as well as for Korea as a whole. She thought it was irresponsible for families to keep having children until they got a son. She had thought about having surgery of her own to prevent any future births. But then her mother-in-law started applying pressure and Mrs. Kim wondered if she really had "failed" in her most basic familial duty. Not long after that she conceived her third child and in due course bore a stalwart son. Only then did the Kims stop having children, though Mrs. Kim later admitted that if the baby had been a daughter they would have had to try yet a fourth time. Being a "good daughter-in-law" turned out to be the most important thing of all, even for an award-winning family planning worker.

Today, the Kims' son is married and the father of two children, a daughter and a son. He lives with his family in the city and not in Poksu District with his parents and grandparents. Both he and his wife attended university, and he has a degree in engineering. The couple's children are also likely to attend college. However, though the family planning worker's daughters are better educated than their mother, neither went beyond high school. Instead, they worked for a short time, married, and moved away to start families of their own. Mrs. Kim herself has advanced to become head of the county welfare department, which includes family planning workers who do what she used to do back in the sixties. She is proud to say that the typical farm family in Poksu now has two or three children. Families with four or more children are very rare.

The story of Mrs. Kim, the Poksu District family planning worker, illustrates several things about the position of women in Korean society, the most important being the power of family interests over individual behavior. Her most important role in life was to be a good wife and mother within the values of the Kim family. The in-laws were willing to accept her having a career, but only after she had performed her primary duty of providing the family with a son.

Once they had a son, however, the Kims did not treat their three children equally. The boy was prepared from childhood to take responsibility for the family line. He got the best education and stands to inherit most of the property from his grandparents and parents. His sisters, on the other hand, "married out," and will be taken care of by their husbands' families. Though they often visit their parents in Poksu, their homes are with their husbands.

Korea today presents incomparably more opportunities to girls and women than it did a generation ago. Public education has made it normal even for country girls to finish high school and the colleges and universities are full of female students whose families work and sacrifice to send them to college. Korean women are shedding many aspects of second-class citizenship but they remain subject to rigid controls and expectations. Their lives are directed toward the goal of marriage and family, and whatever work or career they pursue takes second place to that. Though more and more young women are breaking free of these expectations, they are the exception rather than the rule. Even women who are university professors and elected government officials find that "normal" family life is essential in order for them to have public respect. A professional woman in a high-status position still must subject herself in private to the ancient limits that define her as her father's daughter, her husband's wife, and her son's mother.

KOREAN WOMEN: STEREOTYPES AND PARADOXES

Back in Poksu District on the eve of modernization, the health workers often went visiting to get to know the people and find out about their health needs. On these occasions they would often find no one home except an elderly woman, usually the grandmother, doing chores in the courtyard. Their introductory conversation would go something like this, beginning with the typical Korean "hello," which means "Are you in peace?"

"Good afternoon Grandmother! Are you in peace?"

"Yes," she would answer. "Do come in and be welcome."

They would go into the courtyard and trade comments on the weather, the splendid house, and the fineness of the ox tied in the pen in the courtyard corner. Then they would get down to business.

"We are from the Poksu District health center visiting our esteemed neighbors. We want to ask you some questions about your household."

"Yes," she would say, "but I don't know anything. I'm just an old woman. You should come back when my son is here."

"It's all right," the health workers would try to assure her. "Our questions are quite simple. Though it may be a bother and we apologize, we are sure you can answer them."

They would then ask her about the number of people living in the house, their age and gender, the name of the household head, who was usually her son or son-in-law. She would answer their questions and then they would ask, "And Grandmother, what is *your* name?"

"*My* name?" she would answer.

"Yes, your own name. What is your clan?"

"My clan? I think it's Pak—the Pak clan from the town of Miryang."

"Good. And what is your own name?"

"My *own* name? Goodness! It's been so long. I don't remember my name. It's on my identity card, but I can't read and my son keeps all the cards. Just a minute! I think he's out back in the next field. I'll call over and ask him."

She would go over to the wall, climb up on a step, and bellow out to her son working in the nearby field,

"Hey, they want to know my name! What is it? Can you remember?"

Taking surveys in Poksu demonstrated that Koreans do not use names the way Westerners use them, and that women's names, especially the names of older, illiterate women, are used so seldom that they can actually be forgotten by the women themselves. This is because from childhood they are called "the baby," then by a nickname like "Little Treasure," and then when they marry and have a baby they are *Aegi ŏmma* ("the baby's mother"). If a mother has a child named Ch'ŏlsu, she is called *Ch'ŏlsu ŏmoni* ("Ch'ŏlsu's mother") while he is growing up. After that people call her *Ajumma* ("Auntie"), and finally *Halmŏni* ("Grandma"). Avoiding direct mention of a woman's name is part of the aversion to using anyone's name in ordinary speech. People avoid using men's names too, preferring to address them by their titles (e.g., Honorable Teacher, Honorable Section Chief, Honorable Pastor), with "Honorable Teacher" being the default title in polite conversation with strangers. But at least men's names are known: they are printed along with proper titles on the name cards (*myŏngham*) that every businessperson carries to hand out upon meeting anyone new.

In 1968, the government passed a law requiring every citizen to register and get an identification card. This made it necessary for everyone, including the grandmas of Poksu, to rediscover and use their names. However, the "namelessness" of Korean women up to that point does not mean that they were invisible or without position. Rather it is a clue to the fact that Korean

Poksu village women and girls washing clothes the old-fashioned way in the 1960s.

women have always derived their identities from their male relatives. In traditional times, Korean women had to practice the "three submissions:" to submit to their father, then their husband, and finally their sons. These male relatives protected and provided for them. Well-bred Korean women were supposed to live in seclusion in the "inner rooms" of the house, never to be seen (and certainly never to be touched) by men outside the family. Even their relations with adult men in the family were supposed to be formal. In the "inner rooms," however, women had considerable power. They dominated domestic life, ran the household, and were the dominant influence on the children. The image of the Korean woman as "nameless" and oppressed, therefore, has to be modified to reflect the fact that within their own sphere, women wielded considerable power even in traditional times.

The paradox of public submission versus domestic power is further complicated by the fact that different classes of Korean society have always dealt differently with the ideal. Working women, for example, have never been able to live without going out in public. In a job, however, the more unregulated contact there is between a woman and unrelated male customers, the more harmful it is to a woman's reputation. Thus, though not working is the best situation of all, a bank teller is more respectable than a bar hostess.

Thus employers house the thousands of "factory girls" who work in their plants in special dormitories that are locked and supervised, ostensibly to protect them from harmful influences and the loss of reputation that would come from their living on their own. It is understood that they are saving up for marriage to a young man who does not need to be inexperienced himself but will require a chaste bride. Or, in some cases, they are sending wages home to aged parents, or to finance their brothers' college educations. Whatever the reason, they have to function in public while trying to preserve their reputations in a moral system that is still full of Confucian ideas about women.

Another dimension of the paradox is the way the rules change for women who are past childbearing age. A woman above the age of fifty whose children are grown is excused from many of the rules. She is still not free to associate with unrelated men, but she may go out in public as she pleases and engage in behavior that would be forbidden to a younger woman. She may smoke tobacco and drink alcohol. She can join groups and associations and express herself without anyone else's permission. Women with a little extra money often join *kye*, revolving credit associations, playing the stock market and financing small businesses. Women of all classes enjoy outings with their women's associations, picnicking and entertaining each other on spirited outings. On the highway one has only to follow a bus full of slightly inebriated elderly women singing and dancing in the aisle while the vehicle rocks from side to side to understand that older women do not have to obey the same rules as younger women.

FAMOUS MODELS OF KOREAN WOMANHOOD

Korean literature is full of stories about virtuous women who embodied the Confucian ideal of the three submissions. The stories emphasize sacrifice and self-effacement for a greater good. In the ancient capital of Puyŏ a pavilion marks the Cliff of the Falling Flowers, where a group of maidens employed by the royal palace threw themselves into the river to avoid being defiled by invading foreign forces. There is a shrine in Chinju recalling the beautiful Non'gae, a Korean entertainer who once killed a Japanese general by dancing him off a cliff there, losing her own life in the process. One also recalls the lovely Ch'unhyang, the faithful young woman who waited for her lover to come back from Seoul and was thrown in jail for refusing the advances of the evil governor. The "Falling Flowers," the dancing girl Non'gae, and the faithful Ch'unhyang all paid dearly for their virtue and only

Ch'unhyang's story had a happy ending. But all three are models of a woman's duty to preserve honor at all costs.

Korean society granted women much more freedom in the years before the Confucianized Chosŏn dynasty whose state philosophy explicitly justified male privilege. Under the preceding Koryŏ dynasty, newlyweds often went to live with the bride's parents and the women often functioned as heads of their households. But the Chosŏn dynasty's conscious adoption of Confucian ethics for Korean society meant imposing new restrictions on the freedom of women. These included heavy penalties for those who failed to practice the "three submissions." Under the Koryŏ dynasty, it was tolerable for women to have lovers. The Chosŏn-dynasty Confucianists attacked this as destructive of human order and emphasized their reform by finding women who were guilty of adultery and executing them. New rules restricted the freedom of women to travel and move about. Upper-class women were ordered not to go out during the daytime and their male relatives were punished if they allowed them to violate the order. Thus men were obliged to enforce the restrictions on their wives and daughters.

The ethical basis for restrictions on women lay in Confucian ideology. Limits on freedom for women were expounded in numerous Confucian texts and treatises by important thinkers in the early Chosŏn dynasty. In Confucian ideology everyone had a proper place and role to play. It was important to define the proper spheres for men and women in society and to enforce their adherence to the rules of propriety. Among the ideals, or "proprieties," set forth for women were modesty, seclusion, faithfulness, sacrificial motherhood, and even loyalty to husbands after death. Women were not permitted to divorce their husbands, though there was a list of reasons why husbands could divorce their wives. Nor could a woman remarry after her husband's death, or inherit his property. A widow remained a member of her husband's family for the rest of her life and was prohibited from seeking a new husband and transferring membership to his family. When her husband died, the surviving widow immediately fell under the authority of her eldest son, who took on the role of family head. Rules like these guaranteed that a woman would remain dependent upon her husband's lineage throughout her adult life.[1]

Many of these values and customs have survived intact into the modern era, but the blatant unfairness has not gone unnoticed. The education of Korean women beginning in the 1880s has brought a powerful reform movement and demands for better protection under the law and more freedom for the individual. Along the way, a number of women have won public acclaim for their battle against injustice. Some of them are famous as women but also recognized for their sacrifice in the old-fashioned Confucian way. Yet alongside their accomplishments there remains a certain sense of contrivance: that their reputations are used to maintain male-dominated morality. A few examples of modern Korean heroines will suggest how this is so.

Yu Kwansun was a sixteen-year-old student at Ewha Girls' School when the Korean uprising against Japanese colonial rule erupted in March 1919. Kwansun was from the city of Ch'ŏnan, and at the time of the uprising she smuggled a copy of the Korean Declaration of Independence from Seoul, where she was going to school, to her hometown where it was read and used to spark a local demonstration demanding freedom for Korea. The Japanese police arrested and imprisoned her for spreading seditious documents. They molested and abused her in prison and eventually she died, one of the estimated 7,000 Koreans who lost their lives in the unsuccessful attempt to free Korea from Japanese domination. As such she is a symbol of the patriotic spirit of Korean youth. She also represents something that was new then but common now: the participation of young women in public political movements.

Kim Chŏngsuk was a young Communist, a woman who joined the guerrillas who fought Japan in the mountains of southern Manchuria, just over the border from northern Korea. Here she married Kim Il-sung, the guerrilla fighter who was destined to become the "Supreme Leader" of North Korea after World War II. In 1942 she bore him a son, Kim Jong-il, who became the Supreme Leader following his father's death in 1994. Kim Chŏngsuk herself became a martyr to the Korean Communist cause, an especially tragic figure because of her death during childbirth at a relatively young age, in 1948. Her story belongs in the chronicle of Korean womanhood because of its reinvention over the years, canonizing her as a model of patriotism, motherhood, loyalty to husband, and ultimately sacrifice for the "revolutionary family" of North Korea.

Yuk Yŏngsu was the First Lady of South Korea from 1963 until her tragic death during an assassination attempt on her husband, President Park Chung-hee, in 1974. "Madame Park," as she was called by Westerners, was an unusually beautiful woman, gifted with a smile and physical grace that made her perfect for the part of First Lady. Whereas her husband was a stern and humorless person with a reputation for discipline and even harshness, Madame Park was known for her softer womanly traits, her love of children, her care and concern for family, and her sympathy for the poor. Like Kim Chŏngsuk in North Korea, her public persona was the product of political image-making, but the images were Confucian as well as modern. Her death greatly enhanced public sympathy for her husband, who was under criticism for dictatorial ways and undoubtedly enhanced his ability to rule in the last years before his death in 1979.

Lee Taeyŏng was Korea's first female lawyer and founder of the Family Legal Aid Center, a pioneering effort to improve the rights of women under the South Korean constitution. She was born in 1914 and her father died when she was a baby, but her mother made sure that she got a good education and she graduated from Ewha Women's College in 1936. She married an influential politician and raised a family, in the process becoming an advocate for women's rights. At the height of her career in the 1960s and 1970s she was an important member of the South Korean democracy movement, maintaining as her specialty the needs of women for protection under the law. Through her Family Legal Aid Center she mounted a successful lobbying effort to get the government to create a family court that would hear cases involving domestic abuse and help wives file actions, including divorce, against their husbands. The center was the first institution in South Korea to study family violence, the tension of living with in-laws, conflicts between generations, and conflict resolution. Her efforts earned her an international reputation and an honored position in international women's rights conferences. At home they contributed to passage of a new family law that went into effect in 1990 and provided better guarantees of property and inheritance rights and autonomy within the family, a law that she characterized as a single step on the long road to complete equality for women. Lee Taeyŏng died in 1998 at the age of 84.

RITUALS OF COURTSHIP

Korean young people traditionally have relied on their families to arrange their marriages. Until the late twentieth century there were reasons for this pattern. With life expectancy in the range of forty years, people married and started families much younger, usually in their teens, and sometimes were betrothed, or "spoken for," before puberty. But more important, marriages were alliances between families, the joining of two ancestral lineages. Young people were in no position to make the calculations and decisions that went into a marriage. Adults needed to consider the astrological signs of the two young people, the histories of their clans, and the finances of the marriage. Only after these matters had been considered were the young couple given permission to get married. Even then, it was the custom for the bride and groom never to meet but to remain strangers until the wedding ceremony itself. Many older women in Korea today can remember peeking through their wedding veils to get their first glimpse of their husband-to-be. All this has changed dramatically in recent decades. Young people marry much later and have often finished their educations when they get engaged. "Love marriages" rather than arranged marriages are now common. Education, independence, and modern ideas have all revolutionized the customs surrounding marriage, redirecting the focus to the bride and groom instead of keeping it on the union of two family lineages.

During her career as the family planning worker in South Valley Hamlet, Mrs. Kim had an informal side-job as a *chungmae*, or matchmaker. Because she traveled the entire district by foot, bicycle, and bus visiting households in faraway pockets of the valley, she knew who was of marriageable age and was in a position to make suggestions to young people and their parents. The following conversation with the mother and aunt of a twenty-one-year-old boy who was coming home from service in the army was typical of Mrs. Kim's career as a matchmaker.[2] The young man had told his family that he was ready to settle down, and he was a prime candidate for marriage.

"You say he's twenty-one and finished with the army. Is he the eldest or a younger son?"

"He's our eldest," the mother said. "I do wish we could find him a good match." She was thinking about her own need for a male grandchild.

"Yes," said Mrs. Kim. "But nowadays girls are reluctant to marry eldest sons. They have too many responsibilities. Their mothers-in-law work them like slaves and they have to entertain the whole family so often it wears them out." Mrs. Kim was speaking from experience.

"I know," said the mother. "My husband is an eldest son too. But we still have to think about our old age, and our son needs a good wife. Do you know anyone?"

"Well," said Mrs. Kim. "I do know a house in Dragon Pass Village where the daughter has just graduated from high school. Her parents are impatient with her because she hates farm life and wants to marry a city boy. Is your son going to be a farmer?"

"We have been talking about selling the farm and moving to the city," said the mother. "But city life seems so dirty and dangerous and you have to live in a small apartment. We have many problems to solve before we can make our decision. So for the time being we'll have to stay here and our son will help us do the farming."

"So you're asking me to find you a farm wife for your son," remarked Mrs. Kim. "It won't be so easy!"

Mrs. Kim looked around the room and made a quick inventory. Electricity. A small radio. A fan. No other conveniences. But the floor was very well laid, the wallpaper was better than in most houses, and she had heard that the family made a good living from a ginseng field on the hillside. She decided that the farm would be worth a lot of money when it sold. She knew she could take this back to the girl's family, which was actually not very well off.

"Is your son handsome? Is he strong? What's he like?"

"Oh," said the mother, "he's always been an obedient and loyal son. When his grandmother was living he used to carry her across the stream on his back so she could visit her church friends. He's always helped his father with plowing, transplanting, and harvest. He's even gotten up on occasion to help me with the breakfast rice."

"And how far did he get in the army?"

"Actually, he was sent to fight in Vietnam and now he's a sergeant. He's done very well. By the way, what's this girl like?"

"She's kind of ordinary. She's healthy, though, and won't have any trouble bearing children. Except for her overbite she's actually somewhat pretty, I'd say. The teeth themselves are white and strong. I wish I had a picture. When's your son coming home? Maybe you can send him over to South Valley Hamlet so I can see him. Meanwhile I'm planning to visit Dragon Pass tomorrow and I'll see how the family is doing with plans for their daughter. They might be really interested in this. I'll get back to you."

Mrs. Kim had many such conversations with families in the Poksu valley. They often led to serious negotiations and marriages. Matchmaking is a vital part of the marriage process even in the most contemporary urban settings because no one likes to be embarrassed when things go wrong and someone gets rejected. It is much better to have a friend in between, carrying messages of encouragement or discouragement to the families.

But modernization has also created new situations where young people see and get to know each other directly long before there is any thought of getting married. College classrooms and campus clubs are prime places for seeing who is available. University districts in Seoul are alive with young people dating with no need to check with parents. Churches and sports events are also places where young people make contact. Their first dates take place in coffee shops where they talk. Often they meet in parks and get to know each other. Korea today affords opportunities that the older generation never dreamed of. These things have led to a rapid increase in "love marriages."

But even in this much freer atmosphere, at some point in the relationship the family always gets involved. All young people recognize their accountability to parents and the parents' need to be part of the final stages of courtship, if for no other reason than the social display that seems to be required in the engagement and wedding ceremonies. These ceremonies are enormously expensive and serve as occasions for extended family members and business associates of the parents to get together and pay their respects.

THE TRADITIONAL KOREAN WEDDING

The traditional Korean marriage ceremony—the one where the bride and groom never met before their wedding—consisted of three phases: the betrothal, the presentation of the wild goose, and the bride's move to the groom's house. These phases took place over a period of time, and the element most closely approximating what we would call a wedding "ceremony" was the exchange of gifts, the series of bows, and the trading of wine cups that happened in the house (or courtyard) of the bride.

It was never too early to start looking for a potential spouse. By the time children were nine or ten their parents were fully involved in searching, and if two families decided on a suitable match there was no reason to wait until the bride and groom were old enough to get married. The families could arrange an engagement, or even a formal wedding, as early as age ten or twelve, and the bride would go to live with her husband's family, working as a kind of servant or additional child in the household, until at length she started bearing children. Factors to be considered when negotiating a possible marriage included the groom's "eight characters," which were the four pairs of characters that indicated the year, month, date, and hour of his birth. These were essential for divining his fate and could bode ill for a marriage with someone whose signs were incompatible. Prospective mates had to be from different clans, since Koreans practiced strict exogamy. The negotiations, which may have begun orally, passed to a written stage with the exchange of letters of proposition and intent that were signed by family elders on both sides, affirming the interest of the entire lineage in the bargain.

This exchange led to the betrothal, which was a kind of engagement sealed by an exchange of gifts. The groom's side sent silks and various domestic items in a box that also contained a wedding contract to be signed, which sealed the bargain and constituted the legal basis for the marriage. The betrothal, which could precede the actual wedding by a considerable time, was in many respects more important than the wedding itself. It was then that a young woman became committed to her groom's family, and if the groom died after the betrothal but before the actual wedding, and even if the couple were still children, the bride's commitment to the groom's family could not be broken and she could not marry anyone else. There are many stories of Korean girls whose husbands died before the marriages were consummated and were required to live as virgin widows for the rest of their natural lives.

Some months after the engagement, the two families organized a wedding ceremony. By this time the groom would have been "capped"; that is, his long boyish braid would have been tied into a topknot and he would have been given a man's proper headband and hat. The hat was a dignified symbol of male adulthood, and any man without one advertised himself either as a member of the laboring class and/or as an unmarried "boy" no matter what his age. Thus fitted with the trappings of mature manhood and after having announced his marriage to his forebears at the family's ancestral shrine, the groom was ready for his wedding.

On the day of the wedding the groom would ride a horse to the bride's house, accompanied by male relatives and servants carrying gifts for the bride's family, one of which was a wild goose, either real or wooden, for the bride's parents. The wedding ceremony would take place in the courtyard, sometimes under a tent, where the bride, elaborately dressed and made up, would be led to a position opposite the groom before a ceremonial table laden with ceremonial foods featuring nuts, cakes, and fruits. The bride would then bow four times, the groom would bow back—but not as many times—and the pair would sip from a cup of wine that would be passed back and forth. A feast would follow, and after that a night of celebration and good-natured harassment of the newlyweds who would be left together in a room of the house, surrounded by people making ribald comments and occasionally poking holes in the paper covering the door, removing the couple's only privacy. The party would not stop until the following day.

The groom would then remain for three days and nights in the bride's home before going home, usually alone. Though he might return several times to visit her, in upper-class tradition the groom did not actually collect his bride and take her home to live with his own family until a further ritual exchange of gifts, which might occur over a period of many months. The groom was supposed to make three visits to the bride after the wedding, and only after the third would they begin married life. The amount of time that had to pass was determined by the age of the couple and the time needed to satisfy everyone involved that all interests had been protected and the success of the marriage assured to the maximum extent through the advice of older relatives. A final set of rituals involved presenting the new wife to the husband's clan members and introducing her to the ancestral spirits in the family shrine.

These elaborate steps are signs that Koreans did not simply marry strangers but in fact began their marriages surrounded by love and support from kinfolk after many negotiations and assurances of happiness. However, it must also be said that life in the new household required a bride to fit herself into a hierarchy of women—mothers, aunts, sisters, and sisters-in-law—in which she had a weak position and could only cooperate and submit or be subjected to many kinds of misery. She was particularly subject to her mother-in-law's direction and there are many stories about new brides becoming virtual slaves of their in-laws. She was also subject to intimidation by wives of older sons and sisters of the household. It was a rare bride who encountered no conflict as she took up life in the "inner quarters" of her new home. This inferior condition abated only after she herself bore children—or more specifically a son—and thus made herself a proper "ancestor" of the lineage.

MODERN WEDDINGS

Weddings in today's Korea retain vestiges of the earlier customs but they differ in significant respects. Most weddings now take place in ceremonial halls (*yeshikjang*) that are commercial buildings with all the necessary facilities. Most have multiple floors where several weddings are going on simultaneously, and there is an amiable din throughout the building as hundreds of guests enter and exit, exchanging gifts and gossip all the while.

Contemporary weddings are, if anything, more elaborate and expensive in terms of gift exchanges and social display than weddings in traditional times. Engagement ceremonies continue to be an essential part of the marriage process, and the feast and gift exchanges at that time are major events. The groom's family still sends a gift box via a raucous delegation of the groom's friends who normally create mayhem as they extort money from the bride's family to complete the delivery. On the day of the wedding itself all invited guests are expected to arrive with envelopes containing cash at the going rate, which increases with the social status of the families involved and the general level of prosperity in the Korean economy. Members of the wedding party record the guests' names and the amount of their gifts as they enter the wedding hall, or chapel.

Korean brides normally wear white, Western-style gowns for this phase of the wedding. These gowns are displayed in store windows in special shopping areas of Seoul, notably the streets leading to Ewha Women's University and in the fashionable Myŏng-dong district. The dresses are grand and beautiful and very expensive. Grooms have less expense: they are dressed in business suits, though these too may be of an expensive cut and fabric. Neither the bride nor the groom has attendants, but there is music, usually provided by a pianist or organist who comes with the wedding hall.

Presiding at the wedding is a master of ceremonies, or *churye*, who is usually a dignified friend of the groom or his family, often a professor from the groom's university or a senior business associate of the groom's father. The *churye* announces the beginning of the ceremony, signals the bridal couple when it is time to enter, leads the pair through the exchange of vows and pronounces them married, and gives a speech or sermonette reflecting on the fine character of the two families that are being united and the solemn importance of marriage. The *churye* is almost never a woman.

Following the formal ceremony in the chapel there is often a second, more traditional-style ceremony called a *p'yebaek* in another part of the building that is furnished in Korean style. For the *p'yebaek* the bride and groom don Korean clothes and the bride is fitted with special celebratory accessories including a crown and long sleeves that are typical of dancers in the royal court. The central element of the *p'yebaek* is the bowing ritual, where the newlyweds perform the kowtow before their parents, kneeling and bowing far enough to make their foreheads touch the floor. Current custom calls for the parents to "endow" the bride with chestnuts and other fertility symbols to promote the birth of children, especially male children. Other relatives and well-wishers may also request bows from the bride and groom, and often they present an additional amount of money on a tray, as the "bowing price." The accumulated revenue of the wedding is immediately applied to the vast expense of the entire project, which includes the feast that will follow in the wedding hall's basement restaurant or in another suitable location, and the newlyweds' honeymoon trip. It also helps pay for the gifts the newlyweds are expected to bring back to their parents from their honeymoon trip.[3]

Honeymoon destinations have grown more elaborate with Korea's rising incomes. Thirty years ago, young couples went to provincial sight-seeing spots. Twenty years ago they went to the mountain resorts along the east coast. Ten years ago they flew to Cheju Island off the south coast and enjoyed the delights of "Korea's Hawai'i." Now they go to Hawai'i itself, or to Guam or Hong Kong. An impressive amount of social display goes into these expensive arrangements. From time to time the Korean government has officially disapproved of the consumption that is involved and has called for more frugal rituals. These appeals have not been taken seriously for very long.

THE WOMEN'S MODERNIZATION MOVEMENT

Couples whose weddings follow the modern pattern usually are educated at least as far as high school and are in their early twenties, having been on their own for several years working and going to school. Since boys stay in school longer than girls, it is the girls who have been in the workforce longer when it comes time to get married. Young women between the ages of sixteen and twenty-two are the backbone of the labor force that assembles microwave ovens, TV sets, and VCRs for the electronics industry, that operates the high-speed sewing machines that produce Korea's textiles, and that makes running shoes for the world's athletes. Being young and healthy they are ideal workers, docile and obedient, with quick reflexes and the stamina necessary to produce impressive amounts of whatever they make. Since their "careers" in such jobs are meant to be short, lasting only long enough to save money for marriage or family debts, there is no need for employers to pay elaborate fringe benefits or provide pension plans for them. And best of all, from the point of view of the employers, they are a renewable resource. By the time they get several raises and start thinking about organizing a union, it is time for them to quit and get married. The outgoing twenty-two-year-olds are replaced with fresh, hardworking sixteen-year-olds.

This remorseless labor pattern in light manufacturing is a paradigm for women's labor throughout the economy. A young woman who graduates from high school or college is welcome in the workforce, but it is assumed that she will quit when she gets married, and there is no point putting her on the career track by investing expensive training in her future. In this situation also, there is little point in objecting or demanding better working conditions, because the labor pool contains replacement workers and there are a great many overeducated candidates for entry-level white-collar jobs. All college students face employment uncertainties, but the uncertainties for liberally educated women are especially bleak. They are forced to begin work in positions that are socially and economically disadvantaged.

As the Korean economy has developed in sophistication and there has been a need for experience and judgment as well as quick reflexes and good eyesight, this has begun to change. Many organizations in the public sector especially have women in responsible positions. Even certain enlightened companies have women in middle management positions. However, in both the public and private sectors, it is rare for any woman to rise above the assistant director level. "Chiefs" are men, and their organizational thinking is still tightly tied to male modes of work and interaction. It takes a unique trait—knowledge of a foreign language or a particular system, or a valuable advanced degree—to lift a woman into the upper levels of a Korean organization. Gender is the single, simple reason.

There are exceptions, of course, one of which is the field of education. There are many school principals who are women, though usually in girls' schools. There are many women on college and university faculties. And it must also be noted that there has been sustained improvement in the position of women in the Korean workforce over a period of many decades. The earliest attempts to grapple with this problem grew out of a reform movement in the late nineteenth century and proceeded along two main tracks. The first was the beginning of education for women, first in Christian missionary schools and later in the school system that was developed by Japanese colonial authorities. Though neither of these school systems provided much education beyond the elementary level, the mere acquisition of literacy was a revolutionary step for women. The slow development of opportunities above the elementary school level continued the trend. Ewha School for Girls, a missionary school that began in 1886, eventually became a college and then a university. The royal family sponsored a girls' school that became Sookmyung Women's University. Many other women's colleges were chartered after 1950, and coeducation made it possible for women to earn degrees at the most prestigious national universities such as Seoul National, Yonsei, Ewha, and Koryŏ.

The second "track" for the emancipation of women was legal, beginning with items in the reform program proposed by Pak Yŏnghyo and other cabinet officials in the short-lived government of 1894–95. These proposals included laws forbidding husbands to mistreat their wives, ending plural marriage (concubinage), granting permission for widows to remarry, and guaranteeing access to schooling for women.

The first women's association was founded in 1898 by a group of upper-class women who banded together to start a school. The Independence Club, a reform association, made women's rights an element of its short-lived program before it was disbanded in 1898. At the turn of the century, small women's associations were founded to protest excess taxation and other political injustices. Women organized a "debt-redemption" movement in 1907 in hopes of raising enough to purchase Korea's financial independence by repaying money that the government had borrowed from Japan. Yu Kwansun was just one of 531 women who were arrested in 1919 during the independence uprising against Japanese colonialism.

As access to education for women expanded in the 1920s and 1930s, demands increased for equal protection under the law. Women's associations and women's magazines proliferated and became essential elements of the women's liberation movement. Women continued participating in the independence effort with such innovations as the Patriotic Women's Association (*Aeguk pu'inhoe*) and the Chosŏn Women's Cooperative Society, which had branches throughout the country and sponsored discussions and publications on women's issues. Women's organizations were especially important to the effort to buy Korean products, increasing economic independence for Koreans by reducing reliance on imported products, especially from Japan, and boosting the success of Korean businesses.

The 1990s brought an eruption of indignation in Korea and around the world following the publication of documents and testimony regarding the World War II phenomenon of the "comfort women." "Comfort women" (which translates from the Japanese term *Ianfu*) were women drafted by the Japanese army during the war to provide sexual services to the soldiers on the front lines. The women were part of a much larger pattern of forced labor under Imperial Japan that included hundreds of thousands of Koreans being taken to Japan to work in mines and sweatshops and other unsavory workplaces in the 1920s and 1930s. However, comfort women were qualitatively different, occupants of a labor category that essentially robbed them of their humanity and ruined their future chances for any kind of a satisfactory life. The violation of the comfort women by the Japanese army, and Japan's systematic effort to cover up the phenomenon and escape accountability for it, has been the source of international outrage since the story broke in 1990.

One of the most troubling aspects of the comfort women story in Korea was that even though the facts had been known for many years, the Korean government had done nothing to repair the damage. There had been no investigation, no attempt to locate the victims and attend to their needs, or to support their demands for justice from Japan. Rather, as the anthropologist Choi Chungmoo has written, male-dominated Korean institutions connived at keeping the story quiet. Choi suggests that the cover-up in Korea was part of a much older habit of thinking, going back hundreds of years. Any Korean woman who left home and the protection of her male relatives risked being looked upon as a "returned woman" (*hwanhyang nyŏ*), one who, *it had to be assumed*, had lost her chastity while away from home. Rather than being greeted and welcomed, she was put away and hidden as a shameful secret. Comfort women, like the *hwanhyang nyŏ* of olden times, were Korea's shameful secret, and the institutions of Korea were more interested in hiding them than winning justice for them. Koreans *themselves* despised the Korean victims, and the victims were so terrified about being identified that they maintained their silence.

Korean women have always been taught that losing their chastity was a fate worse than death. Getting them to come forward and testify against their Japanese tormentors has been one of the biggest difficulties. The evidence suggests that there were perhaps as many as 60,000 comfort women serving the Japanese troops in World War II. Of these, many were laborers—cooks, laundry workers, and the like—but a large number were "sex slaves." Japanese witnesses have testified that they were shipped to the front under false papers, with cargo labels reading "ammunition" and "medical supplies." It has developed that in some cases they were taken in place of male relatives who, it was thought, were more valuable if kept at home. As Choi writes, "Raised from birth as daughters who had no rights because they were expected to marry out of their families, they were expendable; yet they performed the supremely sacrificial act of becoming 'comfort women' with no hope of benefit or honor in return."[4]

The outcry over the comfort women was part of a heightened consciousness among educated women about the need for unambiguous objection to the assumptions and practices that have supported the ongoing structure of discrimination against women. A by-product of this effort is a vibrant women's literature, with writers such as Kang Sŏkkyŏng pointing out that Korean women are still reduced to being, by their country's economic system, not only sweatshop workers making cheap electronics for foreign customers but also commodities in their own right. Around American military bases in Korea, for example, are camptowns called *kijich'on*, with strips of bars and brothels that earn dollars from off-duty troops and are tolerated by U.S. and Korean authorities as a way to divert the troops and make their tours of duty in Korea slightly less boring. The *kijich'on* phenomenon goes far beyond entertaining the troops, however. The women who work in the *kijich'on* are tainted for life and unlikely ever to be able to return to normal society, not only because of their trade but also because many Koreans look down on their contamination by foreigners. In the years just after the Korean War there was an additional human tragedy in the form of children born of the liaisons between Korean *kijich'on* women and American soldiers. Birth control methods and abortion have largely eliminated this part of the problem, but the institutional exploitation of Korean women as part of the U.S.–South Korean defense arrangement continues to be an irritant to Koreans generally and a human tragedy to the women themselves.[5]

The women's movement in Korea today is powered by educated people who are smart enough to recognize the institutionalized abuses in their country's system and are determined to do something about it. The fact that laws exist on the books does not mean that they will be enforced, and one major effort has been to seek the enforcement of laws equalizing opportunity and income in the workplace. Korean women workers make just over half of what is normally paid to men in the same jobs. Companies explain the inequality by noting that women are "temporary" workers while the men are "permanent." Courageous union organizers have organized classes for women workers to teach them how to talk to management and negotiate effectively for better wages and working conditions, basing their arguments on the national constitution and the many laws that proclaim South Korea's commitment to equal justice. The Korea Women's Development Institute and the Alternative Culture Movement for women are examples of organizations that stand behind this effort to assert human rights for working women, as does the Family Legal Aid Center founded by the late Dr. Lee Taeyŏng. A radical feminist movement emerged in the late 1980s to attack the structure of the Korean economy as essentially antiwoman, arguing that the South Korean economy feeds on the exploitation of female labor and would collapse if it were to stop. In other words, the entire basis of the South Korean economic system has to change before women can expect to realize true justice. Such positions, which make the South Korean government nervous, belong to only a few people in the Korean women's movement. Yet given the structure of Korean capitalism and the male-centered traditions in Korean culture, it is hard to quarrel with the radical feminists' analysis. True equality of opportunity for women is something that must remain on the agenda for the twenty-first century. Meanwhile, many observers say that disadvantages for women are so basic a part of the Korean system that Korea as we know it will never give women the equal chance they deserve.

NOTES

1. Martina Deuchler, *The Confucian Transformation of Korea* (Cambridge, MA: Harvard University Press, 1992), pp. 231–281.

2. This is a reconstructed conversation overheard by the author, with his attributions of the speakers' thoughts.

3. For the contemporary Korean wedding scene, see Laurel Kendall, *Getting Married in Korea: Of Gender, Morality, and Modernity* (Berkeley: University of California Press, 1996).

4. Chungmoo Choi, "Korean Women in a Culture of Inequality," in Korea Briefing 1992, ed. Donald N. Clark (Boulder, CO: Westview Press, 1992), p. 104.

5. For the *kijich'on* camptown phenomenon, see Katharine H. S. Moon, *Sex among Allies: Military Prostitution in U.S.-Korean Relations* (New York: Columbia University Press, 1997).

9

Greater Korea: Looking Ahead

FOR ALL KOREANS north and south of the Demilitarized Zone, reunification has been the number one national problem since the 1950s. All Koreans profess to want reunification, but the fact is that the long national division has created powerful interests that actually benefit from continued separation of North and South Korea. The governments in Seoul and P'yŏngyang are rivals, and it is hard to imagine any formula for reunification that would not eliminate or at least diminish one or the other. Each government maintains very large military forces with officers whose careers have been made, in effect, defending the status quo. Although the large conglomerates (*chaebŏl*) in South Korea would like to have access to cheap North Korean labor, they are oriented to the world market while North Korea is a closed market that would be thrown into an uproar by the introduction of free trade with the much more prosperous South. Moreover, Korea's neighbors seem none too keen to see Korea reunited and in a position to emerge as an even greater influence on the strategic balance in northeast Asia. Koreans who dream about reuniting their country, therefore, have to overcome some powerful vested interests in continued division.

There was a time when Koreans compared their situation to that of divided Germany. For a short time after the reunification of Germany the Koreans thought that a sudden collapse of the North, the way East Germany collapsed in 1989–90, would be a good beginning for the long-sought reunification of their own country. On second thought, however, noting the vast costs involved in the reunification of Germany, the Koreans began to see more differences than similarities in the two situations. The complete isolation of

North Korea from the South has meant that the two are really much more different than East and West Germany. Reunification would require reintegration of two zones that are badly mismatched in terms of population, productivity, and infrastructure. Moreover, the closed society of North Korea, having been schooled in the unique ideology of the Kimilsungist system, has a world view that differs radically from that of the South Koreans. One of the most interesting problems involved in any future unification is the fact that the two sides tell completely different stories about their modern history. For half a century each side has been telling a version of Korean history that demonizes and refuses to concede any legitimacy to the other. In the process of reunification it will take a long time to revise and coordinate the stories. The North Koreans will have to admit that South Korea, for all its problems and stretches of military dictatorship, is a successful capitalist democracy in its own right and not merely a puppet of the United States. South Koreans will have to concede that the Communist side really did play an important part in the resistance against Japan and that the experiment in building a socialist society in North Korea was an authentic Korean effort to modernize the nation. It will not be easy to coordinate the stories and to find common ground on which to build a shared national identity. Koreans claim to be one family. The family feud, however, runs deep.

Included in the mix is a great deal of "face," especially for the North Korean leadership, which might fare poorly in any honest appraisal of its performance over the past five decades leading up to the disastrous economic situation in the 1990s. It is hard to imagine the North Korean military acquiescing in a reunification formula that would put them completely out of business. Nevertheless, in South Korea there have been many scenarios for reunification that assume a "defeat" for North Korea. Some of the more aggressive visions see the South simply taking over the North Korean economy, abolishing every trace of the Kimilsungist system, and reducing the North Koreans to clients and drones to serve the capitalist economy of the South. Some of South Korea's more militant Christian denominations dream of the day when they can "occupy" North Korea with missionaries teaching and converting the North Koreans and bringing them out of their "spiritual darkness." The people of North Korea, however, though poor and stressed, are nonetheless talented and well educated, and many (if not most) of them are committed to the ideals of their Korean brand of socialism. They may become deeply disturbed when they discover the extent to which their leaders have misled and even betrayed them by keeping their country in a relatively backward state. A sudden and uncontrolled flood of information from the outside world might serve to destabilize the northern regime and throw the country into an uproar, conceivably bringing on a violent revolution or something else that is worse than the present system. However, it is inconceivable that they would abandon every vestige of their own pride and identity and simply turn themselves over to the South Koreans for moral and political rehabilitation.

The militant voices that ring in South Korea are slightly muted by the fact that the North Korean state has survived against all odds and seems less and less likely to collapse in the manner of East Germany. This is a good thing. It has bought time for the South to think more clearly about how the transition might actually be effected. The administration of President Kim Dae-jung has instituted a "Sunshine Policy" that assumes the continued existence of Kim Jong-il's government and seeks to work out ways to communicate and even to accord it a little respect. This South Korean posture has already been useful in restraining some of the more hysterical reactions in Japan and the United States regarding North Korean diplomatic missteps. Not long ago, the South Korean government itself was the force trying to push North Korea over the edge. Under Kim Dae-jung, the watchword is patience. Nature is supposed to take its course. As economic stakes between North Korea and the outside world grow, new interests are being created on the side of peaceful change.

OTHER TRANSITIONS AT THE TURN OF THE CENTURY

Korean identity is an essential element of the reunification issue, and Koreans on their home peninsula are not the only ones thinking about what it means to be Korean. The 2 million ethnic Koreans in China, most of them just over the border from North Korea in the Jiandao district of Jilin Province, have had their own modern experience. The People's Republic of China regards them as Chinese citizens but accords them a special status as a recognized minority. Being concentrated in the Yanbian area means that they are able to maintain a lifestyle that is a kind of hybrid between the Chinese and Korean. They maintain their language in Korean schools, they have a Korean university, and they observe Korean as well as Chinese holidays and festivals. The 750,000 Koreans in Japan likewise have their own special status as "Chōsenjin," composing an ethnic minority that is famously discriminated against and denied Japanese citizenship on grounds of ethnicity. In the central Asian republic of Kazakhstan, the colony of Koreans forcibly transported there in the 1930s speaks a variant of the Korean language, intermarries with the local people, and seems to be slowly dissolving into the local population. And in the United States, nearly a million ethnic Koreans, many of them

Learning Korean music at Seoul's International Montessori School.

naturalized or natural-born American citizens, struggle with the many issues of transition and acculturation. Many of them live in concentrations drawing mutual support through business groups and churches. Others have dispersed into the heartland and raised families, often appearing to be a "model minority"—that is, causing no trouble, working hard, and quietly putting up with the endemic racism in American society. For many thousands of college students attending the annual Korean-American Student Conference (KAS-CON), the issues of history, identity, and place are crucial matters for discussion and mutual reinforcement. The students' parents worry that the younger generation has lost the best of Korean values and culture in the process of becoming American. The young people themselves face all the normal questions faced by young adults but they bear an added burden also: the duty, imposed by their parents, to succeed in America and justify the radical act of emigrating from the homeland to seek a new life overseas.

Back on the Korean peninsula, the South continues to face formidable challenges of its own. The economic slump that hit the South in 1997–98 was a reminder that the economy there is not as rich or stable as many had come to assume. The concentration of wealth in the hands of the business elites and the unhealthy flows of money between industrialists and government officials ("crony capitalism") created imbalances and led to risky economic decisions that sent the South Korean economy into a tailspin within a few short weeks in 1997. At the heart of the crisis was a spate of unwise borrowing from foreign sources that Korean banks suddenly discovered they could not repay on time. So many debts came due so suddenly that it took a massive rescue effort by the international financial community led by the International Monetary Fund (IMF) to make the payments. Korea's credit rating sank suddenly to junk bond status. This was a serious humiliation and it led to significant restructuring, part of it necessitated by the conditions imposed by the IMF. President Kim Dae-jung did much to restructure the banking industry and straighten out the investment practices of the *chaebŏl* conglomerates, but labor unions continue to resent bearing so much of the pain of the crisis and the conglomerates are reluctant to part with their inbred dealings. South Korea has entered the twenty-first century on a much more stable economic footing, but if the reforms do not go far enough South Korea will remain dangerously vulnerable to outside forces that can cause another cycle of boom and bust.

Glossary

Chaebŏl. Conglomerate of companies, usually owned by one family or small group of investors. *Chaebŏl* conglomerates may have their own manufacturing, construction, trading, and financial components. Leading *chaebŏl* include Hyundai, Samsung, the LG Group, and Daewoo. Smaller *chaebŏl* such as Hanjin specialize in transportation, running airlines (Korean Air) and Hanjin container freight shipping.

Cheju Island (Cheju-do). Island off the southwest coast of the Korean peninsula. A province of the Republic of Korea (South Korea).

Chesa. The family ceremony that honors the memory and spirits of departed ancestors. Usually performed on one of Korea's feast days, such as New Year's and *Ch'usŏk* (the Autumn festival) and on anniversaries of the death of parents and grandparents.

Ch'ŏndokyo. The "Religion of the Heavenly Way." A religion of Korean origin (nineteenth century) that stresses the value of the individual under Heaven; also, the religious ideology underlying the Tonghak uprising of the late nineteenth century.

Chosŏn. Ancient name for Korea, derived from Chinese. Also, the name of the last royal dynasty, from 1392 to 1910. Though South Korea uses the term "Han'guk" for "Korea," the term Chosŏn is still in use in the North.

Chun Doo-hwan (Chŏn Tuhwan) (1931–   ).   South Korean army general who seized power in 1980 and served as president of the Republic of Korea from 1980 to 1988.

"Comfort women."   Term referring to female conscript laborers from Korea and other countries who were used as sex slaves by Japanese military forces during World War II.

Demilitarized Zone (DMZ).   Established by the 1953 armistice agreement that ended the fighting in the Korean War, the DMZ is a strip of land across the Korean peninsula that separates the forces of South Korea and the United Nations Command in the South, and North Korean forces in the North. The DMZ is 158 miles long and 2.48 miles wide, with a line exactly in the middle that is called the Military Demarcation Line (MDL). Though there are considerable fortifications in and around the DMZ, it has been largely undisturbed since the Korean War and has developed into something of a wildlife refuge, especially for migratory birds.

Democratic People's Republic of Korea (DPRK).   Established in 1948, the DPRK is the northern part of the Korean peninsula under the governing control of the Communist Korean Workers Party (KWP) led by Kim Il-sung (1912–1994) and his son Kim Jong-il (1942–   ).

Hanbok.   Korean term for the Korean national costume.

Han'gŭl.   Korean term for the phonetic alphabet presented to the people in 1446 by King Sejong of the Chosŏn Dynasty.

Hanyak.   Korean term for traditional Asian (Chinese) herbal medicine.

"Hermit Kingdom."   A nineteenth-century term used by Westerners to refer to Korea's resolute refusal to open relations with foreign nations. Korea's first modern treaty with a foreign power was the 1876 Kanghwa Treaty with Japan. Korea's first treaty with a Western nation was with the United States, in 1882.

Inch'ŏn.   Port 22 miles west of downtown Seoul that serves as its access point to the sea; famous for the amphibious landing in September 1950 that turned the tide of the Korean War in favor of General Douglas MacArthur and the United Nations. Urban growth has effectively merged Inch'ŏn and Seoul into a greater metropolitan area whose population exceeds 15 million.

Juch'e (chuch'e).   The "self-reliance" philosophy that is central to the political ideology of the DPRK (North Korea) and the theoretical basis of the Kim Il-sung cult (Kimilsungism). Originally articulated by Kim Il-sung to assert North Korea's neutrality, or independence, during the years of the Sino-Soviet split, devotion to the *juch'e* idea today is the principle that underlies North Korea's reluctance to open its doors to foreign influences.

Kim Dae-jung (Kim Taejung) (1939–   ).   President of the Republic of Korea (South Korea), elected in 1997. Originally from Korea's southwest, as a National Assemblyman Kim Dae-jung ran for President against Park Chung-hee in 1971 and did surprisingly well, winning 45.3 percent of the popular vote. Thereafter, as he emerged as a leading critic of the military-led government, he was subjected to heavy political persecution including house arrest, imprisonment, kidnapping, and attempts on his life. Surviving these, he ran again for president in 1987 and 1992, then won the election in 1997 as the South Korean economy was undergoing a serious collapse. Kim's leadership is credited with creating conditions for the post-1997 recovery and for a more conciliatory South Korean attitude toward North Korea known as the "Sunshine Policy."

Kim Il-sung (Kim Ilsŏng) (1912–1994). Born in P'yŏngyang during the Japanese colonial period, Kim Il-sung grew up to be an anti-Japanese guerrilla fighter on the Manchurian border and eventually became an officer in an ethnic Korean unit of the Soviet Red Army during World War II. Soviet authorities installed him as the leader of their occupation zone in northern Korea in 1945, and he emerged as leader of the DPRK when it was founded in 1948. His decision to reunite the Korean peninsula by force led to the Korean War, 1950–53. After eliminating rivals and challengers after the war, Kim continued to rule in North Korea until his death in 1994. His personality cult became a major motif of the North Korean state and he lives on as a legend in the political culture of the DPRK.

Kim Jong-il (Kim Chŏng'il) (1942–   ).   Trained by his father Kim Il-sung as an operative of the Korean Workers Party, Kim Jong-il emerged in the 1980s as a contender for the succession, being given progressively greater responsibilities in the ruling party. By the early 1990s he was clearly in position to continue his father's rule in North Korea within the philosophy of Kimilsungism which provided for a monarchial-type succession in the KWP and national leadership. Though sometimes derided in the West as a lightweight, Kim Jong-il apparently commands the loyalty of the party leadership and of most, if not all, of North Korea's citizens.

Kim Young-Sam (Kim Yŏngsam) (1927–   ).   Longtime leader of opposition to military rule during the 1970s and 1980s, Kim Young-Sam joined forces with the ruling party in 1990 and emerged the winner in the presidental election in 1992. The first civilian president of South Korea since the early 1960s, he did much to open the South Korean political system to true democracy. However, his term in office was also marked by controversies and corruption, and he was widely blamed for the poor economic leadership that contributed to the crash of the South Korean economy in his last year in office (1997).

Kimch'i.   Korea's national dish; a spicy condiment made from vegetables such as cabbage and turnips laced with red pepper and fermented in brine. Eaten with rice, various types of *kimch'i* are staples of every Korean meal.

Kimilsungism.   The central element of North Korea's political philosophy, Kimilsungism is a belief system that glorifies the legacy of the Great Leader Kim Il-sung and organizes the loyalty of the Korean Workers Party and the North Korean population in support of the government and its decisions and policies. Kimilsungism justifies the succession of Kim's son Kim Jong-il to national leadership and the transfer of the loyalties reserved for the elder Kim to his son and heavily discourages dissent and opposition. Supported in art and literature and with icons such as statues and portraits of Kim Il-sung across the country, Kimilsungism in many ways resembles a religious cult.

Koguryŏ.   Located in southern Manchuria and northern Korea, the state of Koguryŏ was one of the Korean Three Kingdoms with a founding date traditionally set at 37 B.C. In the early seventh century Koguryŏ forces successfully repelled repeated Chinese attempts to impose their control over Korea. Koguryŏ was finally conquered by the Kingdom of Silla in A.D. 668.

Koryŏ.   The state of Koryŏ (A.D. 918–1392) was based in the capital city of Kaesŏng north of Seoul. The name "Koryŏ" is the basis for the national name "Korea."

Kyŏngju.   Capital of the Kingdom of Silla, in southeastern Korea. Now a "museum without walls," the city is famous for its ancient royal tombs and monumental Buddhist art.

New Community Movement (Saemaŭl Movement). An initiative to raise the standard of living in rural South Korea begun by the military-led government of President Park Chung-hee in the 1970s and continuing in the 1980s. Largely successful, it brought better agricultural yields and important improvements in infrastructure such as electric power, irrigation, communications, and transportation.

***Ŏndol* floor.** The traditional heating system for Korean homes, consisting of hollow passages under the floor that carry hot smoke and gases from the kitchen fire the length of the house to the chimney on the opposite end, warming the floor and heating the rooms. Requires tight sealing of floors to prevent carbon monoxide from entering the room. Modern improvements to *ŏndol* floors include circulation of warm water in pipes under the floor, a system popular in modern apartment buildings.

Paekche. One of the Korean Three Kingdoms, Paekche was located in the southwestern part of the peninsula between its traditional founding date of 18 B.C. and A.D. 663. Served as a conduit for continental influence on Japan (e.g., Buddhism) during the period.

Paektu, Mount (Paektu-san). Extinct volcano in the Ever White (Changpai) Range on the border between northeastern Korea and China, Mt. Paektu is a national symbol for the Korean people, reputedly the location of the founding of the Korean race (*minjok*) and recently claimed to have been the birthplace of North Korean leader Kim Jong-il. Mt. Paektu is more than 9,000 feet high and is topped by a caldera that contains a very deep lake called Ch'ŏnji (the Heavenly Lake). Mt. Paektu is a favorite tourist destination for overseas Koreans as well as Koreans from the northern and southern republics. The Yalu and Tumen Rivers emerge west and east from its slopes, as does a stream that eventually joins the Sungari River in Manchuria.

P'anmunjŏm. The village on the battle line during the Korean War that was used for cease-fire negotiations and eventually became the site for the signing of the July 1953 armistice that ended the fighting and since then, a meeting place for delegations from the Communist side (North Korea and China) and the United Nations side (represented until recently by the United States but also including South Korea). P'anmunjŏm is located in the Demilitarized Zone and sometimes serves as a transit point for persons passing across the line separating North and South Korea.

P'ansori.   An operatic style of storytelling; the performance genre for many of Korea's best-known literary works.

Park Chung-hee (Pak Chŏnghŭi) (1917–1979).   Former schoolteacher and army officer during the Japanese colonial period, became a general during the Korean War and took power in May 1961 in a military coup that ended more than a decade of civilian rule in South Korea. Presided over the economic development of South Korea in the 1960s and 1970s. Park was an authoritarian ruler who lost patience with the democratic opposition and ended up ruling by decree. He was assassinated by one of his own deputies in Octoer 1979, an event that opened the way to a further decade of military dictatorship in South Korea under General Chun Doo-hwan.

P'yŏngyang.   Located on a bend of the Taedong River in North Korea, Korea's oldest major city and the capital of the DPRK since 1948.

Republic of Korea (ROK).   Term denoting the government of South Korea with its capital in Seoul.

Rhee, Syngman (Yi Sŭngman; also Ri Sŭngman) (1875–1965). Educated at American mission schools in Korea and then in the United States, Syngman Rhee was an important leader of overseas Korean nationalists during the Japanese colonial period, especially in the United States. After returning to liberated South Korea in 1945, Rhee maneuvered himself into a leading position with apparent American support and won the presidency of the Republic of Korea in 1948. As president during the Korean War and the period of reconstruction in 1950s, Rhee often resorted to authoritarian methods and was ousted during a student-led people's revolution in the spring of 1960. He died in exile in Hawaii, in 1965.

Saemaŭl Movement.   *See* New Community Movement

Seoul.   Located on the north bank of the Han River near the Yellow Sea on a site once occupied by a regional capital of the Kingdom of Koryŏ (918–1392), Seoul became the capital of Korea's Chosŏn Dynasty in 1396. It continued as the Japanese colonial capital city after the fall of Chosŏn in 1910 and became South Korea's postwar capital in 1945, first as the location of the American Military Government (1945–48) and then as the seat of the Republic of Korea (1948–present).

Shamanism.   An ancient belief system of the Koreans related to versions of Shamanism in China, Siberia, and Japan, whose variants usually involve communication with the world of spirits, including the spirits of the dead, seeking to enlist the spirits' help or to avoid their wrath.

Silla (Shilla). The longest-lived of the Korean Three Kingdoms with a traditional founding date of 57 B.C. Silla conquered its counterparts, Paekche and Koguryŏ, in the seventh century and was the first to rule most of the Korean peninsula as a unified state. It gave way to the rise of Koryŏ (which was in some respects a revival of ancient Koguryŏ), in 935. The capital of Silla was the ancient city Kyŏngju, in southeastern Korea.

T'aekwŏndo. Korea's most famous contribution to the world of martial arts. Stresses spiritual discipline, physical conditioning, and moral virtue as well as fighting skill.

Thirty-eighth Parallel. The arbitrary geographical dividing line across the Korean peninsula that was proposed to the Soviet Union by the United States in August 1945 as the limit of Soviet military advance during the final phase of Japan's defeat in the Second World War. The original proposal was for Soviet forces to occupy the peninsula down to the 38th parallel and for American forces to occupy the southern zone up to the same line. In their respective zones, Soviet and American forces were to disarm the Japanese military and repatriate all Japanese personnel to their home islands, then establish interim occupation governments to keep order pending U.S. and Soviet negotiations to create a government for the unified Korean people. When the negotiations broke down over the mutual unacceptability of candidates for leadership, the Americans organized the creation of a separate government in South Korea under United Nations sponsorship, while the Soviets organized the creation of a Communist-led state in North Korea. In 1948, after creating the two rival Korean republics, American forces withdrew to Japan and Soviet forces withdrew to Russia. Though there have been many proposals to reunify the peninsula and one attempt to reunite it by force (the Korean War), Korea remains divided roughly along the 38th parallel where the fighting stopped with a cease-fire agreement on July 27, 1953. It is often said that the border between North and South Korea is the most militarized place on earth.

Yalu River. River that rises from springs on the western slope of Mt. Paektu, on the Sino-Korean border, flowing westward to the Yellow Sea. Forms part of the boundary between North Korea and the People's Republic of China. Famous in the Korean War as the limit of the United Nations army's advance before the intervention of the

Chinese Communists and the reestablishment of Communist military control over North Korea.

Yangban. Term denoting the aristocratic class of landlords and officials particularly during the Chosŏn Dynasty (1392–1910). Usually a term of respect, it can sometimes simply mean "gentleman" as opposed to "commoner." Yangban lineages still carry great prestige and are documented in carefully-preserved genealogical records.

Suggestions for Further Reading

A Note on Sources and Readings

THIS BOOK is based on a wide variety of published sources by scholars and colleagues in the field of Korean studies. Below is a bibliography of sources on Korea, including many that were used for this book, grouped roughly by topics that are covered in the various chapters. A number of the works listed also contain extensive bibliographies that can point the reader to more specialized sources in fields such as politics, economics, society, and Korean communities overseas.

Korean History, Geography, and Civilization

Cumings, Bruce. *Korea's Place in the Sun: A Modern History*. New York: W. W. Norton, 1997.

Eckert, Carter J., et al. *Korea Old and New: A History*. Seoul: Ilchokak Publishers for the Korea Institute, Harvard University, 1990.

Hart-Landesberg, Martin. *Korea: Division, Reunification, and U.S. Foreign Policy*. New York: Monthly Review Press, 1998.

Hoare, James E., and Susan Pares, comps. *Conflict in Korea: An Encyclopedia*. Santa Barbara, CA: ABC Clio, 1999.

Howard, Keith, et al. *Korea: People, Country and Culture*. London: School of Oriental and African Studies of the University of London, 1996.

Korea Overseas Information Service. *A Handbook of Korea*. Seoul: Samhwa Printing Company, 1994.

Lautensach, Hermann. *Korea: A Geography Based on the Author's Travels and Literature*. Trans. Eckart and Katherine Dege. Berlin: Springer-Verlag, 1988.

Macdonald, Donald S., and Donald N. Clark. *The Koreans: Contemporary Politics and Society*. 3rd ed. Boulder, CO: Westview Press, 1996.

McCann, David R., ed. *Korea Briefing, 1994–96: Toward Reunification*. Armonk, NY: M. E. Sharpe, 1997.

Savada, Andrea Matles, and William R. Shaw. *North Korea: A Country Study*. 4th ed. Department of the Army Pamphlet DA Pam 550–81. Washington, DC: U.S. Government Printing Office, 1994.

———. *South Korea: A Country Study*. 4th ed. Department of the Army Pamphlet DA Pam 550–41. Washington, DC: U.S. Government Printing Office, 1992.

Suh, Dae-sook. *Kim Il-sung: The North Korean Leader*. New York: Columbia University Press, 1989.

KOREAN RELIGION AND THOUGHT

Clark, Charles Allen. *Religions of Old Korea*. New York: Fleming H. Revell, 1932; repr. New York: Garland Publishing, 1981.

Clark, Donald N. *Christianity in Modern Korea*. Lanham, MD: University Press of America, 1986.

Grayson, James H. *Korea: A Religious History*. Oxford: Clarendon Press, 1989.

Kalton, Michael C. *Korean Ideas and Values*. Elkins Park, PA: Philip Jaisohn Memorial Foundation, 1979.

Kendall, Laurel. *The Life and Hard Times of a Korean Shaman*. Honolulu: University of Hawaii Press, 1988.

———. *Shamans, Housewives, and Other Restless Spirits: Women in Korean Ritual Life*. Honolulu: University of Hawaii Press, 1985.

Lee, Peter H., ed. *Sourcebook of Korean Tradition*. 2 vols. New York: Columbia University Press, 1993–96.

Lee, Peter H., and Wm. Theodore de Bary. *Sources of Korean Tradition*. New York: Columbia University Press, 1996.

Palmer, Spencer J., ed. *The New Religions of Korea*, volume 43 of the *Transactions of the Korea Branch of the Royal Asiatic Society*. Seoul: Korea Branch, Royal Asiatic Society, 1967.

Sorensen, Henrik H., ed. *Religions in Traditional Korea*. Copenhagen: The Seminar for Buddhist Studies, 1995.

KOREAN ART AND LITERATURE

Ahn, Junghyo. *Silver Stallion*. New York: Soho Press, 1990.

———. *White Badge*. New York: Soho Press, 1989.

Ch'ae Mansik. *Peace under Heaven*. Trans. Chun Kyung-Ja. Armonk, NY: M.E. Sharpe, 1993.

Choi, Chungmoo, ed. *Post-Colonial Classics of Korean Cinema*. Irvine, CA: Department of East Asian Languages and Literatures, 1998.

Haboush, Ja Hyun Kim, trans. The Memoirs of Lady Hyegyŏng. Berkeley: University of California Press, 1996.

Hwang, Sunwŏn. Shadows of a Sound. Trans. J. Martin Holman. San Francisco: Mercury House, 1990.

Kim Ah-jeong, and R. B. Graves, trans. The Metacultural Theater of Oh T'aesŏk: Five Plays from the Korean Avant-Garde. Honolulu: University of Hawaii Press, 1999.

Ko Un. The Sound of My Waves: Selected Poems of Ko Un. Trans. Brother Anthony of Taizé and Young-Moo Kim. Ithaca, NY: East Asia Program, Cornell University, 1993.

Lee, Peter H. Anthology of Korean Literature: From Early Times to the Nineteenth Century. Honolulu: University of Hawaii Press, 1981.

———. Modern Korean Literature: An Anthology. Honolulu: University of Hawaii Press, 1990.

McCune, Evelyn B. The Arts of Korea. Rutland, VT: Charles E. Tuttle, 1962.

Oh Yŏngsu. The Good People. Trans. Marshall R. Pihl. Hong Kong: Heinemann Asia, 1985.

Pihl, Marshall R. "Contemporary Literature in a Divided Land." In Donald N. Clark, ed., Korea Briefing 1993, 79–97. Boulder, CO: Westview Press, 1993.

Pihl, Marshall R., and Bruce and Ju-Chan Fulton, trans. and eds. Land of Exile: Contemporary Korean Fiction. Armonk, NY: M. E. Sharpe, 1993.

Sŏ Chŏngju. Unforgettable Things. Trans. David R. McCann. Seoul: Si-sa-yong-o-sa, 1986.

Yi Chŏng-jun. The Prophet and other Stories. Trans. Julie Pickering. Ithaca, NY: East Asia Program, Cornell University, 1999.

KOREAN PERFORMING ARTS

Videotapes

Aak, Korean Court Music and Dance. New York: The Asia Society, 1979.

Buddhist Dances of Korea. Seattle: University of Washington Press, 1971.

National Center for Korean Traditional Performing Arts. The Survey of Korean Music Video Program Set. Seoul: National Center for Korean Traditional Performing Arts, 1996.

Pongsan Masked-Dance Drama from Korea. New York: The Asia Society, 1977.

Shaman Ritual from Korea. New York: The Asia Society, 1983.

Sun Ock Lee: Korean Dancer. New York: The Asia Society, 1981.

Yangju Sandae Nori: Masked Drama of Korea. Seattle: University of Washington Archives of Ethnic Music and Dance, 1966.

Sound Recordings

P'ansori: Korean Epic Vocal Art and Instrumental Music. Produced by David Lewiston. 1972. Nonesuch H-72049.

Samul-nori: Drums and Voices of Korea. Produced by Herbert Harris. 1984. None-such 72093–1.

Publications

Heyman, Alan C. *Dances of the Three-Thousand League Land.* Seoul: Seoul Computer Press, 1981.

Howard, Keith. *Bands, Songs, and Shamanistic Rituals: Folk Music in Korean Society.* Seoul: Korea Branch, Royal Asiatic Society, 1990.

Korean National Commission for UNESCO. *Korean Dance, Theater, and Cinema.* Arch Cape, OR: Pace International Research, 1983.

Lee, Byongwon. "Contemporary Korean Musical Cultures." In Donald N. Clark, ed., *Korea Briefing 1993*, 121–38. Boulder, CO: Westview Press, 1993.

———. "Korea." In *The New Grove Dictionary of Music and Musicians*, Vol. 10: 192–208. London: Macmillan, 1980.

Provine, Robert C. "Korean Music in Historical Perspective." *World of Music* 27, 2: 3–13.

Van Zile, Judy. "*Ch'oyongmu*: An Ancient Dance Survives." *Korea Journal* 12, 3 (Fall 1991): 10–21.

———. "The Many Faces of Korean Dance." In Donald N. Clark, ed., *Korea Briefing 1993*, 99–120. Boulder, CO: Westview Press, 1993.

DAILY LIFE AND CUSTOMS

Brandt, Vincent S. R. *A Korean Village: Between Farm and Sea.* Cambridge, MA: Harvard University Press, 1971.

Janelli, Roger L., and Dawnhee Yim Janelli. *Ancestor Worship and Korean Society.* Stanford, CA: Stanford University Press, 1982.

Kwak, Jenny, with Liz Fried. *Dok Suni: Recipes from My Mother's Korean Kitchen.* New York: St. Martin's Press, 1998.

Lee, O-Young. *Things Korean.* Rutland, VT: Charles E. Tuttle Co., 1999.

Rutt, Richard. *Korean Works and Days.* Rutland, VT: Charles E. Tuttle, 1958.

KOREAN URBANIZATION AND ECONOMIC DEVELOPMENT

Amsden, Alice. *Asia's Next Giant: South Korea and Late Industrialization.* New York: Oxford University Press, 1989.

Koo, Hagen, ed. *State and Society in Contemporary Korea.* Ithaca, NY: Cornell University Press, 1993.

Woo, Jung-en. *Race to the Swift: State and Finance in Korean Industrialization.* New York: Columbia University Press, 1991.

KOREAN WOMEN

Fulton, Bruce, and JuChan, trans. *Wayfarer: New Fiction by Korean Women*. Seattle: Seal Press, 1997.

———, trans. *Words of Farewell: Stories by Korean Women Writers*. Seattle: Seal Press, 1989.

Kendall, Laurel. *Getting Married in Korea: Of Gender, Morality, and Modernity*. Berkeley: University of California Press, 1996.

Kendall, Laurel, and Mark Peterson, eds. *Korean Women: View from the Inner Room*. New Haven: East Rock Press, 1984.

Kim, Elaine, and Chungmoo Choi. *Dangerous Women: Gender and Korean Nationalism*. London: Routledge, 1997.

Mattielli, Sandra, ed. *Virtuous Women: Tradition and the Korean Woman Today*. Seoul: Korea Branch, Royal Asiatic Society, 1977.

Moon, Katharine H. S. *Sex among Allies: Military Prostitution in U.S.-Korean Relations*. New York: Columbia University Press, 1997.

Moon, Okpyo. "Urban Middle Class Wives in Contemporary Korea: Their Roles, Responsibilities, and Dilemma." *Korea Journal* 30, 11 (1990): 30–43.

Spencer, Robert F. *Yŏgong: Factory Girl*. Seoul: Korea Branch, Royal Asiatic Society, 1988.

KOREAN-AMERICANS

Abelmann, Nancy, and John Lie. *Blue Dreams: Korean-Americans and the Los Angeles Riots*. Cambridge, MA: Harvard University Press, 1995.

Choy, Bong-Youn. *Koreans in America*. Chicago: Nelson-Hall, 1979.

Kim, Ilsoo. *New Urban Immigrants: The Korean Community in New York*. Princeton: Princeton University Press, 1981.

Light, Ivan, and Edna Bonacich. *Immigrant Entrepreneurs: Koreans in Los Angeles, 1965–1982*. Berkeley: University of California Press, 1988.

Patterson, Wayne. *The Korean Frontier in America: Immigration to Hawaii, 1896–1910*. Honolulu: University of Hawaii Press, 1988.

Yu, Eui-Young. "The Korean American Community." In Donald N. Clark, ed., *Korea Briefing 1993*, 139–62. Boulder, CO: Westview Press, 1993.

Index

About the Author

DONALD N. CLARK is Professor of History and Director of International Studies at Trinity University in San Antonio, Texas. He has written and edited a number of works on Korea, including *Christianity in Modern Korea* (1986).